Toddling to the Kingdom

Editor
JOHN COLLIER

Contributors
MARCIA BUNGE
JOHN COLLIER
JAMES GILBER
BILL PREVETT
CARLOS QUIERO
ARIOVALDO RAM
JOHN WALL
KEITH WHITE
HADDON WILLME

GW00578293

Child Theology Movement

Copyright © 2009 The Child Theology
Movement Limited
First published 2009 by
The Child Theology Movement
10 Crescent Road, South Woodford,
London E18 1JB, UK
Charity registration no. 1106542

Email info@childtheology.org
Website www.childtheology.org

ISBN 978-0-9560993-0-3

All rights reserved. No part of this
publication may be reproduced, stored in
a retrieval system, or transmitted, in
any form or by any means, electronic,
mechanical, recording, or otherwise,
without the prior permission of the
Publisher in writing.

Scripture quotations from the Holy Bible,
New International Version® copyright ©
1973, 1978, 1984 by International Bible
society. Used by permission. All rights
reserved.

Design by
Tony Cantale Graphics
Printed in India

CONTENTS

CONTRIBUTORS

Marcia Bunge
Professor of Humanities
and Theology: Christ College,
Valparaiso University, USA

John Collier
Company Secretary:
Child Theology Movement,
London, UK

James Gilbert
Visiting Professor:
Centro Evangélical de Missões,
Viçosa, MG Brazil

Bill Prevette
Missionary and Professor of
Missiology: Assemblies of God
World Missions and Southeastern
University, USA

Carlos Quieroz
Executive Director:
World Vision in Brazil,
Ceará, Brazil

Ariovaldo Ramos
General Director: Latin American
Faculty of Full Mission (FLAM)
Pastor, Reformed Church and
Baptist Church of White Water,
São Paulo, Brazil

John Wall
Associate Professor of Religion
and Childhood Studies:
Rutgers University, USA

Keith White
Visiting Lecturer:
Spurgeons College and MBTS
London, UK and Malaysia

Haddon Willmer
Emeritus Professor of Theology:
Leeds University, UK

The Child Theology Movement acknowledges with
gratitude the substantial and continued support from
Compassion International which has made possible
both the printing of this book and many of the meetings
mentioned.

FOREWORD

I can't remember the last time I heard a sermon in church on children. In fact, I can't recall hearing one at all. We are familiar with well-trodden verses about Jesus and his openness to children and His wrath at those who would do them harm. Often these are the texts used to try and rope unwilling members of the congregation to volunteer for children's church or Sunday school.

We have a strange paradoxical relationship with children in the church. Many parents' choice of church is influenced by the quality of the children's programme, especially in the USA where I live. Huge resources are allocated to facilities, youth pastors, classrooms and teaching curricula. We know that children are important. We want to do all we can to help them grow and flourish. However, our understanding of children from a theological perspective: their roles in God's covenant with us, or as signs of the kingdom are subjects that preachers rarely touch upon.

Why should we be concerned about child theology? After all, don't we know all there is to know about children in the Bible? We should protect and care for them. Welcome them. Not frustrate them. Teach them in the way they should go. Our traditions tell us, perhaps shaped by culture and context more than careful exegesis, that children are sinful or innocent. We discipline, baptize (or not as the case may be), stereotype and ask for confessions of faith from children.

But try placing a child in the midst of all that we do, including our theology. What changes? Children have a knack of asking the most awkward questions. Questions that get to the heart of what we believe and expose our real core values. Questions that don't fit neatly into the categories we have learned. Dig deeper into the text, Biblical history, and the practical outworking of child theology with some of the most at risk children in the world, and you'll be surprised at what you may discover about God. A group of theologians and childcare practitioners have been doing just that. Over the past 8 years, they created a movement that began to explore theological questions raised by people working with some of the most vulnerable children across the world.

This book is not 'just' for those who work with children. It is for all Christians who are not afraid to walk with children into some relatively unexplored areas of God's kingdom. It charts a journey of some of those who did just that. There is much here to ponder and reflect on. There is still much to learn. With discernment and grace we too can toddle to the kingdom.

Paul Stephenson
Director: Children in Development,
World Vision International

PREFACE

Since 2002 the Child Theology Movement has promoted with the help of others a series of extended conversations or 'consultations' to explore what 'Child Theology' might be in various locations and contexts. Such meetings have been held in: Penang, Malaysia; Cape Town, South Africa; Houston, USA; Cambridge, England; Prague, Czech Republic; Addis Ababa, Ethiopia; São Paulo, Brazil; Quito, Ecuador; Kathmandu, Nepal; Newcastle, Australia.

Although reports were produced of all of these consultations, there is much in them that deserves a wider audience. This book is the result. I have selected key contributions to the consultations from various participants and arranged them in chapters. Some of the chapters are accounts of experiences and challenges children face today. Others are summaries of questions generated by group discussion. Still others are papers presented by individual participants. Together, the chapters offer an introduction to some of the central questions of and approaches to Child Theology.

I have sometimes edited the contributions from the original presentations. They were given orally to a particular group, at a specific time and place. My intention has been to make the presentations more accessible to those who were not at the meetings, to avoid repetition and to introduce some stylistic continuity in this volume. I believe I have not materially changed the sense of what was originally given.

The term 'Child Theology' may not be familiar to many readers. Perhaps it is worth pointing out here, at the beginning, that it is *not* a theology which has children and the issues relating to them as the primary foci. So, in that respect, it differs from a 'theology of childhood' or 'theology for children' and therefore is of interest to *all* Christians who speak of God, not just those who work with or are otherwise interested in children.

The focus of Child Theology is 'God in Christ' and the role of 'the child' is to bring a new perspective on the way God does things. We aim to have a child 'with us' as we do our theological work[1]. In this, we consciously try to follow Christ's example in Matthew 18:1-5:

> At that time the disciples came to Jesus and asked, "Who is the greatest in the kingdom of heaven?" He called a little child and had him stand among them. And he said: "I tell you the truth, unless you change and become like little children, you will never enter the kingdom of heaven. Therefore, whoever humbles himself like this child is the greatest in the kingdom of heaven. And whoever welcomes a little child like this in my name welcomes me."

As children are relatively inept at analytical thinking, our approach might be thought to lead to a 'dumbed down' theology. However, with Jesus' example before us, we are confident that the process in fact reveals a more challenging understanding of the Gospel: one that is relational and concrete more than analytical and abstract, that points us to Jesus' mission, upends our hierarchies and upsets our cherished categorisations and systems of thought.

In this way, Child Theology is akin to other new theologies that have brought new questions to the Bible based on the experiences of those who had long been marginal to formal theological reflection: the poor, the women, the marginalised races that have brought to us liberation, feminine and black theologies.

When we picture marginalised and oppressed children, it's easy to fall into the trap of pulling into focus the stereotypical child soldier or prostitute. But we should think more broadly than that. I remember several years ago that proponents of abortion law reform in the United Kingdom did so using a slogan 'Every child a wanted child'. If that had been achieved, the sacrifice of so many foetuses might have been redemptive though still abhorrent but, as should have been expected from a policy that trivialised human life, the opposite has happened and we have in the UK a generation of lonely, alienated and unhappy young people. Our culture superficially celebrates children, with an unprecedented number of products aimed at them, while denying them what they really need. Predatory producers out to 'accessorise' our children are sometimes called corporate paedophiles. Circumstances differ and the type of oppression varies but the plight of children is global.

As Jesus did something highly significant with a child in Matthew 18, as children make up about half the world's population, as they are the most oppressed social group and as we all are or have been children, isn't it time that we brought this perspective to bear on our understanding of what is meant by 'the Kingdom of God' and how we are to live in God's way?

John Collier

Jesus and Children: Serome Ching, age 10 yrs

NOTE

[1] It needs to be made clear at the outset that this does not necessarily, or even usually, mean that we have a child with us in the room 'in the flesh'. Later chapters will show how we try to do this.

Part One
INTRODUCTION

IN THIS section, I give a taste of the approach to Child Theology that we have used in the Child Theology Movement. Later, the book addresses in greater detail many of the matters raised. This overview might serve to dispel at the outset some misconceptions of what we mean by 'Child Theology' and its relevance to everyday Christian life, thought and action.

Not all the people involved in our meetings would have called themselves 'theologians'. Indeed, some might have been quite apprehensive to be found in the same room as professionals who, to their mind, have a reputation for dismantling and undermining faith! I hope and believe that many left the consultations reassured that theologians can and do have sincere and lively faith in Christ.

There has always been an attempt to get a mix of persons in the meetings, especially of 'professional' theologians and those working with children in practical ways. Wherever possible, we tried to get a mixture of gender and cultures and did our best to include in the mix pastors and church leaders, not only those Christians concerned with children. We believe Child Theology is not just about how the church cares for, evangelises, teaches and worships with children. It has an impact on every aspect of church life. For example, it should affect how the church conducts its business or worships, *whether or not children are actually present*. Unfortunately, it has often proved quite difficult to interest pastors and church leaders. Maybe the title 'Child Theology' signified to some that the meeting was not appropriate for the senior pastor but was 'only' suited for the children's pastor or youth leaders. If so, this would serve to show the need for what we are doing!

A more important omission in the groups, in nearly all cases, was 'the child in the midst' – a child such as Jesus placed in the midst of an earlier group of disciples having a theological discussion. Several participants raised this with us but it is difficult to see how we could actually bring a child or children into the group without somehow abusing them. Many would be intimidated if brought into such a gathering of serious adults. We might attempt to prepare them for the experience but in so doing, would we undermine their childlikeness just by explaining our adult processes and purposes? Perhaps we could find ways of *appearing* less serious (while still doing serious theology)!

To make up for this deficit, we brought real life stories of children, our own experiences and imaginations, and did the best we could to place a child there with us in spirit if not in flesh. Chapter one is an example of one way we did that. We have always found that bringing a child into the room, even in such a way, changed the dynamic and opened a perspective that demanded from our faith a new response. Chapters two and three introduce our own response to such situations, which we call "Child Theology". Chapters four and five attempt to show what impact it has, or might have, and how it differs from other theologies connected with children in some way.

One
Oppressed Child

"FOR I KNOW THE PLANS THAT I HAVE
FOR YOU, DECLARES THE LORD, PLANS TO PROSPER
YOU AND NOT TO HARM YOU, PLANS TO GIVE YOU
HOPE AND A FUTURE."
Jeremiah 29:11

The following story from Romania was passed on to us
by Bill Prevette at a consultation in Prague.[2]

"**I REMEMBER** when I first met Adina. She seemed like a scared child. She didn't dare look me in the eye and could hardly speak to me. I talked with her for only a moment, just enough time to arrange to meet with her for a doctor's appointment the following day. She never showed up. Just knowing a little of her background, I hoped and prayed that she wasn't pregnant. Due to her circumstances – living on the streets – I couldn't see a positive future for herself and a child.

As a social worker working to prevent newborn baby abandonment in Romania, I come across very impressive cases. Incredible stories of people whose lives, you would be tempted to think, had been lived unnoticed and somehow overlooked by God. I would like to share with you a story that has remained close to my heart, because it was one that opened up a series of similar success stories.

Adina was a part of the street kid subculture in Bucharest. Together with some of her other street friends she attended a Teen Challenge outreach where she came in contact with a missionary who began building a relationship with her. This lady asked if I could come to the coffee house **13** one evening to meet Adina. She thought that Adina was pregnant and needed help.

Two months went by until one day I found out that Adina had been hospitalized in the maternity hospital I worked in as a social worker. She had given birth prematurely to twins: a boy and a girl. I located the room she was staying in and this is when I found out the details of her courageous life story.

Adina had been born into a family with many children. When she was two years old she was abandoned in an orphanage, never to be visited again by her family. When she was 11 or 12 years old, she was transferred to another orphanage in a different town. At this orphanage another child raped her when she was 16 years old. The boy was expelled from the centre and Adina was moved to another institution. She gave birth in a maternity hospital and raised her baby until he was 13 months old. Then, she said, she was forced to give up her child.

She was moved back into an orphanage where she continued going to school and where she received training as a seamstress.

When she turned 18 she had to leave the orphanage where she was staying. She was dropped off at her biological parent's home where her parents didn't recognize her.

She lived there for only six months. She was physically abused and forced to work beyond her strength until finally she was driven away from home again. Only now she was grown up she could understand that this was not the place for her. She says, "It was hard for my family, nine people living in a three room apartment, trying to make ends meet living off of the Romanian welfare system."

So in the spring of 2002, driven away by her family circumstances, Adina had no choice but to try to survive on the streets of Buzau. Her hope was that maybe she would finally find a family there. But not even on the streets was she left alone. The police picked her up many times, took her the police station and beat her because she was begging to earn a living. Unable to bear the situation, she left for Bucharest together with another homeless girl, in hopes of being left alone and being able to blend in with the multitude of other street children.

Adina desperately tried to make a future for herself but no matter how hard she tried it felt like she was fighting an uphill battle. Shortly after she came to Bucharest she was taken advantage of by a street boy addicted to drugs and became pregnant. Wanting very much the support of a family, she became part of a street child gang that was receiving help from various humanitarian organizations. Through one of these groups she managed to get a job making candles, which is how I ended up having contact with her, two months before she gave birth.

Adina didn't expect to give birth so soon, and certainly not to two children. She didn't know what to do and felt confused. She was struggling as to whether or not to keep the babies and try to provide a future and a better world for them. She wished that she could at least keep the boy as a comfort for the one who was taken away from her when she was 17 years old. I stood with her when she saw her children for the first time and witnessed one of the greatest miracles of life: a mother allowing herself to be captured by two little lives that God had allowed her to give birth to.

I believed in my heart that, with help, Adina could be a mother to these little children and provide for them. Though, to prevent their abandonment, I would have to find a way to get Adina off the streets. I went to work right away!

Because Adina's babies were born premature, they needed to stay in the hospital until they reached a normal weight. However, Adina had to leave the hospital because she didn't have money to pay for extended hospitalization. So we made use of this time to obtain copies of legal papers that she needed to obtain her children's birth certificates. When we went to register her children Adina asked me to name her baby girl. The name Esther from the Bible came to mind – the woman that had been used by God to save a nation!

All that I had left to do was to find a maternal centre where Adina and her children could live and receive the support they needed to be integrated back to society. I searched all over Bucharest to find such a centre but couldn't find one. It had been almost a month since the children were born. They were normal weight now, so they were ready to leave the hospital. I began to worry but then realized that it wasn't in my power to provide a future for them. I started to pray for the situation and asked others to pray with me also.

It was then that the Lord brought to my mind Jeremiah 29:11. He showed me that He had Adina and her babies' future in His hands. My simple human ability to help them came into being because of what God had purposed for them long ago. It wasn't my job to prepare a future for Adina and her babies but His.

As I write Adina's story, it has been over a year since we found a maternal centre near Timisoara for her and her babies to live in. The children have grown, they are beautiful and healthy and loved by everyone who knows their story. Adina is considered a model mother and a hero for making the courageous choices she did. She is the pride of the maternal centre. By God's grace, a shy, awkward girl who once didn't know how to feed, change or care for her children is now teaching other mothers how to do this. Adina and her babies are preparing to be integrated into society to live independently from the maternal centre.

And as for me, I have learnt that my part is to love and to do all I can to reach out a hand to help those God has put in my life. And in doing so, to be a reflection of His light and life to encourage mothers to put their hope and future in Him."

Jesus and Children: Ng Joe Yee, age 6 yrs

CHAPTER NOTES
2   The story is as told to him by Simona Pop who graduated in sociology and theology from the Baptist seminary in Bucharest.

CHAPTER 2

Our Response

KEITH WHITE AND HADDON WILLMER

FOR SOME years, Viva Network has organised international 'Cutting Edge' conferences for people working with children such as 'Adina' in the previous chapter. Having attended the first two of these and being on the programme committee, I (Keith) became concerned about a lack of theological depth in the midst of much splendid Christian activism on behalf of children. So I was given the task of giving a paper to address this issue at the third conference, held in the year 2001. That paper is reproduced in the next chapter.

The result of the presentation was an outpouring of over two hundred questions, for God and for the Scriptures, arising out of the worldwide church's work with children. These questions are outlined in more detail in chapter seven. I was given the task, along with Ken Harder, of coming up with some responses. We decided to call together a small number of theologians and workers with children for a 'brainstorm' session in Penang in June 2002. It quickly became clear that this was a task with wide ramifications that could not be resolved in five days. So the task became a project and one meeting turned into a series of consultations and round tables which are still continuing around the world.

First Steps

At that, our first consultation, we read Matthew 18:1-5 and talked about it in its wider context in the Gospel. We deliberately, by an act of imagination, set the child among us so that our thinking should never fly off into general theology or into one or another of the kinds of Christian thinking in which the child is invisible, unheard and without impact. As we understood it, if we were to do Child Theology, we had repeatedly to be bringing our theological sayings back to the reality of the child.

As we did so, we took time to identify the *key questions* that we had brought with us, such as:

why are Christians not concerned with children outside the church?

why do great social evils (AIDS, genocide, abject poverty, etc.) persist in spite of the massive missions efforts of the 19th and 20th centuries?

children ('4/14 window') are the most receptive people group and make up nigh on 50% of the population, so why have most missiologists and theologians ignored them?

what range of children is available? Are we looking for the child within all children, the typical or average child, or each individual child?

We also took time to try to identify *pitfalls* that might hinder our work:

that we circle around the issues and do not get to the heart of them;

that we allow our pet ideas of child development to control our discussion;

that we forget teenagers when we speak of children;

that we continue to be controlled by the notion that children should not be involved in church affairs;

that we come to this meeting as professionals rather than as children of God;

that we deal with the issues by making children a 'tag-on' rather than a natural part of the programme.

Childhood is most commonly contrasted with adulthood. This has a number of *undesirable outcomes*. For example:

children are seen not as individuals in their own right but as pre-adults, a human becoming (not yet) human, "an adult-in-waiting";

it sets up opposites: dependent/independent; mature/immature; etc. in which children come off worse;

it is assumed that children should become adults as quickly as possible;

it is assumed that the real world is the adult world;

there is talk of "youth and community" but what is community if we've taken the youth out? Isn't the world composed of children and adults?

Working from such presuppositions, children's Bibles are produced that take for granted that children could not possibly understand the Bible as given – as if adults can! Authorities look for "normal development" and monitor families to impose received standards of normality. Every society has a legitimate desire to ensure that its norms and values are transmitted to the next generation. This has Old Testament endorsement. Liberal notions pay scant attention to the commercial pressures of capitalism/materialism, rampant in children's TV, books, films (with associated money-spinning merchandising) etc. From a Christian perspective, this also is abuse of children.

Luther said: all our language has to go through the bath of the Cross. Similarly in Child Theology all our talk of God has to meet the test of *the child in the midst*. As the poor transformed theology in Liberation Theology, and as women transform it in feminist theologies, so in Child Theology it is the impact of the child that transforms theology.

At that first consultation a seven-year-old boy was with us. We did not inflict our discussions on him – that would have been a form of child abuse and would not have been of any assistance to our theological work – but he ate with us and enjoyed our boat trip and there were frequent references to him. He reminded us of our principle, a vivid orientation point, more impressive than an idea made present in word only. One child in the company stimulated everyone to bring into the discussion the reality of what they knew of children.

This particular child in the midst served as liturgy serves, even when it is done in a routine way: we can pray and read the word without our hearts being strangely warmed and with no fire falling from heaven. Nevertheless even such an apparently arid performance of the liturgy involves us in a publicly enacted restatement of the substance of faith and **19** serves it by rehearsing it. It brings the dry bones together, with sinews and skin on them, all ready for the breath of life to be given. *The child in the midst* is like a sacrament, as a visible word. When Jesus placed a child in the midst, it was indeed more than a liturgical routine: it was a crisis of conversion, a shaking argument.

Our placing the child in the centre of our theological work cannot produce such a converting effect as a matter of routine. Rather our routine is a service, by which we stand and wait in readiness. Sometimes, the waters are troubled. Sometimes, the critical moment opens up. Then we are found watching, ready for the gift we cannot command.

Toddling

Child Theology is a method for 'theology in process', grass roots in a sense. When we started, we wanted to set the child in the midst and see what happened – a deliberate discipline of critical consciousness of seeing and setting the child in the midst and letting that impact our discussion.

Child Theology definitely holds that Jesus did not set the child in the centre of the circle of disciples for them to admire or to make the focus of attention. Neither did he place the child there as one in need of some kind of care, education, feeding, respect, friendship or whatever. There is no sign that the child needed or was given anything in this narrative – except to be remembered for ever as a child who was useful to God in the service of his Kingdom.

The child is placed there by Jesus as a move in the theological game. Jesus did not put his case in words merely, or in signs which could be translated into words. He argued by putting people into challenging and promising situations. That Jesus made theology so serious and drew all of life and all creation into his theological argumentation does not allow us to conclude that Jesus was not theologically engaged.

In terms of being human, we are continually trying to understand that which we cannot fully understand, not just for the child but in general. The Spirit's work in the heart regarding children is a mystery that lies at the heart of understanding and interpreting human relations. But the lack of full understanding need not prevent us from making progress: one's spouse interprets one in an acceptable way even if not fully.

Given that we understand our discussions as experiments, we may press on despite doubts. We are not teaching an orthodoxy but trying to see and to learn. Putting the child in the midst of any and every theological issue goes beyond what Jesus did but may nevertheless be in his spirit, in his way and may be justified by its fruit.

Child Theology and the Kingdom

Child Theology is thinking and speaking *about*, or even more importantly, *from, to, with, for*, God.

It is thinking about God and his kingdom with the child in the centre. There are many valuable ways of thinking about, observing, analysing, theorising, celebrating, lamenting, advocating children which are not Child Theology. Child Theology is distinct.

It is necessary in the first place to be itself. In cultures which are methodologically, practically or ideologically atheist, Child Theology will have to work hard simply to be itself. Many Christians have already concluded that theology is not necessary or that it is a distraction. So Child Theology will also have to battle against untheological religion as well as secular exclusion.

It is necessary to emphasise that the child should not be the primary focus or criterion in Child Theology, because the child is not God. There is a danger of inadvertent or practical idolisation of the child, so that in child-friendly religious discourse the child in effect takes the place of God. Then, rather than the child being upheld and justified by the truth of God, the child would subvert and block the truth of God and our thinking for children would be deprived of the help of God.

This distinction of God and child is merely precautionary not systematic and substantial. For God and the child go together, as a significant relationship within God and his creation. This was made clear by Jesus when he took a child and set him or her in the midst, as a clue to the nature of the kingdom of God and the way into it. In order to speak of God, the Word of God used many human words and many components of human experience, amongst them the child.

Child Theology in its positive substance therefore takes the child as set in the midst by Jesus to be a theological clue. The child set in the midst by Jesus tells us something of great importance: it is a clue to the Kingdom of God. The kingdom of God is important because it is *God's* kingdom and because it is God's *kingdom* – God over all and for all.

Furthermore, if the child is a clue to the nature of the kingdom of God, which is over all the world, the child must also be a clue to *the way into* the kingdom. The kingdom of God is not a kingdom with guarded borders, designed to keep people out. The kingdom of God is open, it is *intended to be entered.*

But not all ways get us into the kingdom. Some obvious ways lead us into destruction. There are simple ways into the kingdom but not easy or obvious ones. Finding the way into the kingdom always involves us human beings in learning. The learning required to enter the Kingdom involves us in knowing ourselves, in seeing ourselves as those who do not know the kingdom truly enough to enter it, in short, in being converted. We are invited into what we cannot understand until we get inside it – and not even then fully. We have to change and be converted in order to be able to see and understand what is on offer. The child is a clue to the kingdom not because the child gives us information, by example or symbolism, but because the child puts us into a crisis, dissolves our existing certainty and assurances and draws us into unexpected possibilities.

It may, however, be a little unusual to make Jesus' setting the child in the midst our methodological hinge. We have not merely quoted this and similar texts (Jesus embracing and blessing the children) in support of child-friendly practice. We have taken the text and lived with it. Jesus took a child and set him in the centre of this theological argument. So we said, we will not do Child Theology without the child and we will not talk about the child without theology.

CHAPTER 3

What is 'Child Theology'?

HADDON WILLMER

CHILD THEOLOGY is the name we give to the work we are doing. As far as we know, no one has ever used the term before. We want to make it clear that we do not have a proprietary attitude to Child Theology, as though it is our invention, so that we can or should be defensive about what happens to it, as others take it up in their own way. What we hope to do is make a contribution to an open conversation.

It is Theology

Child Theology is not an overall Christian theory of all activity around children. Nor is it just a reaction to the child unfriendliness of much of modern life. It also reacts to the massive secular and Christian child *friendliness* which are to be found in the world now – for example, as set out by the United Nations Convention on the Rights of the Child. The Gospel can be ignored or distorted not only in activities that are child-unfriendly. Child friendliness can take forms that have the same effects. Secular humanism can be concerned for children without God and the Gospel. To care for children, it's not just a matter of adding God into the programme. There can be Christian activism for children which obscures the Gospel because it is insufficiently theologically articulate.

Theology is thinking and talking (*logos*) about, from, towards and with God (*theos*). Not all religion involves theology. Even if the talk about Child Development, for example, uses religious language and categories but makes no mention of God, then it is not theology. Child Theology takes the view that theology is important and should be worked at, even though talking about God can never substitute for God and theology as talk is not a substitute for faith in action. Child Theology has only a small corner in the totality of God's world but in and from that corner it must let its light shine.

Our Approach

One approach to Child Theology that I have taken with Keith White is to reflect on some Gospel stories and sayings of Jesus in relation to children.

First, helped by Matthew 18, we aimed to follow Jesus who *put a child in the middle of a theological argument*! The disciples thought the Kingdom of God was such that it was possible and proper to have a competition for greatness in it. Jesus does not merely attack the proud ambitions of the disciples by inviting them to become as children but changes the language in order to speak more precisely about the transcendent difference of the Kingdom of God from the kingdoms of our earthly experience. In God's kingdom, the language of greatness ceases to be competitive. To enter the kingdom is enough – and even the great people on earth cannot take entering the kingdom for granted.

Secondly, we reflected on what it means to *receive the child*. Jesus tells us that we cannot enter the Kingdom unless we become as children. Does this mean we are to attempt the impossible: to go back on our adulthood – the adulthood it seems God implants in every child by nature? Jesus does not expect adults in themselves to become children. They become as children when they receive the child, real children, so that they live with and for the child, so that they walk at the pace of the child. They become like a child, without ceasing to be adult, when they let the child they receive be a child. As they do this, they provide what the child needs as part of its child-ness: reception. This way of reading the Gospels is controversial, and will be disputed by many child-friendly theologians. Our approach is not to be wholly conventional and unprovocative!

Thirdly, we found we had to attend to child suffering, to the massive *despising of little ones* which is all around us. Jesus said they should not be despised because their angels always behold the Father's face. This is certainly a theological saying: it invites us to think that angels and God's face might be helpful and consoling to little ones who are despised. This challenges the widely held view that God is only of value to us if God-talk correlates with and symbolises effective justice and goodness on earth.

Child as Sign

Even in spite of Christ, God has done so much to preserve his invisibility – he preserves the mystery and hiddenness, even while revealing himself. We can never grasp God but we have to go on babbling as we attempt to speak about him (Augustine). A lot of life is about waiting in darkness, waiting in faith. *"The people that walked in darkness … ."* Like Simeon waiting in the Temple, until Christ is brought in.

The child was put in the midst as a sign of the Kingdom of God but this is not the same as the presence of the Kingdom. The child is often a sign of hope but she can also be a sign by pointing to the darkness that is still waiting for the Kingdom, rather like the canaries taken down the mines to detect poisonous gases. Faith does not oblige us to be cheaply optimistic about every situation.

Adina was rescued but what about those that were not? Adina helps us to remember them but they still suffer. People still say: there's no God or if there is, he's not around when you need him. So, many social workers are quite hostile to the involvement of Faith Based Organisations – they think faith only complicates the problem. Many Christians also feel the weight of this question.

The Children's Angels

Perhaps Jesus offers us some help in resolving these issues when he admonishes us not to despise the children because their angels always see the face of God (Matthew 18:10). Despising here is very broad: an unfriendly word is a despising, and death is a despising. Jesus says: don't join in with this. Why? Because of the angels! God's face being open to them is a Biblical symbol of God's acceptance and favour. So how seriously and purely do we take this, the fact that God is for them? Does our concern for children, our receiving them, stem from God? Or are our motives and modes of action largely secular? There is a strong humanist **25** case for doing good for children. Christian action for children is often actually based on secular, sociological sensibility, science and concern. We just add a religious gilding to it.

What comfort is it that angels behold the Father's face? This is a basic issue, which all believers in God feel: Where is God when children suffer? And further, if comfort can be found in God's open face, who and where are the angels? Could, for example, the United Nations Convention on the Rights of the Child be an angel, who represents the child to God and with the affirmation of God?

Standing with the Angels

But we can't leave the angels to do all the representing of children before the Father's face. Even though they're despised, God is still on their side. This in itself doesn't alter the fact of their being despised in the world. We must see this text in the context of receiving a child, which means we should attend to them. So then it would be inconsistent for us not to be on their side, just like God with his angels. Throughout the Bible, God's people are to be as God is. Even when the darkness is deep and it seems that it will never yield, we can still hope that the Kingdom is coming.

In exceptional cases, the angels don't merely behold the Father's face but come with timely help. The story of Hagar and Ishmael is an example (Genesis 16.7-14; 21:15-21) but even stories like this are not to be used to excuse our leaving it to the angels. They strengthen our sense that God is for the despised and abandoned and so make clearer to us what we have to do.

A Pentecostal hermeneutic of the passage might see it in the context of 'spiritual warfare'. The gap between social and spiritual, Pentecostals would like to fill with Holy Spirit, the power of God. Children can be caught in the middle of two worlds in conflict.

Some churches wouldn't help Adina as she wasn't 'one of theirs'. And if she were one of theirs, they would throw her out because of church discipline! What do we actually believe about God? An article in the Baptist Times suggested we shouldn't preach the love of God in the world but only in the church. How much do we believe that God is active in the world just now?

Is there anything in Creation that represents mystery better than a child? The story about angels might be more about God's care and involvement; reminiscent of stories from the desert fathers which suggest that things are not the way they often appear. And in this way, children may begin to expose the gap between the theology we say we believe and the theology that we actually practice.

Questions to be Answered

For those working with children, and to all who would wish to follow this analysis, many issues arise. Here are some that were suggested by participants at a Child Theology consultation:

What do we mean by 'child'? Must he/she be young or can the text stand for any powerless or marginalisebout children before they meet the child? How do we complete the following sentences, in the context of our own particular cultures:

Children are …

Children like to …

Children should …

The child is part of …

Does receiving the child presuppose a movement of the child towards us?

The child should be received as into a family, so openness, patience and willingness to be changed oneself are important. It is the start of a new relationship.

It might mean to open one's home for the child; but that is a serious matter because it means opening a private space.

Receiving is complementary to giving. Who is the giver? The identity of the giver may affect our response to the gift.

Reception must be on the child's terms

There is a price to pay in receiving

CHAPTER 4

Developing Child Theology

HADDON WILLMER

WHAT IS the most popular and influential story or saying from the Gospel that connects the child and theology? Various answers are given, including: the child in the midst; the feeding of 5,000; 'let the children come to me' (Matthew 19).

Traditionally, the most popular text has been *"let the little children come to me"*. The second most popular text is Matthew 18:6 – the millstone. It is now used against child-abusers but such a text should always be read for oneself and not for others.

Our Key Text

Child Theology would like to offer an alternative text: Matthew 18:1-5 the 'child in the midst'. This story has been far less fashionable.

A 'theology of childhood' encases the child in our own thinking. Jesus did something else. The child is capable of breaking through our theologies and habits of mind. Where did Jesus put the child? In the midst of the disciples. Yes, but that's not the whole answer. What were the disciples doing? Arguing – about the Kingdom of God. So it's a theological argument. And the child was put in the middle of that. Perhaps to show them up for the kind of people they were. Instead of respecting God and his authority, they were turning it into an opportunity for self-advancement. Peter asks, what's in it for us? We've given up so much for you.

Aristotle spoke of the unmoved mover, the perfect circle – all Creation moves towards God but God himself is unmoved. In Aristotle's judgment, for God to have moved would have been a mark of imperfection. But Jesus reveals a God who is not like that and is rather a God who creates and loves the world, always moving towards us in invitation.

Although God is perfect and has no need of us, he is not ashamed to put himself in a position where he desires his creation, in which he is specially represented (imaged) by human beings. By enrolling us into his project, he lays himself open to the possibility that we will subvert and pervert his plan. With us and against us, God persists in his project in creation and his persistence culminates in Jesus, who proclaims his kingdom and is seen as the express image of God in humanity. And, in his revelation and service of God, Jesus places the child in the midst of an argument about greatness in the kingdom of God, expecting the child to make a crucial difference to the argument.

The Difference the Child Makes

So, perhaps we should pause now to ask ourselves what difference might the child have made in this story and how. Don't worry too much about which child, or what type of child. The story is vague about this and probably deliberately so. In our understanding, the important thing is to bring a child into the discussion, in imagination, and we are free to choose the child. The text gives us that liberty.

Here are some answers that others have given:

> The child is small, powerless and easy to look down on. The disciples probably got angry and indignant because children lack power and knowledge;
> Children are receptive, like the lamb in the middle of wolves;
> The Kingdom of God doesn't work in hierarchical way: don't worry about status;
> Children are vulnerable and open;
> Children deal with real concrete questions, not the abstract;
> The disciples' argument was very childish! It's the kind of thing children argue about! 'I'm the king of the castle!';
> The child is a model – the text mentions the humility of the child.

The child makes a difference because the disciples are in competition and it's very clear that the child is not in competition with them. The child apparently doesn't stand a chance in the contest but Jesus says the child will win. The child points to a Kingdom that we were meant for, a place where we long to be, but it's a place that runs on quite different lines from what we are used to. The disciples compete to be greatest. Jesus talks about simply 'entering'. Just to get inside the Kingdom is enough, it does-n't matter what position one is given there. *"I'd rather be a doorkeeper in the house of God ..."* (Psalm 84:10).

Understanding True Adulthood

Children are often thought of as incomplete adults and it may be that Jesus intended to teach us something about adulthood through placing a child in the midst. He did not, in modern fashion, chide the disciples for thinking of the child as incomplete, not 'there' yet. He rather worked with their view of children, in order to question their adulthood.

It is not that children are as complete as adults but rather that adults are like children in being incomplete, though adult incompleteness differs from children's incompleteness. Adulthood is much closer to being deceived into denying incompleteness, as though adulthood could be one long sigh of relief to have, at last, escaped childishness. Children open up awareness of our own incompleteness. We all, to the end of our days, have to live in our incompleteness and therefore in our need of others and God. Paul writes, *"I don't count on myself as having attained ..."* (Philippians 3:12-16).

The temptation to seek greatness besets us from all sides: we can even use the resurrection to cancel out the Cross. We don't know how to run the world or to be ourselves without competitiveness and control. This text is not just directing us how to become better people, improving ourselves, e.g. by becoming humble. Rather, the child tells us something fundamental about the Kingdom, about the total and ultimate and press-ingly present framework within which all things exist and all is held together.

The Basic Meaning of the Child

Various qualities of children, such as humility, spontaneity etc, are offered as the aspect that Jesus had in mind for us to imitate. But children aren't humble in a moral sense. And most children aren't purely spontaneous – look at a child who hasn't been given stimulation. These qualities may not then identify what is the basic meaning of the child, as placed by Jesus in the midst of this theological and very practical argument.

But every child needs to be received. In needing to be received, the child reminds us of what is true of all humanity and indeed even of God's own being. God has need of nothing, yet in Jesus, whether as a baby or a man, living and dying, he becomes manifestly dependent on being received. In his resurrection, the one who was so little received by men who nailed him to the Tree, is received by the Father in glory.

Matthew alone talks about becoming like the child. All the Gospels, in their slightly varying versions of this incident, say that receiving a child is a way to receive Jesus and the one who sent him and thus to enter into the Kingdom of God. What then does it mean to receive the child? It is in the nature of a child to be received. Adults might survive alone on a desert island but an abandoned and exposed child will not survive. They must be received to continue in existence.

So reception is a central and fundamental theme in theology, in our understanding of God in Christ and our relating to him. Receiving the child has what some might well see as sacramental significance in this context. It is a theme which leads us to reflect on our various activities on behalf of children. How are we receiving children?

CHAPTER 5

What Child Theology Is and Is Not

MARCIA BUNGE

WHEN I had my own children I was teaching in Sunday School and I realised how poor the resources were. There were a few good materials for religious education but they were hard to find. I began to wonder why theologians spent so little time thinking about children – especially since they were thinking seriously about other issues, such as reproductive technology, abortion, and homosexuality. This led me with some colleagues to put together the book *The Child in Christian Thought*. It turned out that many famous Christian leaders and thinkers in the past had written much about children. Now another book with essays from biblical scholars has been published entitled *The Child in the Bible* (Grand Rapids: Eerdmans, 2008). A third book will look at Jewish, Christian and Muslim perspectives on children.

Because Christian theologians approach children and childhood in a number of ways, each with particular emphases and interests, we need to be clear what we mean by 'Child Theology' and to ask ourselves how it is distinct from other more familiar considerations of children, such as:

Theologies of Childhood
Children's theology
Children's spirituality

Theologies for children

Children and religious education.

For example, we can compare and contrast Child Theology with theologies of childhood.

They both:

Put children at the centre of serious theological reflection;

Prompt action on behalf of children;

Have implications for the church and children themselves,
especially in the areas of:

Children and family ministry

Religious education and faith formation

Child advocacy.

Although similar in these ways, Child Theologies and Theologies of Childhood have distinctive aims.

Theologies of Childhood:

Provide sophisticated theological understandings of children and
childhood and our obligations to children – not just of the
parents but also church, state, etc.;

Should take into account various perspectives on children and
childhood from the Bible and the Christian tradition;

Should honour the dignity and complexity of children –
recognizing that they are both fully human and also developing
beings and that they are both sinful moral agents and also
models of faith. This full view is essential if children are to be
treated well – neither oppressed nor sentimentally idolised.

Child Theology:

Builds on theologies of childhood but with a broader task, looking
at doctrine and practice as a whole;

Re-examines fundamental doctrines and practices of the church
using the "lens" of the child;

Provides new insights into central themes of the Christian faith,
e.g. how would we redefine the doctrine of the church if we took
children seriously?

The approach to Child Theology adopted by the Child Theology Movement reflected in this publication has the following features:

> It involves an international network of professional theologians and practitioners.
> It uses a distinctive approach for putting a child "in the midst".
> It recognizes that child theologies will be diverse, building on the Bible, authoritative texts in particular traditions, research in social and national sciences and experiences of individuals and faith communities.

To take one example of how we need to redefine theology, the most glaring need is in theological anthropology, our understanding of human nature. As currently defined, it is often just about adults, and even just male adults. It takes no account of development particularly of children. This is reflected in our structures: Churches are sometimes scary places - not even a square foot of space for play, no child sized chairs. Religious education materials do not always take into account the creativity and developmental needs of children. Children's ministries are often the last priority of congregational budgets. A robust theological anthropology that takes children into account could positively impact our worship services, educational materials, and many aspects of child and family ministry.

As we work to revise and to redefine these and other doctrines and practices in the light of serious reflection on children, it is wise to keep in mind that child theology is an on-going and open process and conversation. Erasmus thought that the best the best translation of 'logos' was 'conversation'. This gives a very different feeling, much more open-ended, than 'word'. We are invited to be part of a conversation.

Part Two
SITUATIONS
CHILDREN FACE

WHEN THE Child Theology Movement attempts to 'put a child in the midst' of a theological reflection, what is that child like? Who is the child? It would be only too easy to assemble in our imagination an idealised or romanticised child. We try to avoid this. Neither would it be appropriate to bring in the 'average' child or a 'normal' child. Such creatures clearly do not exist!

It was a real child that Jesus 'placed' and the Bible studiously avoids saying much about him (or her). No, we don't even know the gender! When we try to place a child among us, he/she should be appropriate for the context or culture in which we are meeting. That is one reason that we sometimes speak of "Child Theologies". Each child brings a different perspective. Is this a recipe for developing several mutually incompatible theologies? We guard against this by ensuring as far as we can that our thoughts are also informed by the Biblical text and by the long tradition of Christian theology. A particular strength of this process is the opportunity it gives us to develop a contextualised or indigenous theology, speaking to the issues and circumstances that are alive in the place where we meet.

In this section of the book, the various chapters describe some of the children we 'met' along the way and the questions they brought to us.

The situations they describe are often dire. There are the obvious ones: street children, orphan children who are heads of families, child soldiers and child prostitutes. But affluent, comfortable children are often seriously oppressed too, although in different ways. Along with a superabundance of material things, there is often spiritual and relational poverty. It is important to remember, too, that the child 'in the midst' could just as well be well cared for, happy and contented.

Chapter six tells the stories of some of the participants at our meetings and shows their own diverse childhood experiences that they brought with them. Chapter seven describes a number of questions asked by a group of people, drawn from across the world, who worked with children and attempts to draw out some of the issues that they raised. In chapter seven, we hear about the different experiences introduced into the lives of children through a variety of non-western cultures. Many of the problems described in these stories occur when societies fracture, through war, disease, famine, family breakdown, etc. But some types of oppression are culturally mediated and occur in strong cohesive societies. This is a sensitive area, as people are rightly protective of their cultures. But the Bible confronts all cultures, so-called Christian ones not excluded. In chapter eight, various anecdotes describe cultural forms that affect children, chapter nine focuses specifically on the problems introduced by increasing urbanisation and chapter 10 takes the issues more broadly, attempting to form a framework in which to categorise them.

CHAPTER 6

Some Stories

THE FOLLOWING STORIES
WERE SHARED BY PARTICIPANTS
AT OUR MEETINGS[3]

Upside down Kingdom

ONCE I was in a church in Calcutta where the pastor asked for an offering. People brought forward their gifts. There was a pile of paper money. After everyone had left, a woman at the back dressed in rags and with a leprous arm went forward and left a couple of copper coins. A visiting businessman asked if he could have these two coins. He said, "This means more to me than all the money our business has given away (which was millions of dollars)." Pentecostals love resurrection power but at this moment I began to understand something about the upside down kingdom, that it's not about power and control.

I had grown up in an orphanage with a lot of violence and religion in my life, but I knew nothing of God. I became a Christian at the age of 26 in a Pentecostal church in California, full of people like me, ex-hippies and people who had lived violent lives. Later I went to Fuller Seminary where I did a mission course and there I learnt about the Kingdom of God. This transformed my thinking. Now I have a passion to encourage young people to wake up to a spiritual world that sometimes invades this world. Jesus is always speaking about this other world.

Last night some of us went out and met some of the gypsy girls working the streets, many of them trafficked from their homes and sold into prostitution. Afterwards I couldn't sleep, I just was thinking about God's heart for the kids. This is how the kingdom works – it doesn't come out of heaven like a thunderbolt. Jesus invites us into this world that's around us all the time.

Abusive stepfather

WHEN I was 2 my parents divorced. My stepfather was an evil man but my mother never stood up for me against him. I remember he always had an angry face. I felt confused, lost and unwelcome. I thought I was a burden. I wasn't allowed to eat with the family but had a place of my own in the kitchen. They called me names and falsely accused me of stealing. I was forced to confess but when the stolen stuff was found they never apologized.

I ran away when I was 7 years old. It was wintertime and I had no shoes. So I lived first with my aunt and later with my grandmother. She was a Christian and because of her I went to Sunday school. I liked to listen to the songs, see the pictures, and hear the Bible stories. All of the people there were friendly and kind to me. Then I had to go back to live with mother. She forbade me to go to Sunday school but I went anyway, even though I was punished for it. I couldn't understand why, since Sunday school was so good to me.

When I was 11 years old my parents moved to Australia. I said I would come later but I knew I never would. Instead, I stayed with my grandma. She was a poor and simple person but she loved me. Material things were not so important, but relationships were.

I simply believed what I was taught in Sunday school and I knew that I could pray to God whenever I wanted. The church was my refuge. Jesus was my friend when all others rejected me. Putting my trust in Christ broke the cycle of evil in my life. My husband has a similar story and God helps us through our difficulties. Through God and prayer, now I can be who I really am.

Material poverty but spiritual riches

I was born into poverty. It was during the depression in the mid-west of the USA. We lived in a railroad boxcar, with the dining room in the garage. We had food because we lived on a farm but there was absolutely no money. My mother made the dresses she wore from feed sacks. My father was not a Christian but was a very honourable man.

There was plenty of family time as there was no money to go out any-where. We always had 3 meals a day and, what was more important, we always shared them together. Mother would read poetry to us but I never owned a child's book, which is interesting because I've now written more than 150 children's books!

My childhood was filled with interaction with nature. Every day I walked a mile to the one room school and one mile back. Perhaps I learnt as much interacting on the way with the hedgerows, birds, etc. I went to Sunday school every Sunday and at age 16 became a Christian.

I got married, had children, and became busy writing and publishing age-appropriate books for children. It was a busy life and we never had any time for ourselves but we wouldn't trade the time we had with our kids for anything. This was an advantage of working at home for 20 years, to be at home for kids both before and after school. Now I have 11 grandkids and all have a deep commitment to Christ.

A struggle to achieve

THE memory of my childhood life is not a pleasant one, as my father passed away when I was about 4 years old. For years I saw life as unfair: if it were a running race, I had the disadvantage of a late start. To make up the gap, I strove to be an all-rounder, to excel in sports and music. This was a kind of survival, I had to be able to perform anything. But it did not answer my deep quest for fairness.

I grew up in a family that adhered to Javanese mysticism. In this sys-tem of belief, God is unknowable, transcendent and lives far beyond any human experience. He is far and hidden, yet so almighty that nothing, great or small could happen without His will. So it was with my father's death – God decided it without communicating His reasons. In such an inner struggle, I heard about the Christian God, who loves all people. In trusting Him, when I was still a "child", my view of life completely changed. Life is a grace not a tragedy. Life is full of purpose and is mean-ingful.

I saw my culture in a different way too. I owe so much to my grand-mother, who in her simplicity taught me so much about life and virtues through simple folk stories. In Eastern culture, an extended family system is the environment where a child grows up. Grandparents, uncles and aunts contribute so much for the growth of a child for good and for bad. Thank God, my grandmother taught me so much about my cultural values. And they too are redeemed and sanctified in the Lord Jesus.

The child who knew Jesus

WE held a number of children's camps in Africa. One girl, Kathy, had been to all four camps. She knew all the right answers and could have told the gospel story backwards but she never made any visible response. As the camps were drawing to a close, one of the leaders asked her if she wouldn't like to be a Christian. She seemed surprised and said she was a Christian already. The leader was concerned to know if she had really made a commitment to Jesus and so asked, "If God said, 'Why should I let you into my heaven,' what would you say?" She stared back blankly and didn't answer the question or say anything about forgiveness and repentance, the answers that were expected. The leader asked again. Still no response. Finally, one more time: "If God said, 'Why should I let you into my heaven,' what would you say?" She seemed quite distressed to be asked again and blurted out: "Why should I have to say anything? He'll recognise me. I'll just run into his arms!"

Kathy had seen something that the leader, for all his training, had not seen. She understood what it means to be a disciple. Though only in her twenties, Kathy died last year. I know she didn't have to answer silly questions, she would have run straight into his arms.

CHAPTER NOTES
3   These stories were told at various meetings convened by the Child Theology Movement.

CHAPTER 7

The Children's Questions

THE PARTICIPANTS at Cutting Edge III in 2001 were asked to offer questions concerning children. The children weren't there and so this was the only way to hear the children's voices. Several hundred questions were received covering a wide variety of topics. Many issues were raised repeatedly. Here are some examples:

What happens to children with disabilities such that they are unable to make a decision for Christ?

Can life in the womb that is destroyed have a life with God in heaven as a fully grown baby? Do two cells have a spirit?

Why does the church of Jesus Christ seem so apathetic in the face of so much global suffering? Is it because they assume that children go automatically to heaven when they die?

How can God love the paedophile as much as the abused child?

The Old Testament talks about God as the protector of children. Why do children have to suffer, for example, sexual abuse?

How do you answer a child that says: Where was Jesus when I was being abused..?

Should we tell children to 'turn the other cheek'?

Are some children damaged to the point that you have to write them off? Should we apply triage? Is there some damage that God cannot/ will not heal in this life? How did Jesus prioritise?

Why do we avoid the Old Testament passages that talk about killing the children of our enemies (Psalm 137:9)? What should we say about these passages?

What happened to God's anger at injustice?

When is it appropriate to remove a child from a family? Is it abusive?

How do you minister fatherly love to the sexually abused?

Is it valid to have ministries that focus just on children or should they always been seen in the context of family?

What role can we give to children in church? Can we involve 'unsaved' children in the same way?

Why is such a large part of the body of Christ apparently indifferent to the needs and suffering of children?

Do children have a natural belief in God? (Matthew 18:6)

How can we awaken the seared conscience of a child?

Categorisation of Questions

As many of the questions clearly overlapped, we wanted to deal with not just the questions but the underlying issues to. So we attempted to categorize the concerns that had been raised. This produced a more manageable list:

God

God – who? What is God like? God as model

Childhood

The childhood of Jesus

Why do we lose touch with our childhood innocence?

Sin and salvation

Sin and children

Predestination and choice: children deciding for Christ: responsibility

Terms and conditions of salvation for children – do they need to 'know Jesus'?

Writing off damaged unhealable children – or reintegrating?

Suffering

Child soldiers

Street children

Dealing with abusers (castrate them?)
Suffering (Why is it allowed? Absence of God/Jesus)
Demonic forces round children

Standards for action – Biblical and secular

Legitimacy of political action for children
Culture or Gospel, in relation to men, women and children
Church indifference to children
What does the Bible mandate?
The Bible and the Rights of the child
Lack of resources for children – is this a Bible question?

Children and church

Religious education of children
Involving children better in whole life of church
Church indifference to children

Children and family and society

Children and humanity/adults – balancing care between them
The unborn child
Family and breakdown of family (removing children, father
abandoning)

Interconnected issues

It quickly became clear that the issues were made more complex by their
overlapping and interacting relationships, by mutually reinforcing
ungodly lifestyle choices.

God:
What sort of God is there?

The Child:
The context, unborn, the church, community, family, society, state,
cultural determinants, gang and friends. etc.

Childhood:
Gender, sexuality, worth, spirituality, eternality, and other
qualities.

Responding to God:

Sin, predestination, conversion, salvation, silence of God, miracles, suffering, transformation, formation, nurture.

At risk:

Definition, abuse, disability, war, streets, irreparable damage?, etc.

Action: Responsibility, engagement, resources, people, money rights, legal conventions, advocacy, political.

Biblical foundations:

Old Testament, Gospels, epistles, other religions, etc.

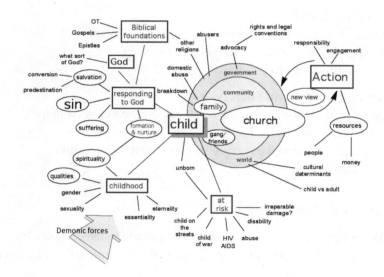

CHAPTER 8

Cultural Perspectives

IN SEVERAL meetings, participants from Europe and North America were obliged to be silent (with some difficulty!) in order to ensure that we heard a non-Western viewpoint. This discussion exposed particular difficulties and challenges of children in these cultures, and it became clear that, in some cases, children are not just 'at risk' but are nearly overwhelmed by all the risks. Responses are classified into clusters around issues facing children.[4]

Rites of passage

In South Africa young boys are initiated from the age of 12. After circumcision they become men. Human rights organizations are outraged by some of these things, but they are part of the culture.

When Brazilian girls reach 15 years of age, they have a special party indicating coming out into the world as an adult, or nearly-adult. Brazil is an ethnic melting pot and the country is still trying to find it's own identity. So there is no "representative" child. The blacks are the poorest. Black children dream of going to Samba school and families save during the year to allow their children to participate in Carnival and other festivals. The middle class are of European descent and some think of themselves as more European than Brazilian. Boys are more important than girls as girls will not make much financial contribution to the family. Large families are valued as a sign of fertility. Children are important in Brazil but also not important. Parenting is viewed theoretically as a joint responsibility but, in fact, fathers have very little role. Mothers are with their children all the time. Even in the church, children's ministry is mostly women's work and they hurry the children out, for the important matters are for the adults, not the children.

Status of children

Children play a great part in Indian mythology and this is reflected in an important role in families and society. Parents accumulate wealth for generations to improve the lot of their children. Parents are especially keen to have their children receive assistance. But parents from lower castes see no value to education. Their attitude is very pragmatic. A large family is not viewed as more mouths to feed but as double the set of hands to bring in money.

In East Africa children are loved but ignored, particularly in the church. Children are important for security in old age and continuation of the family name. The number of children is a status issue. Women are known as "momma Kara", i.e. the mother of the child. There are cases in some areas where children are blamed for the family's continued poverty. They are accused of being sorcerers or witches and chased away from their homes. This is more often associated with 'New' churches.

In Southern Africa children are expected to be silent. Ancestor worship is still common, so the elders and the dead are consulted about everything, but children have no role.

In Africa, a son may not be allowed to look his father in the eye or allowed to speak directly to his father. There is a view that one is a child as long as one has a living parent! These attitudes may be taken into Christian ministry.

Children were linked to the social transformation of South Africa. in 1976 Soweto school children took a militant stand. The children were politicised and this still affects society. The change in world demographics means that South African children now represent a much larger proportion (before AIDS about 1 in 6) of all the world's children.

In Indonesia, children have more freedom to speak and may express their feelings but the child and adult worlds are vastly different. Javanese culture is dualistic, not between good and bad, but between smooth and refined, between coarse and rough. The spirit world belongs to the refined world, the physical to the coarse and rough. The objective is to move from the coarse world to the more refined world. The culture recognizes the three aspects of being: physical, spiritual, and soul. For the soul, one must discipline oneself to have a more refined soul, reflected in art and dancing. Asceticism is practiced to refine the spirit. Children are born into the unrefined world and are expected to move into the other world. This covers every area of life, for example, children use one language with each other and a different language to adults.

In the Philippines, daughters as young as six are given responsibilities at home: housework, looking after younger siblings etc. Sons have more freedom. Age discrimination is common: the children are given the chicken feet, wing, or head; the best parts are for grandfather, father, or other adult.

Gender and marriage

In East Africa, girls may be taken out of school to be married to an older person and many never even make it to school. Gender discrimination is common. The bride price custom gives girls some status. Most girls would be insulted if there was no bride price or if it was little. There are gender issues: the treatment and value given to boys and girls is often different but it differs greatly from tribe to tribe. In Nigeria girls may not be allowed to speak in the family and may not be educated. They do not share in the father's property and join their husband's group. There is a tribe in Ghana that would sacrifice the firstborn girl. Now it may not happen literally but it still happens mentally. Women are often not allowed to work because it is assumed that they would sleep around.

In India, discrimination is often gender-based: the boys eat and the girls remove their plates. The boys wouldn't even know how to hold a broom! If the household has only one egg it will always be given to the boys or men. Similarly, parents ask "Why should we send the girls to school?" When a girl becomes a woman in India, it is highly celebrated but her status is still low.

In Thailand today, children are generally very welcome. The parents own their children who are highly valued. Gender discrimination is prevalent: "Having a baby girl is like having a toilet in front of your house" but baby boys traditionally provide a path to heaven.

Rituals concerning children

The dualistic way of thinking in Indonesia manifests itself in ceremonies for childbirth and the naming of children. Names reflect the expectations of the parents. If the adults feel the given name turns out to be too ambitious or optimistic, the child's name may be changed. Sickly children may be sold to relatives in order to change their luck; birthdays are celebrated every 40th day (in conjunction with the solar and lunar cycles). The hopes that parents sometimes have for their children often cause them to "sacrifice" them: they go to the mountains where there are spiritual influences and perform certain rituals, making agreements with the demonic powers e.g. family wealth in exchange for one of the children. The child may become mentally handicapped or otherwise exploited for the benefit of the parents.

In Indonesia there is preference for the good-looking child and discrimination against the plain child. Pregnant women avoid looking at things that are ugly as this might make the baby ugly. Children born with disabilities are viewed in a very bad light; families are understood to have done something wrong. This causes a challenge of self-acceptance for children, especially those not so good-looking. This is true for both poor and wealthy families. Large families are welcome as they are understood to give protection, preserve family wealth and provide for the parents in old age – even if they cannot be properly supported.

In India, every child has a "history" and a story, kept by the Brahmins. There are other practices whose aim is to protect the child by confusing evil spirits: e.g. naming the child "garbage" or "rubbish". So the god comes to take the child and thinks, "Oh this child is only rubbish" and leaves without him or her. On the other hand, naming children after people in the Bible can be very powerful.

In South Africa, certain parts of the child's body are used for medicinal purposes: arms, brains, private parts, etc. Body parts may be put in front of the door for prosperity or success. In some tribes, a mother will tell her daughter not to show her teeth to men of another tribe. Sometimes, adult initiation requires killing a man from another tribe. When a child says something unexpectedly profound, it is assumed not to be the child speaking but the ancestors. The child may be treated as an adult because he or she is possessed by the 'Living Dead'. In the Eastern Cape a child prophesied the suicide of a whole clan. More positively, there was a revival which started through a little child praying.

Sexual Exploitation

In East Africa, child or temple slavery is common. Children are often sold for a family's debt and some never escape. It is very common to take a child into the extended family but taking in an unknown child is almost unheard of. There are daily stories in the papers of children being "defiled." The child is sent home, the teacher is transferred. Young virgins are even seen as a cure for AIDS.

Race groupings shaped all thinking in South Africa until 1994 and the different race groups still have their own cultures. Gangs are very common in Cape Town and the result is that adult prisons are full of children. The government is pumping a lot of money into street kid programmes etc, but not with passion or commitment. Because of AIDS children are heading families. They have no education and no future. There is a generation of illiterate children.

In Indonesia the use of boys for homosexual sex is thought to confer more power on the man. Homosexuality is increasing in the Philippines and is being linked to men not having an active role in raising their children. It is ironic: we say children are important, but we don't really mean it.

In Thailand, many families sell their daughters to the sex trade, even when very young. Girls may even sell themselves because of materialistic desires, mobile phones, make up, etc.

Every Indian is part of a caste (except Christians) and several castes are designated to be prostitutes. So they are expected to be prostitutes. Conditions are unspeakable but the government is not bothered. There are no sanctions or stigma and the police are part of the system of exploitation. Parents who cannot afford a dowry may sell girls to the temple for prostitution.

There are almost no controls on Brazilian TV programmes. The content is very sexually explicit and is shown all day. So children are exposed to sexual situations very early and start sexual activity very young. Parents even provide beds and condoms for their children in their own homes, thinking they are providing a safe place for their children to have sexual encounters. Brazilians feel it is one of their cultural features – they are sexual "somethings"!

Materialism

The main concern of Malaysian Chinese is survival as they cannot go back to China. Their children are part of the means: if they have a lot of children it indicates the family will survive. They are very westernized with a great desire for materialistic success. The Christian parents of a man wanting to go into Christian ministry told him: "you have to think about your stomach first." The firstborn is very important. He is expected to inherit the business of the family. Parents have to be very brave to allow children to pursue the Christian ministry.

Philippine culture is a mix of those who have colonized the country. In times past, children had playmates and played lots of games, helping in the socialization process. Now, many children have no friends at all. Their 'playmates' are electronic toys. Before, they would play together and would go as far as one kilometre from home without the parents worrying. Now, the parents are afraid of kidnapping, etc, so they keep the kids in the house with the television and their electronic toys.

Destruction of family life

There is a problem with street children all over Africa; in fact there are now whole street families who have never had any other home but the street. Why are they going onto the street? What can we do to stop it? It is not enough to help them on the streets. A suffering child may also be viewed as an asset, for example to a family for begging or to an NGO for fund-raising. Among the Muslim community there is a belief that there should be beggars on the street to allow others to fulfil the religious duty of almsgiving.

What is our reaction to the disintegration of the traditional family in Africa? In earlier times, no-one could honestly say: "I have no-one to feed me." Every older person was your father or mother; each child was your own. To what extent has or should the church replace the traditional family?

In a meeting of Christian leaders in Pretoria, one of the speakers blamed the collapse of family structures for the problem. "Normal" families no longer exist: in one area five years ago a survey revealed that less than 5% of parents were married. In the absence of parents, who shapes children? Perhaps the key formative influences are gang leaders and radio DJs. In fact, the person who controls the music controls the development of the community. Some years ago, research claimed that 80% of the adult character is formed by the age of three years. If this is so, how should it affect our theologising?

The notion of family in Africa is not just fragile, it is individualistic, isolationist and survivalist and there is no social infrastructure to pick up the pieces. Is the Gospel that is preached one that ignores African realities? Many children are in care because of abandonment and/or abuse by fathers; there is a huge crisis in parenting, particularly fatherhood.

There is much the church can do to counteract this and perhaps Child Theology has an important role to play but it could inadvertently contribute to the problem of family breakdown if it becomes too individualistic. One way to avoid this would be to discuss 'family theology', always seeing the child in the context of the family. A task for Child Theology is to consider what can be done to restore dignity to God's institution of the family.

Education

Traditionally, education in Africa was informal – the boys went with the men to learn men's things. School was not to educate children but to protect them – learning the taboos, the do's and the don'ts, (most of them are don'ts).

Apart from the French colonies, it was the Church that led the way in instituting formal education. The main problem these days is the idea of value-free education: we live in a human rights culture. Most such constitutions and policies are developed from humanistic assumptions. Society is raising materialistic children, with an ever-widening gap between (materially) rich and poor. In this process, children often have their childhood stolen from them. Does the church have a role in revising policies that affect children? If the church does not allow some to specialise in

Child Theology, who will address these issues on behalf of children? Our response must come out of our passion for God. Although we must respect African traditional culture, we must not give it the pre-eminence that belongs to Christ.

Child labour

This has become a prominent issue in the campaigns against globalisation and capitalism. But it is more than an international economic problem. For many families trapped in poverty the ability to gain an income from their children is a matter of survival. However, it is at best only a short-term solution as children lose out on an education that could enable them to become more prosperous.

The issue is exacerbated by companies, governments and families that view children as mere commodities or units of production. At its worst, it encompasses heavy or dangerous work that endangers health, causes stunted growth or even risks the life of the children it exploits. Local systems of bonded labour and slavery commonly connive with Western companies seeking cheap labour for competitive advantage.

The issue is complex because children like to imitate parents in their play. This includes the work that their parents do, perhaps in the house or on the family farm. This is part of their preparation for adulthood. Most adults get much of their sense of self worth from the work that they do. So, why deny children the same benefit? In a society of subsistence farming, where there are no other employment opportunities, work alongside the family on the family farm makes sense for most children. If 'development' is seen as a universal good, then an education that prepares for 'more productive' employment is a benefit only so long as such employment actually is available. The adult coming out of school or university with no employer needing his or her new skills and unable or unwilling to be productive on the land becomes a burden. He or she might migrate to the 'First World' to make up some of the skills shortages there!

Children working is not wrong *per se*. But they should not be expected to carry adult responsibility or to undertake work that puts their present or future life at risk. This implies, among other things, that it should not impair an appropriate education for them.

One project for street children trains the children for a lifetime of employment as part of a full education programme. They do real work: carpentry, metalwork, bakery etc. However, the (progressive!) law of the country forbids that they sell the children's produce. This would be seen as exploitation. Yet doesn't this devalue the work of the children? It would be much more 'progressive' if they were encouraged to earn money (better than begging or stealing) and to put the money that each child earns into an account that would be given to him/her when s/he leaves the project. In most cases, they have no family to help them get started in life.

CHAPTER NOTES

4   These are anecdotal responses given by participants and represent their own experiences and perspectives. They do not necessarily represent the views of CTM or well-researched opinion.

CHAPTER 9

A Child's Dream

ARIOVALDO RAMOS

TIAGUINHO (Jimmy) was seven years old when he showed up at our conversation program with street children. Certainly, he came because of the lunch, the possibility of having a decent meal.

We were drawn to him. He was alive, intelligent, talkative and seemed to have a resilient joy, the type that suffering cannot to destroy, at least not easily. He had left his house and presently was fighting for his space with others over one of the various mocós (hiding places of street children often in holes, construction sites, bridges, plazas and abandoned places) in the downtown of the city.

There are many cases in which the children go to the streets in search of sustenance but at the end of the day return to their houses. Tiaguinho had fled from an alcoholic father and desperate mother. He had fled from beatings, hunger and degradation. He did not want to return home. The street had turned into his home – there he didn't get beaten, he didn't need to see his father beating his mother and he did not have to do what he did not want to do.

Our boy was among those that were far from God. He was one of those victims of a scandal, about whom Jesus had warned in the sixteenth chapter of the Gospel of Matthew. He could no longer understand the significance of God as Father, because the figure of a father was violent. He could not understand the affirmation that 'God is Love', because everything he knew about 'love' was full of exploitation and abuse.

Tiaguinho was another victim of the urban world. His parents were migrant workers; those that leave home, thrown out by hunger, in the hope that in the city they will encounter economic and social liberty. On the other hand, when they arrived at the city they lost their identity, they were converted into numbers. And what these numbers tell about them is that they are unable to overcome the urban environment. And the city is relentless to those that falter.

The Stigma of the City

In the Old Testament, the city is under the stigma of being marked anti-God. It is principally the enemy of the rural world. The city was born, in the scriptures, under the stigma of insurrection and ends up becoming a paradoxical relationship. The first instance of this phenomenon is the city founded by Cain, which is given the name Enoch. This city is born under the sign of rebellion. Cain is a murderer whom God, instead of giving him the death penalty, punishes with a type of banishment: you will wander about the earth and the land will no longer produce. So that no one resorts to do justice with their own hands, he receives a sign by which all will know that he is under judgement from God and nobody should interfere. By creating a city, Cain not only goes against God's judgment, declaring that the protection God offered was insufficient, he also decides to take over the land that was denied him. Cain's city is as much the proclamation of independence from God as it is an imposition on the land, an aggression of the ecosystem instead of integrating ecologically with the land, becoming its servant and reconsidering his "ethos". Thus the city came about as a place centered on humanity and its rebellion towards God and the environment. It is the world in the image and likeness of the human being.

The city of Enoch was taken away by the flood and the next scenario is the City of Shinar. After the flood, humanity settled in the valley of Shinar. The objective was to resist God, who wanted humanity to spread throughout the planet, and to establish a new principle in history: human interest, another rebellion, independence from God reaffirmed. This city became a sign not only because of the disgrace that occurred there but because it became the urban paradigm in the scriptures. It received the name Babylon, the mother of all prostitutes. This city also inaugurated urban segregation, wars and social injustice. She is represented, at the end of the scriptures, as the place of political and economic injustice, as the worshipper of the market, an impersonal self-regulating god which trades in the abuse and autonomy (reification) of humankind. All those that profess faith in the Kingdom of God should leave! But it also appears in Jeremiah as the place where Judah goes to be punished and where they should pray for the enjoyment of peace. It is also the place where the Hebrew prophet interprets the dream of the pagan king about the succession of time.

Other cities appear in anguishing contexts: Sodom and Gomorrah were destroyed because of the oppression with which they treated their vassal states, because of the injustice that they inflicted on the poor and the needy and because in them there could not be encountered ten just people, from which the city could be refounded. Episodes like these tell us that there exists a judge in history. It is always good to remember that the iniquities were always connected with the contempt towards the poor and needy.

Nineveh, another symbolic city, in the first instance, receives a chance to repent because the number of children that it had but it succumbed too in a second judgment by fire, launched for the same reasons as Sodom and Gomorrah. Other cities could be cited with this paradox: Tyre and Sidon will be judged but they will receive in the last judgment more clemency than those cities that rejected the visits of the Apostles. Even cities irrevocably condemned, such as Jericho, know something of this. Although condemned for the atrocities practiced, principally against children, in the same city we find a prostitute that submits to the God of Israel and is saved.

The city with the most distinction is Jerusalem, guardian of the Ark of the Covenant and called the city of the great king. It is the city which the prophets cry over, Jesus of Nazareth being the greatest, proclaiming: "Jerusalem, Jerusalem, which kills her prophets and stones those that were sent, how many times have I wanted to gather you as a hen gathers her chicks, but you did not permit me". This is perhaps the most paradoxical of cities: it is a precious city but it will be sent into exile and will finally be destroyed. It will effusively receive the great king but it will also sacrifice him. Of all the cities it will receive the most promises and punishments but it is unique in that it is graced with the hope of resurrection, coming down from the heavens, becoming the eternal dwelling of the Eternal One.

Tiaguinho dreams of this converted city, where the Garden is in the center and gives tone to the life of the city. He dreams of the new reality described in Isaiah eleven, where a child leads, where its environment is completely beneficial and there are no restrictions, even the possibility that the child can without fear place his or her hand on the serpent. In this city, the simplicity of the child triumphs. It is a city for children, where the most adult-like are child-like. In a city like this, a child like Tiaguinho would learn to want to be a person and indeed be recognized as a person. This is the time when we learn to like to be people so that we can like people.

Tiaguinho dreams of a city where, as Zechariah 8:5 says, "The city streets will be filled with boys and girls playing there. (NIV)" For this to come about there needs to be a new paradigm for the administration of the city.

A Christian Project

According to Matthew 10: 42-45, "You know that those who are regarded as rulers of the Gentiles lord it over them, and their high officials exercise authority over them. Not so with you. Instead, whoever wants to become great among you must be your servant and whoever wants to be first must be slave of all. For even the Son of Man did not come to be served, but to serve, and to give his life as a ransom for many." (NIV)

Jesus Christ recommended a new society in which governmental power is exercised by serving all. Only in a society in which the governor assumes the role of servant for everyone can all be citizens and flourish. For society to fulfill its true vocation, in Christ's society power should be exercised in the following ways:

A society where the use of the land is regulated for the good of all. Isaiah 5:8 says God does not allow that someone could buy house after house and lot after lot until they are the only owner in the place. In Christ's society, the land would be divided among everyone for it is for everyone. This type of thing only happens when the governor is serving everyone.

A society where wealth is distributed with equality. That is, as the Apostle Paul says: God desires that those that harvest extra do not stay with it and those how harvest less do not lack, 2 Corinthians 8:15. A society with the consciousness of collectivity. Where the taxation would be the legitimate instrument for the redistribution of wealth. This only happens when the governor is serving everyone.

A society where the workers can use the wealth of their labor, as it is written: the worker is worthy of his salary, Luke 10:7, and "Do not muzzle the ox while it is treading out the grain", 1 Timothy 5:18. That is to say that the worker is the first to use what he produces. A society of workers for the workers. This only happens when the governor is serving everyone.

A society where the child has priority, for God does not want one of the little ones to perish and threatens harsh penalties on the society that leads children away from their divine provision: the provision of health, education, security, long life, work – that is a life that can be celebrated. This only happens when the governor is serving everyone.

A society where the orphans and the widows, those that have lost everything, do not remain without anything, just the opposite. Part of the production of society would be designated exclusively for them so that there would not be any misery in society. This only happens when the governor is serving everyone.

A society where the elderly are a reference of wisdom, never a weight. In the Bible the elderly are counselors that help the young on their journey and because of this are considered as mentors. They are those that preserve the values that should guide society. They should be honored, as citizens of excellence, who constructed and left success for the succeeding generations.

In the society that Christ recommended, the citizens are the state. Everyone is a citizen. That is why the governor must serve everyone. This signifies that the governor should be under the control of the citizen and human rights are respected carefully. Thus, the future of the citizen would be guaranteed. This foresight would do more than take care of health and the elderly. It would include schooling, security, work, recreation, to the end all that would have a quality life. In this society, the governor would be an agent of foresight. The future would not be something that is better the farther away it is but would be a succession of 'presents', where each day would bring the guarantee of a secure future.

There is nothing worse for Tiaguinho's dreams than a society that does not tackle the question of future security and human rights, which is not a society of citizens. Yes, now there are citizens but very few. The only citizens that are represented and whom the governor serves are those that hold economic power and finance the political class. For them there is no problem of future security or respect for their human rights because all their rights are already respected.

This generates an "apartheid": on one side you have the holders of economic power, on the other side the people. When it is said to the people that they also are citizens, in reality it is a falsity for their votes only legitimize what the few have already decided. The people vote but they cannot obligate those elected to represent them. The consequence is that they will never have their rights respected. Who respects those that only serve as a mass of manpower? And more, the vote of the people becomes subverted by the large marketing companies that elect someone who has no identification with the people, who through another marketing campaign will be able to legitimize all the desires of the dominant class.

During the term of these so called representatives, the people will have to swallow all kinds of falsities such as:

Privatization – the solution that no one explains. Good administration is for the health of the company but certainly not for the health of the employees.

State companies can only fulfill their social role with efficiency if they are profitable. State companies with a social role have to be efficient to be effective. The worker does not pay taxes so that the municipal transport company is profitable but that the he or she can be transported with dignity.

The great problem is inflation, never unemployment, misery, illiteracy, low salaries and hunger. But to resolve the inflation problem, there needs to be more unemployment, lower salaries, more misery and more hunger. The people give in and the problem never gets resolved.

There is never money for social problems and even less for social prevention.

Tiaguinho dreams of a miracle of power, to play on the streets and in

59

his house, and in the school! Not a supernatural miracle, but a miracle of conscientization, the miracle that opens the eyes.

Each worker, every marginalized person has to be conscious that 'the people' is a category that does not exist; either you are a citizen or you are nothing. Each one of them has to be aware that their rights are to be respected, so that the governor does not trick them with falsities. Each one needs to become a citizen. That is, he or she has to turn into someone that the governor has to serve, has to transform the obligation to vote into the right to vote, to vote only for those that pay attention. It is necessary that there be an electoral reform that makes it impossible for the elected to subvert the citizens. The category 'the people' has to be substituted by the category 'society' – a society of citizens where the law is for everyone. Where citizenship triumphs, the 'people' disappear and the citizen and society appear.

Oh, that this would be so in the Name of the Lord Jesus Christ!

Two visions
of the city

CHAPTER 10

Concepts and Practices that Label Children

THE FOLLOWING material derives from a discussion held at a Child Theology consultation[5]. One aim of the discussion was to compare the 'Kingdom of the World' with the 'Kingdom of God'. It was not simply to put them in opposition. It would have been relatively easy but too superficial to identify ways in which the secular adult world shapes vulnerable children and contrast them with a more compassionate child centred approach taught by Jesus. We wanted to open ourselves, as Christians and participants from a variety of religious and non-religious cultures, to whatever it was Jesus had in mind. We were and are aware that the differences we discerned were only provisional and so our brainstorming must continue.

1. To consider concepts and practices that place and label children; this included secular and religious words, practices and institutions;
2. To let the child be set in our midst, where Jesus placed him/her and to let our minds and imaginations be moved by attending to what God places before us. It seemed to us that the Gospel story (Matthew 18.2) deliberately omits mention of any defining characteristics of the child, so that it could be any child – like

the 'Unknown Soldier' it might have been you, me, my child, her child etc;

3. To find the matches and mismatches between our answers to 1 and 2. We expected to find that the ordinary cultural practice of the world is sometimes closer to and sometimes further from Jesus' teaching and that any particular practice includes both match and mismatch. Such is the complexity and ambiguity of life.

The method was, in practice, quite difficult to follow as many areas overlapped and interacted with each other in complex ways. For example, a culture in which children do not do more than deliver newspapers before the age of 12 is closer to Jesus than one in which they are sent up chimneys when they are five or six. But a culture where children do not work at all may be one where they are kept out of the adult world of reality and quickly corrupted into consumerist indulgence.

The results are impossible to describe simply. There were so many and various interconnections between the issues identified. The following is a combined summary of the results posted by the groups, with an attempt at categorisation to help the reader make cross-links. We realise that the following assertions are often generalisations that are only valid in part. However, we believe they represent widely held preconceptions and prejudices of which we should be aware because they affect our practice.

Concepts that place and label children

A place in a society

Children ask questions and adults need to have answers all the time! But they don't have all the answers - the world is changing so fast. So parents often abdicate responsibility to governments who tend to emphasise cognitive development. Even social, emotional and relational development may be neglected, never mind spiritual development. In democratic capitalist societies, persons are sometimes valued as mere economic entities: producers, consumers or burdens. This is mediated principally by education systems which are a function of economic structures, preparing children for a productive role in the economy. But this is aided and abetted by:

advertising which targets children to develop 'brand loyalty', the better to be exploited as adults;'

peer pressure: group identity among children is exploited to sell goods.

The approach to learning is often mechanistic – as if children were like computers where consistent input leads to predictable output but – beware GIGO[6]!

Sophisticated economies require increasingly skilled operatives which requires that education is prolonged. This has an impact at both ends of childhood:

hideously early nursery education;

adulthood is deferred beyond sexual maturity creating the 'not-child, not-adult' world of adolescence.

The concept of children as objects rather than relational beings:

soldiers: "Because they don't feel things as adults do you can train them to do things;"

sponges: empty vessels needing our input to become someone; even in the church they are often taken to be spiritually passive, recipients as opposed to actors.

The educational objective is often subverted merely to enculturate the child in the dominant society's value system and its prejudices. This may also occur even, or perhaps especially, in churches. As one participant observed: if you are Croat, you are a Catholic; if you're not Catholic, you're not a good Croat.

A place of his/her own

The world is a dangerous place so, while it is generally accepted that respect demands that children be accorded a proper 'place' in society, the practical consequences are fraught with difficulties, ambiguities and con-tradictions. So, for example, they are helpless, vulnerable and ignorant and need protection. So children are recipients rather than givers and their play and their worlds are relegated to the margins.

The prevailing individualism of western culture finds value in the 'uniqueness' of each child. Each child is placed on a pedestal. But this overlooks the other truth that children also share common characteristics.

63

Children have rights and must be prepared to challenge the adult world (even when adults are scared to!) Yet we still hear that "Children should be seen and not heard." Is talk of questioning the adult world simply a politicization of childhood?

The transition to adulthood is not clearly defined. In some ways, mental development is the key – even in their twenties, adults with learning difficulties are treated as children. At other times, financial independence may be the key – frequently (Philippines; Indonesia) children marry and have children but are still helped financially by the parents so they are still considered children. But street children often support themselves and are not adults. The place of residence may be the key. While living at home with parents, they may be considered children, even divorced people who return to live with their parents and married couples who are unable to afford a home of their own. And back of all these, there is the driving power of biological development which occurs whatever adults may say. For many if not most, puberty finishes their own childhood, whatever society says.

A place in the church

Do children have a place in the church before conversion? The church uses the concept of an 'Age of accountability' before which the child is not responsible before God. Is there a solid scriptural foundation for this?

A practical outcome is that a Christian vision statement for a ministry to children can state an aim of enabling "[children] to become fulfilled Christian adults." But apparently not fulfilled Christian children!

Characteristics of the 'Child in the Midst'

Capacity

We think of ourselves as the observers: assessing children but they also watch and observe, returning our gaze.

We are familiar with the idea that children may know more about some things than their parents, such as computers, but could they have other insights and abilities that we overlook?

We know that children like stories, but what if the child appreciates the meaning in ways that adults cannot, being able to accept and respond to mystery?

How do children define themselves? Children have different levels
of articulation, etc. They do not necessarily see themselves as
being in any way incomplete

Children are incredibly resilient and adaptable. They find ways of
coping with appalling adversity. Would we let them help us in a
crisis?

Relationships

The way children relate to each other is in some ways a model for
adults. They can often relate across cultures and languages
without difficulty.

They need attention and acknowledgement as persons. They are
often excluded for no good reason; rejection and neglect are
disabling.

They are often trusting and uncomplicated, so it's especially
harmful when their trust is broken. But when children from the
favelas are less dependent and less trusting, are they less
children?

They, like anyone else, need a safe place, physically and socially.

Is innocence a characteristic of childhood? They can also be
naughty, and like to test the limits

They are often sincere and speak frankly, without pretence: "you
look ugly today!"

They can take responsibility for things that go wrong, and do so,
even inappropriately. Maybe God can speak to us through the
child, challenging us to take responsibility

Faith

The 'child in the midst' has a relationship with Jesus.

They are willing to ask God for the impossible.

They often express their feelings honestly to God.

Children are often better dealing with grace: while adults are
analysing it, children are simply happy to accept unconditional
love.

But are there matters of faith which are beyond the child? If so,
what are they?

Do "handicapped" children represent most accurately how adults
are to God?

Activity

Children like (and need) to play.

Even life itself is a game, unstructured, not following accepted
rules but quickly making their own rules and expecting them to
be followed!

They often act out adult roles.

They are curious and like to explore often making sense out of
something unfamiliar.

Match and Mismatch

We used these characteristics to perform an 'audit' of the responses to
children by our various societies and cultures. We found places where the
culture seemed to 'fit' well but other places where it pinched like an ill-
fitting shoe.

These were some of the things brought out as matches and mis-
matches (note: 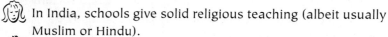 = match; = mismatch):

Education

In India, schools give solid religious teaching (albeit usually
Muslim or Hindu).

Western education often leaves no space for religious
instruction.

In the west, Christians develop alternatives, e.g. home
schooling.

But some opt for the easier short-term solution of making the
child fit the system.

Adults assume they know the meaning but offer children a
hopeless world.

Childhood

We encourage and recognise creativity and curiosity,
empowering children to flourish.

We label the same intrinsic drive as 'naughty' etc. and prefer
children who are passive, harmless, and not disruptive.

Play is squeezed out of children's life with the quest for success
in education.

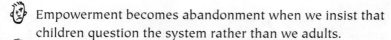

Empowerment becomes abandonment when we insist that children question the system rather than we adults.

Indonesian traditional societies have definite rituals for the transition to adulthood, usually around puberty (12–14 years).

In westernised groups, adulthood follows education and is not clear – at end of high school or University? lack of clarity breeds insecurity and rebellion.

We need to try to identify the values that underlie 'needs' and 'rights' language.

How can this be done without oppressively denying freedom?

Economics

Play and articles of play have become commodified and need to be bought.

Women in Sierra Leone need children if they are to beg successfully on the streets. They can't afford to allow the children to go to school.

Children's fashion. Children are made into little adults. They have their childhood taken from them. Toddler girls wearing bikinis – is this innocent imitation of mother or pressure to be adult?

Parental guilt for their busyness and lack of availability leads to them buying unnecessary things for their children.

Spirituality

There is a romanticised view of children as innocent 'angels' but "The children I work with throw their fish curry and they lie and cheat."

Some ideas of 'Original Sin' and the need to make a personal decision affect attitudes to the evangelism of children so that children are seen primarily as souls needing salvation. We may seem to make more of human choices than the reality of the love of God.

In the Old Testament, the child was viewed as part of the community of faith simply by virtue of having been born into the "household of faith" and the emphasis was on a growing faith relationship to God.

67

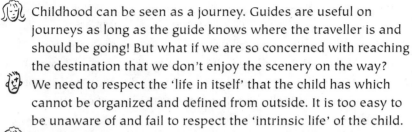

Childhood can be seen as a journey. Guides are useful on journeys as long as the guide knows where the traveller is and should be going! But what if we are so concerned with reaching the destination that we don't enjoy the scenery on the way?

We need to respect the 'life in itself' that the child has which cannot be organized and defined from outside. It is too easy to be unaware of and fail to respect the 'intrinsic life' of the child.

We often assume that children are irresponsible, but look at child headed households! It is true that childhood is taken away but at the same time the children demonstrate that they can be responsible.

Relationships

It is important to remember the family context, which is prominent in both Old and New Testaments. The cult of individualism takes children out of the family, emphasising children's rights against those of parents.

Churches are often seen as places of judgement where there is little grace.

But they can be and should be seen as places of safety.

Organizations can be oppressive and a 'power thing', where the focus is on escaping misery not finding freedom.

But organizations often are liberating and humanizing; whose aim is to put children into community, because freedom is in relationships.

Sometimes our organisations are so rigid there is no freedom not to conform to the system.

Sometimes expectations of parents are unrealistic – the 'perfect parents' required by church and state cannot be delivered!

The place we give to children in the church may be tokenistic and patronising.

CHAPTER NOTES

5 Penang, June 2002
6 Garbage In = Garbage Out

Interlude: Trust Home

JOHN COLLIER

I WAS on the bus travelling to Pokhara to visit one of my favourite places. A place that, more than any other I have seen at the time of writing, embodies in a practical way the values that Child Theology holds dear.

Two or three hours out of Kathmandu, the bus swerved off the road and came to a halt. I had been warned of the hazards – landslides, accidents, requests for a 'donation' by Maoists. I had seen buses that had made sudden involuntary stops – having left the road altogether, they lay at dramatic angles peering down the steep hillside to the beckoning waters of the river below. But it seemed our stop was scheduled – it was time for breakfast! In terraces up the hillside behind the parked buses, I could see a garden and food stalls steaming in anticipation of the travellers. Even now, knowledgeable travellers had alighted and were heading for the loos! Soon a queue had formed and only the first few would have any chance of a sliver of soap to wash their hands afterwards. The idea of washing hands with soap as well as water was one I had been trying, without much success, to implant in the minds of the poor children of Nepal. I decided to leave the loos until later and headed up for a cup of hot spiced tea. With a view to staying healthy (and avoiding the toilets!), I avoided the rice and curry and made do with a packet of biscuits.

At Pokhara, I made my way out of town to a spot where the houses gave way to rice paddy fields shining emerald green with the new spring growth. Along a small lane I came to a sign:"Good Shepherd English Medium School". Turning in by a rusty iron gate, I came to a two storey

69

house set among the fields. Children ran up to greet me and help with my bags. After the long 6 hour bus ride, the peace replacing the insecurity and the order following the uncertainty outside were especially welcome.

"Trust Home" is more than a name. It is a real home to 65 boys and girls, all from broken Tibetan refugee families, in which trust is a way of life. What impresses me each time I visit is that it is a home, not an institution – a home reposing among peaceful rice fields, watered by rapid running streams from the graceful nearby sheltering forms of Himalayan Machhapuchhare and the Annapurnas.

Many orphanages aspire to create a homely atmosphere and no doubt several achieve it but there is something special about this one. I've been coming here for three or four years following the original invitation to do health checks on the children in the home and also those in the school that was attached to it. It was one of these school children that I had diagnosed as an early case of TB and had since been successfully treated in the local hospital. This reassured me of the value of even my rusty medical skills after having spent so much time in medical research administration. My clinics were necessarily very basic, not having X-ray, laboratory, pharmacy, surgery etc. Even so, they seemed to be appreciated and I keep coming once a year.

But, apart from the usual infected wounds and sores common in active children (in a country where soap seems to be a luxury item), the children at the home were remarkably healthy compared to others I had seen in villages in Nepal. I first began to appreciate the difference at the home when Dolma, the mother and founder of the home, invited me to join the children for their devotions at 6.30am.

Early the next morning, bells started ringing signals to sleepy children. Someone started practising on drums. I could hear children's feet running to and from the bathrooms and voices calling to each other. Eventually, by 6.30, the voices and drums coalesced into a recognisable worship song. Dutifully and sleepily, I turned up, realising that I'd be asked to share a thought from the Bible. Not my best time of day! The first surprise was that Dolma was nowhere to be seen. Nor her husband Arjun. Nor any of the staff. I suppose I had expected that one of them would be leading the service and would introduce me. But worship was happening, spontaneously led by the children. The children sat on the floor, girls to the left and boys to the right, the dog lying alternately with boys or girls!

I sat on a bench at the back of the large sparsely furnished room. Shortly after, Dolma joined me on the bench. One of the children ran and brought me a song book. I opened it but the songs were mostly in Nepali and Tibetan – not a lot of help to me! One of the children would start a song and the others would join in. If the song required, two of the smaller children, a boy and a girl, would jump up and run to the front on each side and lead the others in the actions. Some did it seriously as if a sacred duty but probably just concentrating hard to get it right. Others did it with a broad grin, the girls with their straight black hair tied in bunches and the boys with short cropped hair. The song finished, they would run back into their places on the floor – sometimes only to pop up again if the next song also needed an action leader. At some point, one of the children would lead in prayer and perhaps others follow. And then, as if by a hidden signal, the heads would all turn round and look at me sitting on the bench at the back – my time to share a word of encouragement.

Worship over, there would be time for chores as school starts quite late. Some would be in the food hall with a mug of hot sweet milky tea learning homework off by heart. Others might be sweeping out the bedrooms or tidying in the garden, washing clothes in the stream, helping with food preparation and so on. Each one had a responsible job to do.

'Sunday worship' in Nepal happens on Saturday. So the worship time starts later and the children are joined by staff and several adults from the locality. Again, I was interested to see that even on this public occasion, all was led by the children. This time, the lectern on a small raised stage was used and one of the older children stood behind it helping to lead the meeting. Some of the younger children took up an offering. When the time came for teaching from the Bible, one of the adults had been prepared to do this. As we broke up at the end of the meeting, I noticed a small group of children on the floor busy with something. As I approached, I found that they were counting the offering money. This group was responsible for the money at the home. This was revolutionary to me. I had been in churches and homes where children were given jobs to do but generally they were kept well away from the money, as if it were something too important for children! In fact, in most if not all churches I've been part of children were given jobs with little or no responsibility so that if they failed, it wouldn't make any difference to the running of the institution. In this way the subtle message is given that children will fail. Actually, they will, just as adults do!

So how does this home 'work'? Can children really be given significant responsibility without taking away their childhood? I was keen to discover more of the inner workings of the home but before exploring this, first it is useful to learn the history of the home because this illustrates its founding principles, learned from precarious experience not from a textbook.

Dolma's Story

In 1959 the Chinese communist army invaded Tibet. Only about 6 or 7 years old, Dolma fled on her mother's back, crossing through snowy Himalayan mountain passes into Nepal. As they left with many other refugees, they became separated from her father and to this day she doesn't know if he is alive or where he might be. Her mother was a carpet weaver. They were both Tibetan Buddhists and her mother was particularly careful to teach Dolma their faith.

They survived by hiding during the day and walking at night. Eventually, they crossed the border into the Mustang province of Nepal. They stayed there for four years or so and then moved down to Pokhara to the Tibetan refugee camp set up by the UN.

At first her mother worked as a carpet weaver but it was clear that she was ill with TB and by 1967 she was unable to work. They were able to get medicine from the INF hospital in Pokhara. With her mother incapacitated, Dolma got work as a nurse aid in the hospital, along with six other Tibetan girls. She remembers hearing about Jesus but did not accept this new faith. About six months later, her mother died. In 1971, the 'Chinese' Dalai Lama came to Pokhara and all the Tibetan girls were dying to catch a glimpse of him but the INF wouldn't give them the time off. So they all resigned their jobs and went anyway! But they didn't see anything because of the crowds and security. When they went back, INF forgave them and took them back but docked them one month's pay. They were overjoyed to get their jobs again.

In 1972, it was discovered that Dolma also had a TB, in her case affecting her hip. She was treated for 7 months at the "Shining Hospital"

(INF) in Pokhara but she needed more specialist help and was sent up to Kathmandu. She needed a screw put in her leg and spent 5 months with her leg in plaster. Although she had some family there on her father's side, they didn't come to visit her and she felt quite alone. She was in hospital for two years and, with no family visiting, she became very depressed. But a missionary couple with UMN, Mr and Mrs John Dore, began to visit her every couple of days. They brought food, changes of clothes and so on. They also gave her a Bible but Dolma didn't want anything to do with it. She felt that if God was as good as this couple were saying, why had he allowed her country and family to be taken away from her? She felt she wanted to die. "I don't like to pray," she said, "who listens to my prayer?" The couple said that God had sent them to show her that God's love was real.

One day, wanting to know if God really existed, she asked "If you are Lord, today, you speak to me." Opening her Bible at random, she found herself looking at Isaiah 60:15-22:

"Although you have been forsaken and hated, with no-one travelling through, I will make you the everlasting pride and the joy of all generations. You will drink the milk of nations and be nursed at royal breasts. Then you will know that I, the LORD, am your Saviour, your Redeemer, the Mighty One of Jacob. Instead of bronze I will bring you gold, and silver in place of iron. Instead of wood I will bring you bronze, and iron in place of stones. I will make peace your governor and righteousness your ruler. No longer will violence be heard in your land, nor ruin or destruction within your borders, but you will call your walls Salvation and your gates Praise. The sun will no more be your light by day, nor will the brightness of the moon shine on you, for the LORD will be your everlasting light, and your God will be your glory. Your sun will never set again, and your moon will wane no more; the LORD will be your everlasting light, and your days of sorrow will end. Then will all your people be righteous and they will possess the land for ever. They are the shoot I have planted, the work of my hands, for the display of my splendour. The least of you will become a thousand, the smallest a mighty nation. I am the LORD; in its time I will do this swiftly." (NIV)

That day in 1974, she accepted Jesus as her Saviour.

After leaving hospital in Kathmandu, she returned to Pokhara and started work again in the hospital, at first two hours a day. Six years later (1980), to the consternation of her church, she married Arjun, the brother of a friend and a Nepali man from a rich family but not a Christian. This also caused quite a lot of problems with his high caste Hindu family. As she was a Christian and a Tibetan, she was very low caste and the family refused to have anything to do with her. For 9 years, she wasn't allowed into their house. She left the INF hospital and went down to the India/Nepal border where her husband was working as an engineer. They had a daughter and, as is the custom, at 11 days old they went for the naming ceremony but her husband's family refused to allow their name to be given to the child. Her husband was broken hearted. The church stepped in and offered to give their child a name. Although her husband was anti-Christian, he allowed this and the daughter was given a Christian name. A year and a half later, a son was born and the same thing happened. So he also got a Christian name.

When the boy was 4 years old, he developed a brain tumour and they had to take him to a Christian hospital in the Punjab for treatment which took 4 months. During this time, Arjun found a book in the hospital book-shop, written by a converted Muslim, which warned against the Bible saying that reading the Bible from beginning to end would change your mind. So he did and it did! He did accept Christ but, nevertheless, their son died shortly after. He was encouraged by the hospital padre who told him that he would meet his son again in heaven.

Naturally, Dolma was very happy at her husband's decision yet she was devastated by the loss of her son. She became depressed again. She prayed: "If you give life to me, I will serve you." Then she began to realise that there were many children in the streets who could be like 'sons and daughters'. She also began to ask why there were so many missionaries going to Nepalis but none to Tibetans. A leader told her that she could work among her own people. Dolma doubted this as she didn't have any education. Instead, she was expecting God to send someone else. She again opened the Bible at random for guidance and her finger settled on Esther 4:12-14:

"When Esther's words were reported to Mordecai, he sent back this answer: 'Do not think that because you are in the king's house you alone of all the Jews will escape. For if you remain silent at this time, relief and deliverance for the Jews will arise from another place, but you and your father's family will perish. And who knows but that you have come to royal position for such a time as this?' " (NIV)

A woman also pointed her to Jeremiah 1:4-10:

The word of the LORD came to me, saying, "Before I formed you in the womb I knew you, before you were born I set you apart; I appointed you as a prophet to the nations." "Ah, Sovereign LORD," I said, "I do not know how to speak; I am only a child." But the LORD said to me, "Do not say, 'I am only a child.' You must go to everyone I send you to and say whatever I command you. Do not be afraid of them, for I am with you and will rescue you," declares the LORD. Then the LORD reached out his hand and touched my mouth and said to me, "Now, I have put my words in your mouth. See, today I appoint you over nations and kingdoms to uproot and tear down, to destroy and overthrow, to build and to plant." (NIV)

God also spoke to her through Ezekiel 2:4-10:

The people to whom I am sending you are obstinate and stubborn. Say to them, 'This is what the Sovereign LORD says.' And whether they listen or fail to listen – for they are a rebellious house – they will know that a prophet has been among them. And you, son of man, do not be afraid of them or their words. Do not be afraid, though briers and thorns are all around you and you live among scorpions. Do not be afraid of what they say or terrified by them, though they are a rebellious house. You must speak my words to them, whether they listen or fail to listen, for they are rebellious. But you, son of man, listen to what I say to you. Do not rebel like that rebellious house … . (NIV)

At this time, she was visiting all the Tibetan refugee camps, not knowing what to do. In 1996, she was given her first child: an unwanted baby born to a teenage mother and no known father. After a year, she had six such children, given to her in the camps. Her husband was still working on the **75** border with India and supporting her. So she rented three rooms to look after the children. Soon, she had 24 or more children in six rented rooms. It was a very old (and cheap) house and the roof leaked whenever it rained. She didn't know what to do as she had no training or experience. So she asked the children to pray with her.

Someone in America heard about her work, though she had never met him, and a letter came asking how much she needed. He sent $45,000 to buy land and in 2000 the hostel was built. The donor eventually came out to see the land. Later, another Christian leader who had come to Pokhara for a conference heard the story and visited her. Before returning to the USA, he gave her NPR500 (about £4). Three months later, she had a call from a man who said "I have your support." This was out of the blue and she told him he had the wrong number. He rang again and she said the same. Eventually, she found out the money was for her and this person has continued to support 30 children for several years.

How children fit in

I spoke to Dolma and Arjun about the roles and tasks of the children and also discussed the same issues with several of the older children. A key principle for Dolma is that the children are not just recipients of care. In one sense, the home belongs to God – it has all been given by grace and Dolma and Arjun trust God for all their needs. As far as the practical arrangements on earth, the home belongs to the children. Ownership has been transferred to a charitable trust so that when Dolma and Arjun go to give account of their stewardship before God, there needs to be no transfer of ownership. And to prepare for the time when they are no longer able to be actively involved, the children are already learning to take responsibility for the running of the home. Two of the older children, one boy and one girl, are attending college to study management and the intention is that they will become houseparents in due time. Dolma has considered the alternative that she has seen elsewhere, of hiring managers but the trouble with this is that it's difficult to find people with real commitment and vision. Being a parent is different from having a career. She saw one home where they had had seven different parents over 11 years. This is not good for a family or a child.

Children are involved in every aspect of the day-to-day affairs of the community. There are three or four paid staff who prepare meals, do some cleaning, etc but the children are involved in supervising them. Children are given special tasks from about the age of 11 or 12 but even the small ones have a job to do according to their ability. They are not pushed into responsibility but come forward. When they have a particular interest, they are expected to shadow the child responsible for that task. So this means that all the leaders have two or three helpers. Here are some of the various groups and roles:

Finance – one of the older girls controls the accounts for the home. Usually there are two children involved, this is always preferable where money is concerned, but at the time I was there, one of the helpers had moved on and another was being prepared to help. These children would be responsible for purchases of food, clothes, paying school fees etc and would keep an account of income and expenditure.

Pocket money and tithes – They give a lump sum each week to another child who is responsible for distributing pocket money and the tithe offering money to the children each week. Each child has a named envelope in which to give the tithe money. She keeps a record of the money the children give and also the collection at the Saturday open worship service. The money collected in this way is given to poor families as decided by the children's committee.

New building – at the time I was discussing this, the home was in the process of constructing a new hostel for the older boys, so that adolescent boys and girls could sleep in separate buildings. One of the older boys is responsible for supervising this work and seeing that the salaries of the building labourers are paid and that they are reimbursed for building materials. He told me that he checks how many workers come each day and calculates how much they should be paid. He gets this money from Arjun and hands out the payments to each worker.

Pastoral care – although Arjun and Dolma are always available, some of the children are shy and prefer to discuss their problems with the older children. Dolma encourages this and

77

any serious matter would be passed on to her. When children first arrive at the Home, Dolma spends a lot of time getting to know them. She meets them face-to-face in her room two or three times a week to understand their background. This continues as long as she feels necessary, until the child has settled, and it may last as long a s a year.

Medical care – two of the older girls run a small 'clinic' each day where prescription medicines are handed out and first aid treatment is given. One of the girls who had been doing this before is now training to be a nurse. The two girls responsible for this discuss difficult cases together and take them to Arjun or Dolma if needed. They told me they really enjoy being able to serve in this way.

Spiritual life – two older children have the responsibility of teaching the little ones how to pray and worship. They will teach the songs and the any actions that go with them. They meet on Fridays in a group of about 20. One of the leaders told me that she found it quite discouraging at first because the young children were disobedient but God spoke to her through the scriptures about the importance of training younger children and so she carries on. She started this role when she herself was just 12 years old and has been doing it for 6 or 7 years. "When we were small, Aunty and Uncle taught us how to pray and worship God. Now it's our turn to help the younger ones."

Care Groups – there are eight groups, four for boys and four for girls, divided according to age: 4-7 years; 8-12 years; 13-16 years; 16 + years. Some of those in the oldest group are leaders of the groups for younger children. These groups meet for fellowship every night after the evening devotions. In these groups they learn the memory verse for the week, discuss what happened during the day and pray for each other. These groups are foundational in integrating new children into the culture of the home and establishing the values and norms of behaviour. For this reason, any new children joining the home first join one of the groups for the youngest children. Although they might be meeting with much younger children, they are prepared for this and it is explained that it is a temporary arrangement because they have a lot to learn – how to pray, the worship songs and practical things like how to use the toilet, brush their teeth and wash themselves.

Devotional times – there are morning and evening devotions every day. On some days, there are special activities. For example, on Friday nights, everyone in turn has to recite the memory verse for the week. On Sunday nights, there is a time when children can share the blessings they have experienced from God. Monday evenings are given over to special prayer – for the supporters of the home, for their families, for Tibet, etc. Saturday night is a talent night. Children prepare and share a drama, a song or other musical item, either individually or in a group with friends.

Children's Committee – there is a committee of four older girls and two older boys. This is not democracy! The children are chosen rather than elected and are mostly chosen from among the early residents who are well versed in the ways of the home. Decisions are always made by consensus. They keep talking and praying until they agree. They never vote on an issue. They meet about once a month and discuss the running of the home. They prepare the food menus. For something like this, they would gather the views of the younger children before deciding. They may discuss any problems being experienced with particular children. They are also responsible for preparing the cleaning rota. Children are responsible for cleaning their own rooms and every day there will be something that has to be cleaned. The committee will also take care that the children are doing their school homework properly.

Clothing – one of the girls is responsible for giving out clothes to the children. For example, if a child thinks he needs new shoes, he will come to her and she will decide if he really needs them. If so, she will hand out shoes from the clothing store that she manages. She told me that the other children always accept her decision! She lets Dolma know when new clothes need to be bought.

Other stores – another girl runs the general stores: snacks, toothpaste, stationery, etc. Children come to her and tell their needs. If she thinks they really need it, she hands it out. Although she has official 'opening hours' the children tend to come at other times too which makes this job quite demanding.

Kitchen – one of the girls is responsible for supervising the kitchen staff. She will ensure that they don't reheat old food or throw leftovers into the water canal. Children sometimes help with the kitchen work, especially during school holidays and on Monday nights when they cook Tibetan food. This is one of several ways the home has for the children to learn about their own Tibetan culture even though they are living in the midst of a quite different Nepali culture.

Building maintenance – Arjun is teaching three or four of the older boys about plumbing and electrical maintenance. There are some safety issues but simple tasks like changing light bulbs are within their capability.

Garden – the garden is Dolma's hobby but three of the boys help her with the work. It mostly grows flowers but some fruit and vegetables are grown too.

Laundry – the general laundry work is done by paid staff but on Saturdays the children are responsible for washing their own clothes. Dolma checks the washing lines to see how well this is done. She may give some items to the staff to rewash but if it is repeated, she will take the child aside and give some tuition on how to wash clothes properly.

Problems

When you have a group of people from traumatic backgrounds, there are bound to be problems and Trust Home has its fair share of behavioural difficulties. It's not always the newest or youngest children that are challenging. One girl of 21, who had been at Trust Home for seven years, was full of anger and was always hitting younger children. Some of the older girls had tried to help her and Dolma also became involved in counselling her. Dolma called her mother to come and speak to her but nothing helped. She had had a difficult life before coming to the home. She had worked as a servant since the age of six. She might have been intellectually less able as she had had to repeat her school year twice, in spite of studying hard. Given her age, it was felt best that she return home to her mother.

There was a similar problem with another younger boy who had come to the home age 3 and a half. His mother was still a teenager and there was no father in sight. His first question was: "Where's my father?" He had been taunted even at such an age that he had no father. He also was full of anger, hitting the other boys. Counselling and punishments didn't help him. Eventually, he became quite sick and the girls explained to him that his anger would make it worse. Eventually, with persistence he settled and is now doing well.

Another type of problem is stealing. One boy would steal money but also especially food. He would steal food from the bags of other children. Punishments and counselling were of no use. His behaviour was so disruptive that eventually Dolma thought she would have to send him back to his mother but by then both parents had disappeared. In desperation, she cried out to God for insight. She received this idea. Taking him to the storeroom, she threw open the door and said, "Samuel, take what you like. It's not mine. It's all yours." He looked up at her and crying said, "I've been very naughty." After this he settled down and had the confidence to trust that all his needs would be met.

The difference

The children told me "The main thing is that we learn from the work we do." When I asked what makes Trust Home special, they told me "It's not a hostel, it's a home. In other hostels, they don't do it like this." (They meet children from other homes and orphanages in the local schools.) Another child told me that it's the family they have that makes it special. She believes that each child has been called to the home by God. Though most of the children have at least one parent, from day to day they care for each other, even when one is sick.

A major test

Recently, there was a major test concerning the finances of the home which displayed to me the special, perhaps unique, trust in each other and in God that characterises this community.

It came to light that the major financial supporter of the home, a Christian from a wealthy foreign nation, had been raising money fraudulently. There were also other issues concerning his attitude that conflicted with the community's sense that the home very much was God's own work. The issue culminated in a vexing letter that this person sent to Arjun and Dolma. Typically, they shared this letter with the children. (I asked Dolma if they kept any secrets from the children and the answer was that generally no, they don't. The exception is that they do not discuss sexual matters with the younger children.)

The children took the letter away and spread it before God, praying over it. They returned and told Arjun and Dolma that the home should no longer accept money from this source. Accordingly, this was communicated to the donor. It was a painful break with someone who had been a great support over several years. But how would the large monthly sum of money be replaced? It amounted to some thousands of dollars. The whole community and other supporters joined in prayer and God provided. Not only were the existing commitments met but it was possible from the funds received to start work on the pressing need for a new boys' dormitory and training centre.

Trust Home lived up to its name, trusting each other but, most of all, trusting the God who provides.

Part Three
OUR
RESOURCES

OVER MANY years, there has been an outpouring of love and concern from churches in response to the plight of children such as those described in the previous section. From the earliest days, the church has established orphanages, schools and hospitals. Recently, large Christian organisations have established significant ministries to children at risk but, for the most part, the Christian response has been uncoordinated and mediated through small 'one off' projects. Though these are often under-resourced and overlooked, in aggregate they make a major impact.

At least in the western world, it has taken longer for secular organisations to respond to the needs of children. Indeed, the case has been made that recognition of childhood happened relatively recently, in the last 300 years or so. Previously, children seemed to move straight from infancy to mini-adulthood – often married at a young age and helping in the home, farm or cottage industry. It is often supposed that Jesus grew up in this way, helping his father from childhood in the carpenter's shop and taking over the family business, perhaps as an adolescent, to support the family when Joseph died.

But now there are many organisations that seek to help children, many professing no religious motivation. In fact, some of these were started by Christians, in an age and culture when Christian affiliation was taken for granted, but have become secularised in the succeeding years along with the secular drift of the prevailing culture. They continue to serve the needs of children and often are very well funded by governments, businesses etc. perhaps in part because of their avoidance of potentially contentious religious affiliation.

As we attempt to develop a specifically Christian response to the situation of children, we do well to take stock of the resources at our disposal. In this, I am not thinking of physical resources such as the homes, orphanages, clinics, feeding centres and the like, which undoubtedly are of great value in our ministry to children. Over and above the material resources, we have a whole range of assets in the Christian tradition which taken together give us a God's eye view of the problem we are trying to solve or ameliorate.

The need is so great that it is tempting just to roll up our sleeves and get on with the work at hand, helping as we can. I readily understand the impatience of those who shrink from talking, seemingly incessantly and to little practical effect, while children are dying. But before we embark on building our organisations and material structures we should reflect carefully on the insights these resources offer us. And, if we are already up to our eyes in relief and development work, we should regularly programme into our diaries time aside to reflect on 'God's way of doing things' while we are helping.. Child Theology is a brilliant tool in helping us to do just that. In this way, perhaps we will be more likely to reflect God's values, priorities and methods than if we rush in with our best idea, which might possibly be unconsciously modelled, for good or ill, on secular approaches.

However, there is a lot that secular analyses can contribute to our response and we should remember that there have been many Christians working out their faith in these secular disciplines. The most notable, in the sense of being the largest and most recognised by the secular world, has been the development of the Convention on the Rights of the Child (CRC) sponsored by the United Nations and the work of UNICEF. Chapter 11 gives a brief overview of the development of the CRC.

Chapter 12 describes an analysis, based on sociological and psychological insights, that has been worked out in a Christian setting. Following the description of this analysis, the 'Comments and Questions' section suggests some issues that require further attention for this to be a wholly Christian and Biblical approach to children's needs.

These secular analyses and descriptions are a resource for us but we reckon that we do well to give Scripture pride of place. We turn to the Bible in chapter 16. First we discuss some general issues of interpretation and then proceed to overviews of some Biblical material relating to children in chapters 17 and 18. More detailed expositions of two Bible passages are offered: – Psalm 8 in chapter 19 and Matthew 16 to 21 in chapter 20.

As we study the Bible it must always be contextualised. We do this in two ways: looking at the past and the present. Firstly, we remind ourselves of the present contexts in which children live and that we should also be ready to learn from them (Chapter 15). Secondly, we put the Bible into historical contexts – both of theological discussions and formulations and of practical caring projects. Chapter 13 begins with an overview of the way children have been addressed in Christian history and the value of that history to us now is discussed in Chapter 14.

Singing with Jesus:
Yeoh Gi Sean,
age 6 yrs

CHAPTER 11

The United Nations Convention on the Rights of the Child (CRC)[7]

JOHN COLLIER

THE CRC is having an impact. All but two countries have signed up to it and its presence is being felt in child policy, in families, the rights of the unborn child, the right to education, etc. However, some have complained that middle class do-gooders are foisting Western views on other cultures and that this is further abuse of the poor.

The historical context of the CRC is interesting. When Eglantyne Jebb, founder of Save the Children, first drafted a set of 'Rights of the Child' in 1924, she was informed by her sincere Christian faith and spurred to action by the horrors she had seen in Europe in the period before and after the 1914-18 war. The League of Nations took up her ideas and many nations signed up in agreement. The declaration as it was formulated at that time was as follows:

THE DECLARATION OF THE RIGHTS OF THE CHILD (1923)

By the present Declaration of the Rights of the Child, commonly known as the "Declaration of Geneva", men and women of all nations, recognising that Mankind owes to the Child the best that it has to give, declare and accept it as their duty that, beyond and above all considerations of race, nationality, or creed:

THE CHILD must be given the means requisite for its normal development, both materially and spiritually.

THE CHILD that is hungry must be fed; the child that is sick must be nursed; the child that is backward must be helped; the delinquent child must be reclaimed; and the orphan and the waif must be sheltered and succoured.

THE CHILD must be the first to receive relief in times of distress.

THE CHILD must be in a position to earn a livelihood and must be protected against every form of exploitation.

THE CHILD must be brought up in the consciousness that its talents must be devoted to the service of its fellow-men.

This statement is elegant in its directness and simplicity. It is worth noting that, although called 'Rights' of the child, it is actually written as 'responsibilities' of adults. Even so, little was done to ensure implementation and the 1939–45 war only served to emphasise the need for some sort of binding international agreement. The idea was taken up by the United Nations and an agency was formed to oversee implementation.

The Convention on the Rights of the Child was adopted by the United Nations General Assembly in November 1989. Unlike its forerunner, quoted above, it is too long, with 54 separate articles, to reproduce here but the text is readily available elsewhere.[8] It has been ratified by all but two countries worldwide although implementation is far from adequate. It is also subject in some places to the criticism that it is in fact an imposition of 'western' cultural values.

Ironically, given that 'western' values have been greatly if not predominantly influenced by a Christian worldview, some parts of the church opted out of the development of the convention, although the World Council of Churches provided input throughout.

If it is to be more than 'do-goody' wishful thinking, the convention also needs strategies and interventions. Organisations such as UNICEF and 'Save the Children' have worked hard at implementation and it is regrettable that some of the church has stood aloof from this. However, in its own way, the evangelical church tends to support the CRC in practice **87** and works to ensure that children are respected and not exploited.

If we have not got anything better, then we can still as Christians affirm much in the CRC. Just because it is does not come from a Christian source, does not mean we must despise it. The challenge to the church is to maintain Christian input. The original five principles clearly betray their Christian origin. As has been noted, they were not written as 'Rights' to be demanded so much as adult responsibilities regarding the child that were to be given. They included the need to teach the importance of serving others. The redrafting by the United Nations has replaced this Christian emphasis with something more humanistic. Now it is common to talk of four groupings of rights: survival, protection, development, and participation. These are, in a sense, all Biblical and as Christians we can interpret them in this light.

Christians will often want to affirm the importance of the family as the God-given, biblically mandated structure in which the child's rights are to be provided. Though stable affluent middle class nuclear families have their problems, the real challenge comes when family life disintegrates. As one young person said: *"Our parents are our worst abusers"*. What a tragic comment on the state of family life in some communities! Some Christians recoiled in shocked and vocal horror at this statement but we need to consider if there could be any truth in the assertion and, if there is, to develop a Biblical response. In the aftermath of war, bereavement by AIDS, desertion by drug-addled parents, children often find that families are not working for them.

The CRC is gaining influence in many Christian organizations. This may be because they do not have an explicitly Christian alternative - still grappling with the theology of the child – and, in the absence of a better model, they resort to the CRC as a satisfactory rationale or basis for their work. It certainly provides an excellent social minimum standard by which we must operate. Many organisations have found the CRC to be a useful lever, perhaps the only one, by which they can bring pressure to bear on their governments to do something good for oppressed children.

However, if we wish to be authentically Christian in our responses, we should beware of using the CRC as the *sole* or *primary* basis for our ministries or interventions. The concept or model of the child in the CRC is very narrow and, as noted above, the CRC is couched in the language of

Rights. It is possible that it may not be very compatible with a Biblical view of relationships or reflect biblical priorities. There is a challenge here for the church to do further work on this so that Christian organisations may have a Biblically based alternative to the CRC. It may not be very different overall but there could be significant deviations in emphasis and approach. This process is happening not only through the work of the Child Theology Movement[9].

Another concern is that although almost all nation states have signed up to it, has it made any difference? We still have horrifying statistics about the mistreatment of children that all this rights-oriented activity has not stopped. What can be said about the vindication of all the children who still suffer? Is God there for them, even when father and mother, and the CRC, fail them? Chapter two touches on this question but we readily acknowledge the need for further work.

In summary: the CRC is a useful tool for Christian organisations making practical, material interventions in the lives of children. However, when it comes to the profound spiritual problems of the children of the world, the CRC is seriously lacking. For the spiritual, more profound needs of the child in the midst, a developed theology of children and childhood is crucial.

Jesus and Children: Sarah Ong, age 6 yrs

CHAPTER NOTES

7   From Penang consultation June 2002
8   For example, http://www2.ohchr.org/english/law/crc.htm
9   See, for example, *Questioning the Basis of our Work* by Judith Ennew and Paul Stephenson; Tearfund and Black on White Publications (2004)

CHAPTER 12

A Theoretical Typology of Children's Needs[10]

KEITH WHITE/HADDON WILLMER

THIS CHAPTER describes a presentation by Keith White and a critique by Haddon Willmer.[11]

Background

This typology has been developed over twenty years in the context of Mill Grove, a Christian residential community caring for children at risk. It draws from the cross-cultural experiences of this community and from the major insights of psychoanalysis and psychotherapy. In 1999 it was adopted at the Cutting Edge Conference Child Development Group as a standard for assessing the quality of models of intervention.

If a child has lost, or is at risk of losing, consistent daily links, contact and bonds with his or her own birth family and kin the following universal needs must be paramount in assessing the most appropriate potential setting to satisfy as many, if not all, of these needs.

Love, the Overriding Desire and Need

The overriding and overall need of every child is to be loved by and to love one or more significant adults. The five needs listed can best be seen as elements or aspects of this process and relationship. If one or more is not met the capacity of any child to experience and express love will be impaired. If none are met over a substantial period of a child's early years the likelihood is that the child will be emotionally scarred and impaired.

Five Needs that must be addressed if love is to grow

Security

This is the primal need. Without security there is no safe base for exploration, relationships, play and development, and dysfunctional defence mechanisms will develop that prevent the experiencing of love.

In biblical terms we note that a 'safe place' (from Eden to the Ark, the Promised Land and the New Jerusalem) is the most fundamental image of salvation. *"I go to prepare a place for you."*

No intervention, however well intentioned or resourced, will begin to have any effect unless children know that they are safe. This safety can be met in many different ways. At Mill Grove it is represented by an actual place that has remained constant for 100 years and by people who protect the children as their own. In psychotherapeutic terms this is Bowlby's 'secure place'.

All alternatives to and substitutes for a family must provide such security. It is possible in all settings: adoptive, foster and residential. However the security of children in these microsystems will be jeopardised if there are poor meso-, exo- and macro- systems. It is also possible for each of these microsystems to be dysfunctional because of internal conflict or inadequacies. No one type of setting is a guarantee of security.

Significance

Children are people. They are individuals and cannot be treated or dealt with as if they were a group, numbers or statistics. Vital to their development and well-being is the assurance that they are infinitely precious as people, not because of something they have done or achieved but because of who they are. They need to know that at least one adult is committed to them unconditionally. This means that this adult is prepared to be theirs for life and possibly even to lay down his or her life for them.

In biblical terms this is a wonderful dimension of the whole experience of God and His grace described throughout the Scriptures. God is personally interested in us not because of our merits or potential but because of His heart and covenant love. The "I/Thou" relationship is of eternal significance. It is at the heart of the Gospel. It is the ultimate expression of unconditional commitment, in that Jesus Christ sealed the covenant by and through His death.

In theoretical terms this is the essence of child development. The existence of a committed significant other is the sine qua non of 'good enough parenting' and the quality of this relationship determines to a large measure the emotional health of the child.

In child care terms it means that institutions, systems, rotas and training count for nothing unless there is the person and this relationship. The whole dynamic and structure of Mill Grove revolves around this axis. As a consequence it is quite different from nearly all other residential establishments for children in the UK.

The challenge of identifying one or more adults unconditionally committed to a child is the primary task of any intervention and its difficulty cannot be underlined too much. This is why separation from natural family is so threatening to a child's well-being. It is for the vast majority of children, parents and kin who are committed in this way. The very existence of a life-long family name is recognition of this bond.

An obvious response is adoption. But it is problematical in certain ways. Cross-cultural adoption often leads to difficulties of identity and in many parts of the world potential adoptive families are scarce. Assessment is crucial and time-consuming. Adoptive families need supportive meso- and exo- systems and should not be assessed in isolation.

Foster care is increasingly popular worldwide but there can be breakdowns and serial placements. Only rarely does fostering build in an unconditional commitment. (It is most appropriate when there is the prospect of a child being reunited with his or her own family.) Unless there is a permanent fostering arrangement (unusual and difficult) fostering is best seen as temporary or as a complement to other interventions and systems.

Residential settings are many and varied. Large establishments such as refugee camps, asylums and boarding schools, will be unable to provide unconditionally committed carers who can function in the place of parents and family. However, smaller places (like Mill Grove, for example) may be able to do so. Their strength draws from the support of systems and networks of which they are a part.

The role of the local worshipping faith community is a vital element of the personal support system for all offering unconditional commitment.

Boundaries

Every child and human being needs boundaries if they are to feel safe, relate to others and develop appropriately. Some think of rules, discipline or values. All of these are embraced by this term in some measure.

We see the way in which God provides boundaries for His people in the Bible so that they can thrive. There are many: physical, moral, practical, sexual and spiritual. Their purpose is that we might live 'with the grain of Nature', and be at home in God's world. They provide a healthy setting for the development of not only individuals but communities.

In child care terms, the place of firm and consistent boundaries is universally recognised. They can be represented in different ways. At Mill Grove we find that the best boundaries are 'lived' ones, and that they are appreciated and respected by children of all ages, backgrounds and faiths.

The relevance of such boundaries applies to each alternative form of care for children at risk. It is important to realise that external boundaries, like rules and regulations are no substitute for 'lived' boundaries. The adults and peers in the child's life will communicate consistent moral and emotional boundaries by the way they live. It is well to be alert to the many ways in which boundaries can be transgressed consciously and unconsciously. Peer group bullying is one common example and ever-present in large group care settings. Changes of carer are likely to confuse boundaries in a child's mind. Continuity of boundary between the birth family, culture, tradition and the new setting is important. A change of culture, language and norms is likely to be detrimental to a child's development.

Community

There is a recognition in the Bible that we are made for community and for relationships. Families are our starting point but the norm is to find and make bonds beyond kith and kin. The biblical story is of a community or people of God.

In child care terms, the importance of peer groups, play and neighbourhoods is often under-estimated. In Britain, for example, the individual child tends to be seen in abstraction or simply as part of a family. Children need to be and to feel part of accepting communities, especially faith communities. Child care cannot be divorced from the wider world of social relationships. Schools are a very significant aspect of 'community' for children.

The critical element here is the quality of the links between the child's microsystem and the exo- and meso- systems. It is possible for the substitute caring system to be separated from the wider community. The danger is probably greatest in large residential establishments which can tend to become total institutions cut off from the outside world. Once again faith communities are a vital resource because they link and support the different systems

The quality of the political, military and economic conditions of the macrosystems is a factor determining the nature of the community, associations and relationships that are available to a child. Street children worldwide show how the desire for community can lead to dysfunctional or dangerous relationships developing.

Creativity

Children are essentially creative and creators. They are made in the image of God. If they are to fulfil their potential they must be given opportunities and encouragement to create, to make, to shape and to dance. The Scriptures testify to this aspect of humanity. We are to express ourselves with joy and variety in movement, music, work and play.

In child care terms, this is one of the most helpful indications of a child's emotional and mental state and of the group of which the child is a part. It can often be underestimated by adults. Institutionalisation is one of the big stumbling blocks in the way of creativity, as are poverty and deprivation. Education should not be conceived without reference to play and spontaneity.

One of the readiest measures of the quality of any child care is the proclivity of the child to play and create. It is important that routine care and organisation do not stifle play and self-expression. This desire or need can easily be channelled into dangerous and destructive 'play' and behaviour. Children may be attracted to war and prostitution, for example, unaware of the larger meaning and implications of their actions.

Creativity finds its ultimate expression in loving and being loved!

Summary

These needs are universal, although the way they are expressed and addressed will vary from culture to culture and place to place. There is no panacea or single model of intervention guaranteed to meet them.

They can be used as a standard against which to assess the effectiveness of any proposed or existing form of child care. It is possible to link them specifically with theoretical frameworks and also to the understanding of lay people from different faith perspectives. The above has been specifically written with reference to the Christian faith but this is indicative of how the process can work, not an exclusive prescription.

Comments and Questions / HADDON WILLMER

Is this document self-sufficient in its own terms and idiom? It seems to do quite well without extensive explicit theological exposition. Or does it? Could it benefit from theological comment or addition?

Does the sentence: *"The overriding and overall need of every child is to be loved by and to love, one or more significant adults"* need to be evaluated theologically? 'God' is the Name which signifies the overriding and overall in human existence. How does this statement about love fit with the whole biblical revelation and theological understanding focused by texts like 'God is love'?

God pops in and out of this document – does this suggest that God may be seen here as an intruder, a gate-crasher, a discordant note or an irrelevant digression? Or are the mentions of God here to be likened to an underground stream whose waters bubble up in little springs at various points? Could we detect and chart the underground stream in its whole course? What would be gained by making this hidden theology explicit? **95**

What is the relative status and value of 'need' as a defining category for human being as God's creature? What other categories should be taken into account? Is being human a state of needs, or a privilege/blessing, or a calling or task, or an ordeal in the world as 'a vale of soul-making' or whatever else? The needs of children are identified by five words here. What other words might be used for the same purpose? Especially consider words which have an equal or greater theological resonance than the ones used here.

In this document, the needs of the child are described primarily by talking of any individual child and what s/he needs. But it is indicated, more than once, that meeting the needs of the child requires systems: for example, the child's security is presented as dependent on the efficient cooperation of micro-, meso-, exo- and macro-systems, within which individuals exist. All these systems need to work as one child-friendly system. What theological questions, if any, need to be considered here?

How do we understand God to be related to system in the way system appears in this document? Is God present and active through the human systems (which represent best human practice?)? Are systems then to be understood as creation, in which God is everywhere present, as the source and upholder, even in hiddenness or in the reticence of 'common grace'?

Is God present and active despite the systems which oppose God by their disobedience as rebellious powers and do not recognise God but rather squeeze him out of the world to the Cross? God's presence and activity then appears as criticism of and resistance to the world, effected by God who is on his own in the darkness of the world, without the support or the service of systems to his will.

Is God present and active in redeeming the systems and bringing them back to serviceability? Does this redemption of systems mean they are totally freed from all imperfection, indifference, lack of love, inflexibility, contentment with mere technical efficiency even when it does not attain the true end of humanity (e.g. gaining the whole world but losing one's soul when God calls to account)? Or is the redemption of systems never finished, so that it has to be understood afresh in each situation and moment, as God resists and works against it? So God's work on systems would issue in the hope which keeps us going for the next struggle and would keep us praying with joy: *"Your Kingdom come!"* rather than bringing us into a haven where we can rest from our labours. How then do we think about systems theologically? What significant difference would it make to what this chapter is talking about?

Significance here is rooted explicitly in the whole biblical story of God, to show that God gives significance and expresses it ultimately in the unconditional commitment shown in Christ's dying. Then the document switches to another less theological idiom and talks of the necessity of good enough parenting and various forms of institutional child-care. Might the statement not be presented with greater theological continuity? The death of Christ did not achieve significance or salvation at a stroke. It is the hinge in the story, which is continued in the post-Cross life of Jesus, at God's right hand, in the Spirit and Church to the ends of the world.

Consider the presentation of institutions of child care: how do they fit with and realise God's work in making present in each new day, to the end of time, what He has committed himself to in creating and in giving himself for the redemption of the world? If God does not make present what he has done in Christ on the Cross, is God credible?

Boundaries here are said to have the purpose of our *'living with the grain of Nature and being at home in God's world'*. Is not this formulation one-sided? What is the grain of Nature? Nature is not a place where we can simply be at home, is it? When we think of community, we may have a dream of a child-friendly world and the dream can be very valuable. But we live in a world where Christ died and where his little brothers and sisters still die. Do we live in an orderly or disorderly world?

The 'creativity' section bristles with provocations which might be explored. Does creativity spell itself in play rather than work or institutionalisation? Is not this a narrow view of creativity? This document virtually equates play and creativity.

CHAPTER NOTES

[10] From *Celebrating Children*, Section 5.3 by Keith White. There is now an extended exploration of these five themes in *The Growth of Love* (London: B.R.F., 2008).

[11] Originally given in Penang in July 2004

CHAPTER 13

Historical Perspectives on Children in the Church [12]

MARCIA J. BUNGE

MANY PEOPLE today are concerned about the children in our midst and in our wider culture. We wonder:

Are they being raised with love and affection?
Are they receiving a good education?
Are they safe in their homes and schools?
Are they being exposed to good role models?
Will they have a sense of meaning and purpose in their lives?
Will they contribute in positive ways to society?
In the church we also ask: will the children have faith?
Will they live out that faith in service and compassion toward
    others?

Although we express these concerns, we find that many countries fail to meet even the basic needs of children and children around the world suffer hunger, poverty, abuse, neglect and depression. In the United States, for example, 16% of children live in poverty and approximately nine million children have no health insurance. Many children attend inadequate and dangerous schools and solid pre-school programmes, such as 'Head

Start', lack full funding. Children are one of the last priorities in decisions about budget cuts at the state and federal level. Road maintenance and military budgets take precedence over our children, even though politicians pledge to *"leave no child behind"* in terms of health care or education.

Although those in the church certainly care for children and have created beneficial programmes for them, the church also often lacks a strong commitment to children and treats them as truly *"the least of these."* We have witnessed this recently, for example, in the child sexual abuse cases within the Roman Catholic Church. We have been shocked not only by the abuse of children but also by the ways in which financial concerns, careers of priests and reputations of bishops or particular congregations came before the safety and needs of children. Yet the church exhibits a lack of commitment to children in other, more subtle, ways. Here are just four examples taken from our experience in the USA.

Poor quality faith development programmes

First of all, many congregations offer weak religious education programmes and fail to emphasize the importance of parents in faith development. The curricula and lessons of many religious education programmes are theologically weak and uninteresting to children and qualified teachers are not recruited and retained. Furthermore, there is little coordinated effort between the church and the home in terms of a child's spiritual formation. Many parents don't even know what their children are learning in Sunday school and parents are also not given the sense that they themselves are primarily responsible for the faith formation of their children.

Failure of Parents to inculcate the faith

As a result, we find, in the **second** place, that many parents within the church are neglecting to speak with their children about moral and spiritual matters and neglecting to integrate practices into their everyday lives that nurture faith.

This claim is confirmed by many of my college students. I have taught primarily at church-related colleges. My students are bright and articulate and most of them come from Lutheran or Catholic backgrounds, have attended church and are confessing Christians. But they know very little about the Bible and their own faith traditions and they have difficulty speaking about relationships between their beliefs and their everyday lives and concerns. They also tell me that they rarely, if ever, have spoken to their parents about any issues of faith and they regret that they did not even pray together at home.

The experience of my students is confirmed by several recent studies of the Search Institute and Youth and Family Institute. For example, according to one study of 8,000 adolescents whose parents were members of congregations in eleven different Protestant and Catholic denominations, only 10% of these families discussed faith with any degree of regularity and in 43% of the families faith was *never* discussed.[13]

The spiritual formation of children is undervalued

In the **third** place, many churches consider reflection on the moral and spiritual formation of children as 'beneath' the work of their theologians and as a fitting area of inquiry only for pastoral counsellors and religious educators. Consequently, systematic theologians and Christian ethicists say little about children and offer few well-developed teachings on the nature of children or our obligations to them.

Although churches have highly developed teachings on related issues such as abortion, human sexuality, gender relations, and contraception, they do not offer sustained reflection on children or our obligations toward them. Children also do not play a role in the way that systematic theologians think about central theological themes, such as the nature of faith, language about God and the task of the church.

Failure of churches to be public advocates for children

In the **fourth** place, national churches have not been consistent public advocates for children. Mainline Protestant churches support legislation to protect children's health and safety, yet they hesitate to contribute significantly to public debates about strengthening families. Protestant evangelical and conservative churches, on the other hand, are more vocal in nationwide debates about marriage, divorce and the family, which has been positive. However, these churches sometimes focus so narrowly on

the rights of parents to raise and educate their own children w
ernmental intrusion that they inadequately address the respon
parents, church and state to protect, educate and support all cl

Simplistic views of Children

Related to the lack of commitment to children in the church are several simplistic views of children and our obligations to them. Many scholars have argued, for example, that in a consumer culture a 'market mentality' moulds even our attitudes toward children.[14]

Thus, instead of seeing children as having inherent worth, we tend to view them as being commodities, consumers or even economic burdens. The language of children as commodities is most blatant in discussions of reproductive technology, in which 'high quality' donor eggs from an Ivy League female cost more than 'regular' eggs. But we also speak of children as commodities in more subtle ways when we say that they 'belong' to us or view them more as expressions of ourselves than beings with intrinsic worth. In our culture, children are understood to be major consumers and we now market countless goods to children in TV shows, videos and fast-food restaurants. We also treat many children, especially the poor, as burdens and don't supply the resources they need to thrive.

Other scholars have noted that we tend to view children as either all good or all bad. For instance, popular magazines or newspapers tend to depict infants and young children as pure and innocent beings whom we adore but teenagers as hidden and dark creatures whom we must fear. In the Christian tradition, we have often focused on children merely as sinful or as creatures who are 'not yet fully human'.

These kinds of simplistic views diminish children's complexity and intrinsic value and thereby undermine our commitment and sense of obligation to them. These are just a few examples, but they show us how one-dimensional children often are to us.

The tradition teaches a broad and complex view of children

We can do much to overcome these simplistic views of children and thereby strengthen the church's commitment to them by retrieving a broader, richer and more complex picture of children from the Bible and **101** le Christian tradition. Although theologians within the Christian tradition have often expressed narrow and even destructive concepts of children and childhood, there are six central ways of speaking about the nature of children within the Christian tradition that, when critically retrieved and held in tension, can broaden our understanding of children and strengthen our commitment to them.

1) Gifts of God and Sources of Joy

The Bible and the Christian tradition often depict children as gifts of God, who ultimately come from God, belong to God and are sources of joy and pleasure.

Many passages in the Bible speak of children as gifts of God or signs of God's blessing. For example, Leah, Jacob's first wife, speaks of her sixth son as a dowry, or wedding gift, presented by God (Genesis 30:20). Several biblical passages indicate that parents who receive these precious gifts are being *"remembered"* by God (Genesis 30:22; 1 Samuel 1:11,19) and given *"good fortune"* (Genesis 30:11). To be "fruitful" with children is to receive God's blessing. The Psalmist says children are a *"heritage"* from the Lord and a *"reward"* (Psalm 127:3).

All children, whether biological or adopted, are gifts to us. They are greater than our own making and they will develop in ways we cannot imagine or control. Scientists are still exploring the mysteries surrounding conception. Even with great advances in reproductive technology, we still do not understand and cannot control all of the factors that allow for conception and a full-term pregnancy. There is wonder and mystery, too, in the process of adoption. Adoptive parents often relate stories of the spiritual journey they underwent to adopt and they cannot understand or explain the miraculous 'fit' they sense between themselves and the new member of their family.

Children, we should remember, are God's gifts not only to their parents but also to the community. They are members of a community from the start and they play various and complex roles within it. In addition, they will grow up to be not only sons and daughters but also husbands, wives, friends, neighbours and citizens. Viewing children as gifts of God to the whole community radically challenges common assumptions of them as 'property' of parents or 'economic burdens' to the community.

Related to this notion that children are gifts and signs of God's blessing, the Bible and the tradition speak of them as sources of joy and pleasure. Here, too, there are many examples. Abraham and Sarah rejoice at the birth of their son, Isaac. Even in his terror and anguish, Jeremiah recalls the story that news of his own birth once made his father, Hilkiah, *"very glad"* (Jeremiah 20:15). An angel promises Zechariah and Elizabeth that their child will bring them *"joy and gladness"* (Luke 1:14). In the gospel of John, Jesus says, *"When a woman is in labour, she has pain, because her hour has come. But when her child is born, she no longer remembers the anguish because of the joy of having brought a human being into the world"* (John 16:20-21).

Parents in the past perhaps wanted children for reasons we do not always emphasize today, to perpetuate the nation or to ensure someone would care for them in their old age. Nevertheless, there is a sense today and in the past that one of the great blessings of our interactions with children is simply the joy and pleasure we take in them.

2) Sinful Creatures and Moral Agents

The Christian tradition often describes children as sinful creatures and moral agents. *"The whole nature"* of children, John Calvin says, is a *"seed of sin; thus it cannot be but hateful and abominable to God."*[15] Johann Arndt claims that within children lie hidden *"an evil root"* of a poisonous tree and *"an evil seed of the serpent."*[16] Jonathan Edwards writes that as innocent as even infants appear to be, *"if they are out of Christ, they are not so in God's sight, but are young vipers, and are infinitely more hateful than vipers."*[17]

This view is based on several biblical texts. For example, in Genesis we read that every inclination of the human heart is "evil from youth" (Genesis 8:21) and, in Proverbs, that folly is "bound up in the heart" of children (Proverbs 22:15). The Psalms declare that we are sinful at birth and that "the wicked go astray from the womb; they err from their birth" (Psalms 51:5; 58:3). All people are "under the power of sin" the Apostle Paul writes, so "there is no one who is righteous, not even one" (Romans 3: 9-10; cf. 5:12).

On the surface, this way of thinking about children can seem negative and destructive. What good does it do to speak about children, especially infants, as sinful? Isn't this view of children hopelessly out of touch with contemporary psychological conceptions of children that emphasize their potential for development and need for loving nurture? Doesn't this **103** emphasis on sin lead automatically to the harsh and even brutal treatment of children?

Certainly, in some cases, viewing children as sinful has led to their severe treatment and even abuse. Recent studies of the religious roots of child abuse show how the view of children as sinful or depraved, particularly in some strains of European and American Protestantism, has led Christians to emphasize that parents need to *"break their wills"* at a very early age with harsh physical punishment. This kind of emphasis on the depravity of children has led, in some cases, to the physical abuse and even death of children, including infants.

Although this abuse and even mild forms of physical punishment must be rejected and, although viewing them exclusively as sinful often has warped Christian approaches to them, the notion that children are sinful is worth revisiting and critically retrieving.

There are four helpful aspects of the notion that children are sinful that we must keep in mind if we are going to avoid narrow and destructive views of children.

First, when we say children are sinful, we are saying that they are born into a 'state of sin', into a world that is not what it ought to be. Their parents are not perfectly loving and just. Social institutions that support them, such as schools and governments, are not free from corruption and communities in which they live, no matter how safe, have elements of injustice and violence. All levels of human relationships are not the way they ought to be.

Furthermore, in addition to the brokenness of relationships and institutions in which they are born, human beings find a certain kind of brokenness within themselves. As we grow, develop, and become more conscious of our actions, we see how easy it is for us either to be self-centred or to place inordinate importance on the approval of others.

Second, when we say children are sinful, we are also saying that they carry out 'actual sins', that they are moral agents who sometimes act in ways that are self-centred and harmful to themselves and others. We are taking into account a child's capacity to accept some degree of responsibility for harmful actions. These 'actual sins' (against others or oneself) have their root in the 'state of sin' and a failure to centre our lives on the divine. Instead of being firmly grounded in the 'infinite' that is greater than ourselves, our lives become centred on finite goals and achievements, such as career success, material gain, our appearance or the approval of others around us. When this happens, it is easy for us to become excessively focused on ourselves; we lose the ability to love our neighbours as ourselves and to act justly and fairly.

This view of the 'actual sins' of children becomes distorted when theologians mistakenly equate a child's physical and emotional needs or early developmental stages with sin. However, when used cautiously and with attention to psychological insights into child development, it can also strengthen our awareness of a child's growing moral capacities and levels of accountability.

Although it is important to recognize that children are born in a state of sin and are moral beings capable of actual sins against God and others, a **third** important aspect of the notion that children are sinful, emphasized by many theologians in the tradition, is that infants and young children are not as sinful as adults and therefore need to be treated tenderly. They do not need as much help to love God and their neighbour. They have not developed bad habits or negative thoughts and feelings that reinforce destructive behaviours.

The positive way of expressing the same idea is that young people are more easily formed than adults and it is easier to nurture them and set them on a straight path. This is one reason that most theologians who have emphasized that children are sinful have never concluded that children should be physically punished or treated inhumanely. Rather, they view them as 'tender plants' that need gentle and loving guidance and care instead of harsh treatment. For example, A.H. Francke, an 18th century German Lutheran Pietist, claimed that treating children with *"gentleness and sweetness"* instead of *"strictness and harshness"* is the best way *"to present to them the love of God in Jesus Christ"* and thus *"to plant within their hearts a longing for and love of the Word of God," "to awaken faith in them,"* and *"to bend their hearts toward the good."*[18]

A **fourth** and final dimension of viewing children as sinful is that some theologians who have viewed children as sinful also view them as equals and they thereby have shattered barriers of gender, race, and class. For example, Francke responded to the needs of poor children in his community in Halle, Germany. He built an extensive complex of charitable and educational institutions to address their needs. He even allowed gifted poor students and orphans to prepare for a university education along-side children of the upper and middle classes — something unheard of in his time. His notion of original sin provided a kind of positive, egalitarian framework of thought that opened a door to responding to the needs of poor children, seeing them as individuals with gifts and talents to be cul-tivated and positively influencing educational reforms in Germany.[19]

3) Developing Beings who need Instruction and Guidance

A central perspective within the tradition is that children are developing beings who need instruction and guidance. Because children are 'on their way' to becoming adults, they need nurture and guidance from adults to help them develop intellectually, morally and spiritually. They need to learn the basic skills of reading, writing and thinking critically. They also need to be taught what is right and just and to develop particular virtues and habits that enable them to behave properly, to develop friendships and to contribute to the common good.

The Bible encourages adults to guide and nurture children. In Genesis, Proverbs, Deuteronomy, and Ephesians, for example, we find many pas-sages about the responsibilities of adults to nurture children. Adults are to *"train children in the right way"* (Proverbs 22:6) and bring up children *"in the discipline and instruction of the Lord"* (Ephesians 6:4). Parents and caring adults should tell children about God's faithfulness (Isaiah 38:19) and *"the glorious deeds of the Lord"* (Psalm 78:4b). They are to teach children the words of the law (Deuteronomy 11:18-19; 31:12-13), the love of God alone (Deuteronomy 6:7) and what is right, just and fair (Genesis 18:19; Proverbs 2:9).

There are also many examples in the tradition of theologians who took seriously the education and formation of children. John Chrysostom, in the 4th century, wrote sermons on parenting and the duties of parents to nurture the faith of their children. He viewed the home itself as "a little church" and ranked parental neglect of children's needs and their spiri-tual formation among the gravest injustices.[20]

Luther and Calvin also wrote catechisms and religious education materials for parents to use in the home and they emphasized the responsibility of parents to guide and to instruct their children in the faith.[21] In his popular book *Christian Nurture*, Horace Bushnell, the 19th century Congregational pastor and scholar, emphasized that parents are the primary agents of a child's spiritual formation, claiming that *"Religion never penetrates life until it becomes domestic."*[22]

We might say that adults are to attend to the 'whole being' of children and provide them with emotional, intellectual, moral, and spiritual guidance. Thus, in addition to providing children with a good education and teaching them skills that are necessary to earn a living and raise a family, adults are to instruct children about the faith and help them develop moral sensibilities, character, and virtue so that they can love God and love the neighbour with justice and compassion.

4) Fully Human and Made in the Image of God

Although children are developing, they are, at the same time, whole and complete human beings made in the image of God. Thus, they are worthy of dignity and respect.

The basis of this claim is Genesis 1:27, which states that God made humankind in the image of God (Genesis 1:27). Thus, all children, regardless of race, gender, or class, are fully human and worthy of respect. Although children are developing, they are, at the same time, whole and complete human beings.

This theme has often been neglected in the Christian tradition and we find in the tradition the language of children as 'almost human' or 'beasts' or 'on their way to becoming human'.

But there are some theologians who have emphasized the full humanity of children, such as the 20th century Catholic theologian, Karl Rahner. In contrast to those who claim that children are not quite fully human or are beings 'on the way' toward humanity, Rahner asserts that children have value and dignity in their own right and are fully human from the beginning. Thus, he believes that we are to respect children from the start. We need to see them as a 'sacred trust' to be nurtured and protected at every stage of their existence.[23]

5) Models of Faith and Sources of Revelation

The New Testament depicts children in striking and even radical ways as moral witnesses, models of faith for adults, sources or vehicles of revelation and representatives of Jesus.

In the gospels we see Jesus blessing children, embracing them, rebuking those who would turn them away, healing them and even lifting them up as models of faith. He identifies himself with children and equates welcoming a little child in his name to welcoming himself and the one who sent him. *"Unless you change and become like children, you will never enter the kingdom of heaven,"* Jesus warns. *"Whoever becomes humble like this child is the greatest in the kingdom of heaven. Whoever welcomes one such child in my name welcomes me"* (Matthew 18:2-5). He adds, *"Let the little children come to me, and do not stop them; for it is to such as these that the kingdom of heaven belongs"* (Matthew 19:14).[24]

The perspectives on children found in the gospels continue to be as striking today as they were in Jesus' time. In the first century, children occupied a low position in society, abandonment was not a crime and children were not put forward as models for adults. Even today, we rarely emphasize what adults can learn from children.

One of the theologians who did emphasize what adults can learn from children was Friederich Schleiermacher, the 19th century Protestant theologian. He emphasized that adults who want to enter the kingdom of God need to recover a childlike spirit. For him, this childlike spirit has many components that we can learn from children, such as *"living fully in the present moment"* or being able to forgive others and be flexible.[25]

6) Orphans, Neighbours and Strangers in need of Justice and Compassion

Finally, there are many biblical passages and examples in the tradition that remind us that children are also orphans, neighbours and strangers who need to be treated with justice and compassion. For example, biblical passages explicitly command us to help widows and orphans – the most vulnerable in society.[26] These and other passages clearly show us that caring for children is part of seeking justice and loving the neighbour.

There are many examples within the Christian tradition of leaders who have taken seriously the situation of poor children. Martin Luther and Phillip Melancthon influenced positive policies and reforms in Germany for universal education that included girls and the poor. Francke, the 18th century Pietist, attended to poor children in his community and built hospitals, schools and orphanages to serve them and their families. Like Luther and Melancthon, he also influenced positive educational policies and reforms in Germany so that all children could receive a good education.

John Wesley, the founder of Methodism, is another strong example of a theologian who attended to the poor in concrete ways, who inspired Methodists from his time to today to care for the poor and to establish institutions and initiatives to serve them.

Dangers when we retreat from the Bible and the Tradition

Whenever we retreat from this rich, complex, and almost paradoxical view of children found in the Bible and Christian tradition and we focus instead on only one or two aspects of what children are, we risk falling into deficient understandings of children and our obligations to them and risk treating them in inadequate and harmful ways.

On the one hand, if we view children primarily as gifts of God and as models of faith, then we will enjoy them and be open to learning from them. However, we may neglect their moral responsibilities and minimize the role that parents and other caring adults should play in a child's moral development. In the end, we may adopt a 'hands off' approach to parenting or religious education that underestimates the responsibilities of both adults and children. We see the weaknesses of this approach to children in the past and still today. For example, contemporary Christians who emphasize the innocence or spiritual wisdom of children often fail to articulate the full range of adult responsibilities to children, as well as a child's own growing moral capacities. They also neglect building strong educational programmes for children or emphasizing the responsibilities of parents.

On the other hand, if we view children primarily as sinful and in need of instruction, then we will emphasize the role of parents and other caring adults in guiding and instructing children and we will recognize a child's own moral responsibilities. But we may neglect to learn from them, delight in them and be open to what God reveals to us through them. Furthermore, we may narrowly restrict our understanding of parenting and religious education to instruction, discipline, and punishment.

Focusing on children solely as sinful and in need of instruction also has real dangers, since it has often been easier for Christians who regard children solely as sinful to brutally punish them or 'beat the devil' out of them. Even when Christian parenting manuals today emphasize that children are to be treated kindly but continue to speak of children primarily as sinful, they neglect other important lessons of the Bible and the tradition, such as enjoying children, treating them as fully human, listening to their questions and learning from them.

In order to avoid these and other dangers, a solid and biblically informed model of child-adult relationships must take into account all six perspectives on children outlined here. It must incorporate a complex view of the child that holds together the inherent tensions of being a child: fully human and made in the image of God yet still developing and in need of instruction and guidance; gifts of God and sources of joy yet also capable of selfish and sinful actions; metaphors for immature faith and childish behaviour and yet models of faith and sources of revelation.

Implications

If we can avoid inadequate approaches to children in the culture and the church and if we can appropriate and hold in tension all six biblical perspectives of children, then we can strengthen our commitment to children in several ways.

For example, these six ways of speaking about children could strengthen spiritual formation and religious education programmes. If we see children as gifts of God and sources of joy, then we will include them in worship services as true participants and welcome them as full members of the church and we will incorporate more joy and laughter into religious education at home and at church.

Furthermore, if we see children as sinful and in need of instruction, then we will develop more substantial religious educational materials and programmes for children in the church and create Christian education programmes that emphasize the importance of the family in spiritual formation and faith development. We will more readily cultivate growing moral capacities and responsibilities of children, by introducing them to good examples, mentors, stories of service and compassion, etc. We will also include children in service projects, teach them financial responsibility, help them discern their vocations and explore how they can best use their gifts and talents to contribute to the common good.

Finally, if we truly believe, as Jesus did, that children can teach adults and be moral witnesses, models of faith and sources of revelation, then we will listen more attentively to children and learn from them. We will structure our religious education programmes in ways that honour their questions and insights and we will recognize the importance of children in the faith journey and spiritual maturation of parents and other adults.

These six ways of speaking about children could also deepen theological and ethical reflection on children and inform a strong theology of childhood. For example, if we see children as gifts of God and developing beings in need of instruction, then we will no longer see children as 'belonging' to their parents but rather as gifts to them and the whole community. We will also take more seriously our obligations to all children. We will strengthen theological and ethical reflection on the role of church and state in protecting children and the responsibilities of parents. We will also begin to understand spiritual formation as a serious area of inquiry in all areas of theological and biblical studies – not just pastoral care or religious education. In these and other ways, the church could build up a strong theology of childhood.

The six ways of speaking about children could help renew the church's commitment to serving and protecting all children. If we view children as made in the image of God, as fully human and as orphans, neighbours and strangers in need of compassion and justice, then we will treat all children, regardless of age, race, class or gender, with more dignity and respect. We will no longer tolerate the abuse or harsh treatment of children and we will warn against equating 'discipline' with physical punishment.

Furthermore, we will support local, national and international legislation that addresses the needs of all children and families, such as fighting for a truly working wage, parental leave policies and strong educational programmes for all children. As a society, we will provide the resources they need to thrive, including proper nutrition and adequate health care. We will attend to the needs of poor children in our community and around the world, work more diligently to protect and serve all children in need and become stronger and more creative advocates for children in our countries and around the world.

There are many other implications of a complex and biblically-informed understanding of children. A more vibrant view of children can combat simplistic and destructive conceptions of them and thereby strengthen our commitment to them in a number of areas. By appropriating a view of children that incorporates these six central perspectives on children found in the Bible and the tradition, all of us within the church can strengthen our efforts in spiritual formation and religious education; do what we can to facilitate a stronger theology of childhood in the church; and take up more wholeheartedly and responsibly the Christian call to love and care for all children.

Jesus and Children: Teh Hui Wen, age 6 yrs

CHAPTER NOTES

12 This chapter builds on already published material by Marcia J. Bunge, including "A More Vibrant Theology of Children," in *Christian Reflection: A Series in Faith and Ethics* (Summer 2003), pp. 11-19; and "The Child, Religion, and the Academy: Developing Robust Theological and Religious Understandings of Children and Childhood," in *The Journal of Religion* (October 2006), pp. 549-579.

13 Merton P. Strommen and Richard Hardel, *Passing on the Faith: A Radical New Model for Youth and Family Ministry* (Winona, MN: St. Mary's Press, 2000), 14.

14 See, for example, Todd David Whitmore (with Tobias Winwright), "Children: An Undeveloped Theme in Catholic Teaching" in *The Challenge of Global Stewardship: Roman Catholic Responses*, ed. Maura A. Ryan and Todd David Whitmore (Notre Dame: University of Notre Dame, 1997), 161-85.

15 John Calvin, *Institutes of the Christian Religion*: 1536 Edition, translated by Ford Lewis Battles (Grand Rapids, MI:

Eerdmans, 1975), 97. Quoted by Barbara Pitkin, "'The Heritage of the Lord': Children In the Theology of John Calvin," in *The Child in Christian Thought*, ed. Marcia Bunge (Grand Rapids, MI: Eerdmans, 2001), 167.

16 Johann Arndt, *True Christianity*, trans. Peter Erb (New York: Paulist Press, 1979), 34-35

17 Jonathan Edwards, Some Thoughts Concerning the Present Revival (1742), in *The Great Awakening*, edited by C.C. Goen (New Haven: Yale University Press, 1972), 394. Quoted by Katherine Brekus, "Children of Wrath, Children of Grace: Jonathan Edwards and the Puritan Culture of Child Rearing," in *The Child in Christian Thought*, 303.

18 See his "Ordnung und Lehrart, wie selbige in denen zum Waisenhause gehörigen Schulen eingeführet ist" (1702) in *Pädagogische Schriften*, ed. Gustav Kramer (Langensalza: Hermann Beyer, 1885), 162-163.

19 For an introduction to Francke, see Marcia Bunge, "Education and the Child in Eighteenth-Century German Pietism: Perspectives from the Work of A. H. Francke," in *The Child in Christian Thought*, 247-278.

20 Vigen Guroian, "The Ecclesial Family: John Chrysostom on Parenthood and Children," in *The Child in Christian Thought*, 64, 73.

21 For discussions of Luther and Calvin, see Jane Strohl, "The Child in Luther's Theology: 'For What Purpose Do We Older Folks Exist, Other Than to Care for … The Young?'" and Barbara Pitkin, "'The Heritage of the Lord': Children in the Theology of John Calvin," in *The Child in Christian Thought*, 134-193.

22 Horace Bushnell, *Christian Nurture* (New York: Charles Schribner, 1861; reprint, Cleveland: Pilgrim Press, 1994), 63. For a full discussion of Bushnell, see Margaret Bendroth, "Horace Bushnell's Christian Nurture," in *The Child in Christian Thought*, 350-364.

23 See Rahner's "Gedanken zu einer theologie der Kindheit," in *Schriften zur Theologie, 8* (Einsiedeln: Benziger Verlag, 1966), 313-29; translated into English by David Bourke as "Ideas for a Theology of Childhood," in *Theological Investigations, 8* (London: Darton, Longman & Todd, 1971), 33-50. For an excellent discussion of Rahner's views on children and childhood see Mary Ann Hinsdale, "Infinite Openness to the Infinite": Karl Rahner's Contribution to Modern Catholic Thought on the Child," in *The Child in Christian Thought*, 406-445.

24 Some of the most significant passages in the gospels are Mark 9:33-37, Luke 9:46-48, Matthew 18:1-5; Mark 10:13-16, Matthew 19:13-15, Luke 18:15-17; Matthew 11:25 and 21:14-16. For a discussion of these and other passages in the New Testament, see Judith Gundry-Volf, "The Least and the Greatest: Children in the New Testament" in *The Child in Christian Thought*, 29-60.

25 For an excellent discussion of Schleiermacher, see Dawn DeVries, "'Be Converted and Become as Little Children'": Friedrich Schleiermacher on the Religious Significance of Childhood," in *The Child in Christian Thought*, 300-328.

26 See, for example, Exodus 22:22-24, Deuteronomy 10:17-18 and 14:28-29.

CHAPTER 14

How does History Help Us?

MARCIA BUNGE AND HADDON WILLMER

THE ESSAY by Marcia Bunge in the previous chapter and, in greater detail, *The Child in Christian Thought* which she edited[27], provide a helpful review of the way previous generations of Christians approached children and the problems that affected children in their time. However, there is a difference between the 'history of Christian thought' and 'theology'. The following questions suggested by Haddon Willmer draw attention to some important additional work needed for solid theological reflection on children and childhood.

What in general is the relation between the history of Christian thought and practice and our decisions today about what we should think and do?

What is the relation between the history of theology and our theological decision and service today? The history of theology is not theology itself.

Does history confirm the judgment that the Christian tradition generally has failed to follow Jesus in placing a child at the centre of its life and thinking? Is there not a revealing difference between what is disclosed in Judith Gundry-Volf's article[28] and the predominant themes of most of the succeeding articles in *The Child in Christian Thought*?

Do we want Child Theology to be shaped by these resources? Are we not likely to be sucked back into an inconclusive yet dominating discussion about original sin? Does not a serious enquiry into the child and sin today need to be conducted in genuine freedom from this history (but not in ignorance or despising of it)?

For Child Theology today, it is especially important to be aware of recent theological developments, so that we understand the situation we are in, what we have been shaped by and what we are speaking to. The book ends with four articles dealing with twentieth century history but there is still room to ask: what further historical study of the recent past do we need in order to develop adequate Child Theology?

Do we not need a deeper, more comprehensive historical study of the relations between twentieth century theology and contemporary Christian theoretical and practical engagement with children than is given here and elsewhere?

The book is presented as an occasion to re-examine the limits and possibilities of our own current assumptions about children and our obligations to them. It provides resources for strengthening theological and ethical reflection on children, helping to establish it as a legitimate area of theological inquiry. We might therefore ask: What are the signs that the book is having these effects?

In response, Marcia made clear that a key objective of the book was to determine how to build a vital and more complex theological picture of children and its implications for theology. We need both strong theologies of childhood and child theologies, taking account of what we do have: biblical, traditional and historical. This will require collaborative effort from historical theologians, biblical scholars, ethicists etc.

Participants at the meeting responded by starting a discussion around some of the following themes.

The place of history as it relates to Child Theology

The child has not been considered a legitimate theme of inquiry in theology but has been seen as rather beneath the serious theologian and thinker. This might be attributed to various influences such as the feminisation of the care of children, the Sunday School movement and the Industrial Revolution.

Theological discussion with the 'child in the midst' is developing and starting to gain legitimacy. We do not want to develop Child Theology by resurrecting old patterns and history. Dragging historical baggage into the present is like dragging an iceberg to get a cup of water – by the time it arrives where it is needed, it has melted away.

What must be recognized is that, in some respects, the modern western child was not envisioned in the Bible. Moreover, when children are addressed, the focus is much more on males than females. The biblical model was one of, 'my father has a business and expects me to work in it'. The contemporary picture is one of universal education and the creation of 'teenager'. This difference does not diminish the authority of the text for the modern western child, nor does it question the eternal perspective of God who inspired the scriptures. This is merely a statement that the biblical culture was radically different than the present 'Western' culture. The authors of each of the biblical books wrote in the light of their particular culture and this must be recognized when developing any theology, including Child Theology. In the attempt to reconcile the two cultures we run the danger of polarizing our attitudes: sentimentalised child versus working child; romanticised child versus idolised child.

We also run the danger of putting the child in the centre in such a way that Jesus is marginalised. But *Jesus* set the child in the midst to get the onlookers to follow *him* in the way to the cross. This certainly is the spirit of Paul's understanding of the gospel and the Christian life. Deep in the heart of Pauline understanding (Philippians 2) is the way of Jesus witnessed to by the child.

The Question of Perspective

A key beginning to healthy theological development would be to determine how children are to be viewed. It was recognised that 'view of children' could imply observation from a distance rather than child in the midst. The former can feel clinical and remote. If we are to have an accurate and well rounded view of children, we must see them in the context of their culture.

One cause of the difficulty of talking about child in Western Theology is the tension between the high and low views of children. Some have a high view of children and a low view of scripture, leaving children romanticised as lovely, beautiful people needing only development and guidance. But, at what age does development stop and at what point do they no longer need guidance? There is nothing inherent in age that diminishes or enhances one's value in the eyes of God. Others have a low view of children and a high view of scripture in which children must be 'saved' lest premature death take them straight to hell. How do we bring these two streams together?

One answer may be found in different attitudes to love: 'accepting love' vs. 'transforming love'. If we express only accepting love and are not willing to transform there is no challenge, which is the equivalent of ignoring the need for change. If we express only transforming love, we will only experience disappointment because we will never be able to be satisfied. We need to hold these truths in tension. How different would our conversation be if we talked about adults? Don't we need to have a high and low view of persons, not just 'child'?

The Child as Gift and Gifted

Children are a gift that may be disruptive to *everything*. Is this disruption often viewed as a gift? Indeed, we might expand on the idea of 'gift' by developing an understanding of children as not being just gifts *of* God but also gifted *by* God (1 Peter 4:7-11 and Ephesians 4:11-16). God is working in, for and through children. What are children right now in the community? What are the particular skills that children can contribute? Children's cuteness and ability to disrupt could be ministries to us. This is a rich theological concept often missed.

Consider, also, the use of the word 'family'. It has been 'ghettoized' and 'low-churched', being reduced to 'nuclear'. But scripture speaks of something bigger. When the text *says* 'family' it often *thinks* 'generations'! In fact, it frequently meant three generations were present. Separation of children from generational exposure in the faith community, especially in worship, was frowned on. Think of the Jewish family in the Old Testament, which was the only biblical text available at the time of Jesus: where were the children? Was Jesus' placing a child in the midst something foreign to the Old Testament or was it a full expression of where the child belonged as witnessed to by the Old Testament?

Adults, whose worship is so captured and distorted by language, might not appreciate the often non-verbal ministry of children. Even when children speak, adults often don't recognize the 'ministry' in it. Children resonated with Jesus' actions in the cleansing of the temple in Matthew 21:12-17 (not decent and in good order!). The adult religious community was outraged at children shouting out but Jesus quoted Psalm 8:2 *"From the lips of children and infants you have ordained praise because of your enemies, to silence the foe and the avenger".*

The temple clearing account whispers a language of relationship that is perhaps picked up in other parts of the biblical text. There is Mark 2:34-35 – who are my mother, brothers? But the epistles seem relatively silent. Perhaps if we considered Paul to have written as if the child is in the midst of his thinking, we might find more in the epistles. Maybe the child's presence was assumed because it was lived out, therefore there was nothing left to be explained but this could be a dangerous 'argument from silence'.

The Challenge of Doctrine – Sin

How do we connect a view of children as primarily gifts of God and as models of faith with the view of children primarily as sinful and in need of instruction? Is it a real gift if the gift is sinful? How do we work out the responsibility of children for their own behaviour? How do we understand the word 'sinful'? Chrysostom assumed that children are good but must be punished harshly. (He wanted them all to become monks.) Calvin marked the high tide of a low view of children yet, when actually faced with children, he helped them.

The whole question of 'sin' is much more complex than we have allowed it to be. How we view sin, especially in connection with the child, will impact how parents and adults want to relate to children. If we follow Barth's line of thought, there is no need to panic at the evidence of sin in children because there is another truth at work in them of which we are confident. In our times, an important step is to ask: "How do we see the child prostitute and the child soldier in the light of Christ?" How do we see sin in these circumstances?[29]

Some Implications

There needs to be a greater understanding of 'community'.
Have we allowed our concept of child to enrich our theological

understanding of parenting?

What of "family"? There are 120 million orphans. If family is limited to the purely biological, then many are missing out. What do we mean by the church being 'family'? How could the church replace the broken down biological family in a real practical sense, not just the token commitment of two hours on a Sunday?

Getting over poverty involves understanding our identity in Christ. Sentimentalising children doesn't recognize the suffering and pain of children who take on adult roles.

How will we negotiate gift and sinful in light of Augustine, Calvin, Aquinas, and Bushnell? Christianity has the ability to retain the tension of these two, but how?

If it is true that children do not reveal themselves to people who do not enjoy the company of children, does that eliminate the work of theologians who spoke on the theology of children but who themselves did not enjoy children and therefore missed out on the empirical evidence?

Child in the World

What is poverty? What does the child in the world experience in poverty and what does that say to Child Theology?

Poverty can indicate a deficit of one or many different needed resources, such as spiritual, social, material or educational etc; urban or rural; the poverty of affluence. Abject poverty is traditionally defined as absence of any two of the basic needs (shelter; clean water; education; food; medical care). Child Theology might develop its own definition of poverty. Does the 'child in the midst' change the criteria?

What is essential or common to all types of poverty?

Absence of resources and deprivation

Access – Power issues – a common feature is powerlessness – God has something to say about this!

Balance – Poverty is something out of balance – poverty of deprivation and poverty of excess;

Would Child Theology have something different to say about poverty compared to what Liberation theology says? Should there be a preferred option for the child, is that what Child Theology is saying? (cf. Liberation theology) **119**

Child as such

We need to develop our theological understanding of 'child' to include areas such as: child development; sexuality; the ending of childhood and transition to adulthood; child as actor or leader.

In addition, we might develop our understanding of what constitutes a 'Good childhood' from a biblical perspective. It might include:

receiving instruction about God and his ways as emphasized in Deuteronomy

passing on to children a knowledge of God and an invitation to them to enter in

Our understanding of the child in the midst does not mean a child in isolation but rather a child in the midst of tremendous activity and relationships and in the context of the influencing community powers of politics, health systems, policy, law and culture – see illustration.

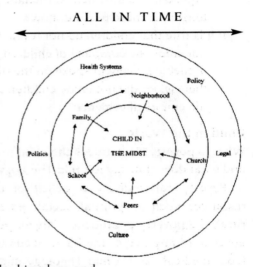

ALL IN TIME

Impact on the Church

When we consider children in the kingdom and the place of the church, we almost need to get the church out of the way just like the Pharisees and the disciples needed to get out of the way.

We need to exercise a Hermeneutics of suspicion in the same way feminist theology did when it asked if the bible marginalized women. We should be looking at all resources with a critical gaze.

CHAPTER NOTES

27 *The Child in Christian Thought*; Wm. B Eerdmans; 2001
28 Ibid; chapter 1: "The Least and the Greatest: Children in the New Testament"
29 This issue is worked out in more detail in chapter 22.

CHAPTER 15

Seeing God in the Child

CARLOS QUEIROZ

Introduction

MY COMMUNITY of faith is a group of 16 or 17 children that go to my house and there they evangelize and humanize me. I meet with them with the feeling that they are going to reveal God to me and not the opposite. However, we cannot take the risk of turning the child into an absolute revelation. What I present here are not notes but some scrawls badly prepared.

We have a formed holistic vision of adults and we want to speak about children from within that perspective. Nevertheless, the child is a focus of theology. If we point out Psalm 8 we will see the figure of the child being used as an example of how to praise God. When we think about perfect praise, we think about liturgy but the Psalm points us to children – who are not even announcing God's glory yet! The child is a projection of the incarnation, of the image and similarity of God in a more original form. He or she learns while he or she plays. We learn while working, using our rationality. The child worries more about relationships, about affection – interpreting scenes and faces and deciding whether they express belonging or rejection. We read from texts and not from the child. Our Christianity has space for children when it baptizes them (obviously, in the Christian groups that baptize children), which in fact is a space complicated to talk about to children. Any religion that becomes big is made rationalistic, bureaucratic and liturgical and consequently marginalizes the popular classes, such as the poor and, in this case, children. However the Christian faith has a much bigger space for the child. The child recognizes the Messiah kicking inside the belly of His mother (like John the Baptist did in Elizabeth's belly). Only Matthew says in his gospel that there were children who recognized Jesus as the Messiah. Matthew's account is not liturgical.

A hermeneutic question

To say that the child is not just another but an absolute revelation would commit the same mistake as liberation theology. The child cannot be made sacred as liberation theology did with the poor. Jesus started to be seen only as a poor person that died wrongfully and who suffered more than others. This ended up rejecting the expiatory sacrifice of Jesus on the cross. Jesus in His teaching on God's kingdom takes the child as a model, as a major indicator of humility, of simplicity, of absolute confidence in God. In this sense, while we should recognize the purity of children we must absolutely affirm that they cannot be made sacred. We cannot stop recognizing that some children act with cruelty, precociously acting like adults. But at the same time we have to recognize that there are adults who, by God's grace, live like children. The child then must be seen as an important mediator of revelation and not as an absolute revelation herself. As a matter of fact, I think that the child should be taken as a most important mediation of the revelation.

We are going to consider a hermeneutical question. Depending on the biblical text that we analyse, the child can be used positively or negatively. For example, from one side, when Jesus takes a child and says: "Whoever receives one of these children in my name is receiving me"(Matthew 9:37), he illustrates a theme. The theme is not the child, it is the Kingdom of God and the illustration is humility, a condition of entry into the kingdom. He makes the child an illustration to show the need for humility to enter into God's kingdom. The lesson is "simplicity", the total surrender, the full confidence in God.

On the other side, children can be used as negative examples. Paul does so when he says: "I could not speak to you as to adults, but as to children"(1 Corinthians 3:1). There is a danger in interpreting an analogy contained in a text and losing the idea. For example: "You are the salt of the earth". This is a very rich figure. The salt serves to preserve the food; then we say that the disciple serves to preserve the society. The salt serves to give taste; then the disciple serves to give taste. However, too much salt spoils the food; then we would have to say that too many disciples would be a destruction for society. And this is not true. The idea of Jesus was about virtue and he gives the illustration of the salt to communicate this idea. But sometimes we lose the idea and instead we interpret the figure. The same thing can happen with the figure of the child. Therefore it is important to notice the intention of the idea when we use an analogy, in order to not devalue or overestimate the analogy.

In the case of Matthew's text, I presume that we overestimate the child because Jesus was speaking about the kingdom of God and of the necessary humility to enter in the kingdom. He presented the child as a great illustration. Jesus, at another time, used the analogy of the Samaritan to talk about a good attitude. We should not interpret the analogy and conclude that all the inhabitants of Samaria were very good people!

Looking at the biblical text, I believe that God wants to teach us that the child, the poor person and those who are on the margins of society have a bigger probability of manifesting God because they have been looted, because of their inner condition, because of the pressure of society. In this sense, they are a more pure demonstration of the human being. In other words, when we see a child we do not see the position, the power, the bank account.

A challenge

The biblical text is the testimony of a given revelation. The demonstration of God's word comes before the text. In other words: God revealed himself, then someone wrote. First there was the revelation, then there was the register, the attempt to interpret the revelation. This is the text: "From the lips of children and infants you have ordained praise" (Psalm 8:2). Before the text the narrator had an experience, a glance of a child at the breast. This scene revealed something to the writer and gave him a perception which he registered. The revelation was before the text. In other words: the text is the evidence of the revelation.

Before registering the experience of Hagar with her son in the desert, someone first perceived it and only then registered it. The subjective, sensory perception precedes the text. The real life event reveals God and someone registers it. Moses had an experience of speaking with God in the desert. The experience is previous to the text and the text naturally refers to the experience. When we refer to the child, we affirm that, in general, the biblical accounts are preceded by the child himself. The child is the form of the revelation. For this reason, I have difficulty in saying which is the priority, if it is the child or the text. But it is clear that the child is the means of revelation. And so it is very clear when Jesus puts the child in his lap and says "who receives this child receives me and who receives me receives the Father who is in heaven" that he is talking about the attitude of welcoming the child, and about the child as God's message for all of us.

Theology is part of life – the theology of life or a theology with life. In this sense the child both announces and denounces. The difficulty and the suffering caused to our children very often creates an indignation. The history of children, the account regarding them, creates in all of us an indignation and a desire to do the will of God. The reality of children today and the facts about the situation of children that are presented to us systematize a real fact that is already denouncing us and announcing what the will of God is for society.

The child as a projection of the human creature

"The child, being at the beginning of her existence, represents the projection of the human creature in its most original and pure phase. Using the same language that the divine Spirit used in the book of Genesis, it usually affirms that the newly born child is soaked by the gracious breath of God. If we do not care well for this contact with God, time gets in charge of snatching from our hearts the gracious taste of the divine breath." This sentence comes from my article in the magazine *Mãos Dadas*. I feel that is what happens with me. I distance myself as I become an adult and lose the divine breath.

It is exactly what also happened in Genesis when the crown of creation stopped being a child. They began to realize their nakedness and thought of clothes as a power, the necessity of garments to appear like adults. So, in this sense, 'child' is not only a chronological age, it can also be a paradigm, a way of seeing life and a way of being seen as a human being. The idea of the nakedness of the child is something very interesting. The fact of an adult seeing him or her, giving him or her a bath, touching him or her, does not inhibit her. (Of course, I do not refer here to the opportunists, to exploiters). The child, in this condition of naivety, of simplicity, is the demonstration of this original purity that we are losing. (I hope the naturalists do not listen to me on that!) This nakedness is a deeper purity of the child. Then in this sense, the wise men of the Orient recognized the Messiah before he had done any miracle. Jesus had not done anything spectacular when they came and adored the baby. And the child was wrapped only in cloth. You have the demonstration of the adoration of the child, a simple glance, looking at the boy.

However when we write about adoration, we generally content ourselves with the liturgy. When Paul says "Therefore, I urge you, brothers, in view of God's mercy, to offer your bodies as living sacrifices, holy and pleasing to God – this is your spiritual act of worship" (Romans 12:1) he talks about worship as a person. He does not talk about liturgy. He says that we are a worship to God. In other words, when we live, walk, work, we are worship. We are a reason of adoration. When we walk, talk, or practice any other action, other persons see God in us. This is an adoration: to show God in existence. The child is, in himself, this constant adoration. When we look at Psalm 8, for example, we see that the child is also a demonstration of perfect praise. We realize that this subjective demonstration which is not liturgical nor bureaucratic is what adores God and that says who God is. Jesus did something very interesting, which leads me to realize adoration is shown in the playful way of children. I refer to the entry of the donkey into the temple. This is something a mischievous boy might do! In playing, children see God manifested. That is difficult in our times, in our worship services and in our liturgies. The boys have no chance to be mischievous. John the Baptist plays football in the womb and his mother, Elizabeth, adores in the kick! The boy shudders and she worships God. This is a very maternal experience.

The child is a paradigm. I presume that Jesus divided human adults into two groups: those who are children and those who are not children. If so, as the children favor more joy than sadness and produce more life than death, so will be also those that become children. They produce more joy, they produce more justice and they produce more life than death. For the rest, who are not children, from Jesus' point of view, death approaches, cruelty approaches, bringing with them everything that provokes pain and sadness. As we distance ourselves from the childlike being, we lose the fragrance of God and come nearer to death. We might call that precocious and voluntary aging. Happy are the men and the women who, receiving a child or in familiarity with children, are invaded again by the divine spirit and enjoy life again, in its most original and singular projection, through God's grace, in the children whom God favors to reveal this mystery of his presence.

Paying attention to children

My father was a very simple man and he had a rule: "if I communicated it in the church so that the children understand, others will understand everything". And he used to do everything that he could. A boy, my friend, who belonged to a family that were very resistant to the Gospel, was helping in the worship service. He was a little boy and used to assist the service seated in the window. When he became an adult, during college, he told me: "Carlinhos, I used to go there because when your father was speaking, I could understand everything but when it was another person I could not understand anything". My father had this way of speaking so that children could understand.

Thinking about that, one day I asked my son and my daughter if they would quickly check whether I had prepared my sermon in such a way that it could be understood by children. I would be going to preach on the blind man of Jericho. Well, in the introduction I said that the blind man was in the entry of the city, with a bowl in his hand, begging from people. Then I was interrupted: "Father, do not speak on that. If you speak on that, you are going to be embarrassed". I asked: "Why?" "Because I remember one day when I was with you, you were going down from the pharmacy where you had made a few purchases and the shopkeeper had given you the change. When he finished, a woman approached and asked you for some money and you said that you had no money but you had seven bills of ten Reais that I saw in your pocket. If you had given her one of those bills, you would have kept six and would have given her only one. Then do not go to speak there in the church, because I am going to say: people do not believe in what this Pastor is saying. No!" My children made hard work for me!

Another time, Kelvinha, when she was quite little had been naughty. When I arrived at home, she began to cry and said: "Father, mother caught me doing something and gave me a few slaps". I said: "Look, if you do the same thing I also would give you a few slaps". My intention was to reaffirm what the mother had done. Then Carlos Filho, little one, said: "Father, you two so big, with a slipper in your hands against such a tiny Kelvinha. This is a lot of cowardice!"

How can we hear our children more? How can we understand children? Naturally, I have to discern that probably he was defending his space. But what he was denouncing was true. When we assume the institutional power of father, we do not respect any more the son and the daughter because we have power. But the truth is that, even though we have authority, we do not have the power in our hands. I think that we need to sharpen our eyes and open our heart to see this manifestation of God in the life of a child.

A Triangle of revelation

I think that we could build a triangle of revelation: the text, this community of adults and children and the collective production. There is no theology produced individually, it must be the result of a community and of our reality.

I find two texts in the Bible that help me in this. There is that moment in which they brought a woman caught in adultery. The accusers bring in the biblical text but the biblical text in that circumstance is not God's answer, nor was it God's word. It was the letter that kills. Then we have the moment where Jesus welcomes the woman into his community. And we have the context that Jesus observes: reading the heart of the individuals; reading what they are thinking; reading the perversity. In the interaction of these three axes you can find the revelation. At Pentecost we see a phenomenon in the community. And the phenomenon is not – Pentecostals forgive me – because they were speaking and were not understanding but quite the opposite: they were speaking and they all understood. The phenomenon is not the same as 1 Corinthians 12 and 14. Since here we are hearing in our own language but only because we have interpreters, we have to imagine the people in that context, who did not need interpreters. There is an external reality that raises the question: "what does this mean?" and Peter goes for the biblical text. There is an interaction between the biblical text and the community. Before the answers of an external necessity, the revelation is shown.

In Child Theology, we see in the child's perspective a holistic vision of the world, like a paradigm, and not only the chronological age. We can think about adults as organic and physiological formations but with this lively, full child inside.

Sin

My father was a widower who married a second time. Then I was born into a family of 14 children. My father was a Pastor who had been converted in the Assembly of God. When I wanted to do something foolish, my oldest siblings would not allow me. When I was with the youngest ones, they would go and tell our father. When I turned 18 years old, I began to work with young persons who were drug addicts. I lived at their home with them. The young guys were telling their histories and I was finding myself the holiest person in the world, because I had not done the foolish things that they did. Then I realised that I had not done the foolish things because my brothers did not allow me, not even my father, not even the church. It is not because I did not have sin in me.

We are saved by God's grace. The child is potentially vulnerable to practice sin but I cannot find that a child of one or two years of age has committed sin. Therefore, when one talks about children's sexual exploitation, in other words an adult from the outside exploits the child, we must recognise that the child in this situation still has no capacity to decide on this. I am not saying that she is not born in sin, because of the fall, and that she does not need the salvation and the grace of Jesus. I recognize that she has sin in herself. Likewise, the poor person needs salvation as any other. This is the difference that we make between liberation theology and the more orthodox evangelical theology in respect of the salvation in Jesus. We are not saying that the child is holy and pure. We need to be careful not to create a condition or an absolute category within a certain chronology of our existence.

Jesus calls a child who participates in his kingdom. Besides saying that the child is an owner of the kingdom, he uses her to teach the disciples who dispute about power. If you want to know if the church is only a great business, ask how many children participate in its activities. Because the child does not contribute money and does not pay towards the accounts, she is not interesting as a business client. So, a large number of participating children shows that God's kingdom is different.

Jesus and the Children:
Serena Chin, age 10 yrs

CHAPTER 16

An Outline for an Exploration of Hermeneutics[30]

KEITH WHITE

Introduction

"HERMENEUTICS" literally means "interpretation". So if there is a picture, a story, an event, a piece of music, there is a question of understanding it, of reacting to it. The issues of interpretation are therefore universal in arts, sciences, politics, theology and ordinary life. Most people, including Christians, don't reflect much on hermeneutics (although we are in fact interpreting life all the time) and if we did, we would find it very complicated.

It involves some of the most important issues of philosophy, sociology, science, history, language and communication. The whole question of "post modernity" revolves around issues of interpretation. Contemporary theorists are questioning and deconstructing accepted interpretations of history, literature and government. Therefore, we do need to understand how crucial hermeneutics is as we seek God's guidance and will in our Christian ministry.

Some Historical Background in Christianity

Western Theology

Roman Catholic and Protestant theology have involved many disagreements (for example, the role of the Church, priests, Scripture, Sacraments and so on) but in both groups theology has tended to be dominated by an academic, rational approach. It takes place in colleges and seminaries and involves reading and study. It assumes that you work from the Bible (interpreted correctly), to principles and then to individual and corporate belief and action. It also assumes that the principles arrived at are applicable to every situation. Denominations are integral to this process as guardians of what they believe to be sound or authentic theology. They all have their statements of belief or creeds. But for an outsider to the West, like Pandita Ramabai, denominations seem a contradiction of the life and teaching of Jesus.

A key text in understanding how different denominations do theology is *The Social Sources of Denominationalism* by H.R. Niebuhr.[31] He traces with sadness how the social background and culture of Christians influences how they select, read and understand the Scriptures. It is a salutary text.

Orthodox (Eastern) Theology
This includes Russian, Greek, Coptic and other traditions. It has always had an emphasis that contrasts with that of the Western churches. It starts from the basis that God can never be fully described in words and so ikons, celebration, spirituality and charity are integral parts of theology. A theologian is one whose life and teaching form one seamless robe.

Radical, Spiritual and Charismatic Movements
All through the history of Western Christianity there have been challenges to the prevailing practice of theology. Monastic orders in the Roman Catholic Church (for example, Francis of Assisi and Benedict) and denominations in Protestantism (for example Anabaptists and Mennonites) have challenged the accepted beliefs, institutions and practice.

There has also been a massive twentieth century Pentecostal explosion that has transcended denominations and challenged rational methods and processes. It stresses worship, celebration, signs, wonders and experiences of God's Spirit. Its "theology" is often done by way of personal testimony, preaching and prophecy.

Radical Alternative Theologies
In addition to challenges within the Western tradition, there have also been challenges from other parts of the world.

The Brahmo Samaj was an early one.[32] It responded to Jesus and understood His teaching in a way that contrasted with "Western" theology. It found Western theology formal, "hard" and lacking in emotion and empathy.

Since the 1968 Roman Catholic Conference at Medellin, Colombia, there have been major and sustained challenges to traditional, academic, Western theology. These include Liberation Theology, Black Theology, Asian Theology, Feminist Theology, Urban Theology. And arising now is what I believe is potentially the most challenging of them all: Child Theology!

These theologies have had immense impact and question the whole basis of traditional theology, the way it is done, who does it, where it is done and what it's all about in the first place!

For this essay, I draw on Liberation theology, Asian theology and Urban theology. This is partly because they are all done by committed Christians who are wrestling with real challenges to their faith from contemporary realities but also because they have been an integral part of my own journey of faith and obedience.

Issues in Hermeneutics[33]

Richard Bauckham is concerned with politics. That is useful for our purposes because he wants to know how to read the Bible so that concrete action can be taken. He is aware of the different historical and geographical contexts in which the Bible has been used as a guide to Christian behaviour and action.

He sets out three initial issues that arise from the area of life he wants to explore. These will vary depending on the field of study, but it is important to clear the ground in this way, whatever we are looking at.

The Old and New Testaments

The social and political contexts are quite different. In the Old Testament Israel becomes a nation with all the associated stages and issues (terrorism, liberation, law, formation of government, land allocation, kingship), while in the New Testament Christians are a politically powerless minority. This is of crucial importance in understanding God's will whatever our particular commitments and field of service.

There is then the question of selectivity in our focus. What tends to happen is that we favour the parts that support our own positions and attitudes. Those who stress social justice find plenty of ammunition in the Old Testament, rather less in the New.

How far does the Old Testament apply today? Is it superceded by the New in some or all respects? If so, how do we decide? How far should the Old Testament be read in the light of the New, and vice-versa?

Bauckham concludes that in general the Old Testament is instructive, but does not provide literal instructions.

Personal and Public

How far is the Bible addressed to individuals in their personal lives, and how far in their public lives? Luther argued that a Christian judge was to forgive and to turn the other cheek in his private life but that, as a judge in court, he was to seek reparation in an identical situation.

But there is also the question of whether the Bible applies to everyone and the whole of life or particularly to Christians. The Anabaptists saw the Bible as a guide for them but not for others. They would not therefore engage in public office.

Permanent or Culturally Relative Norms

There are huge differences between Bible times and the contemporary world. So how do you span the gap? Is it about finding some general and rather abstract principles that don't change? Or is the Bible itself influenced by the contexts of the writers? A good example of this is the introduction of kingship in Israel. R. Bauckham argues for paradigms, analogies or models, that take the specific events or stories of the Bible in context and in detail but can distil a message for our times and situation.

With these issues clearly stated he moves on to matters to do with textual interpretation. I have listed these under three headings that derive from his book, but are not given in exactly the same way.

Text and Context

Pre-canonical/Original Meanings:

Linguistic. What do the words mean?

Immediate literary context. Is the passage part of a poem, a story, narrative, a letter, a chronicle, a prophecy, a proverb?

Wider literary context. What are the conventions of this genre?

Cultural Context. What was normal at the time? What did people take for granted?

Broad historical context. What do we know of the historical situation?

Immediate historical context. Do we know anything about the situation of the writer or group?

What's the point? What is the main moral, issue or teaching, so far?

Canonical Context

How does the interpretation we are working towards fit with the overall thrust of the Bible?

Is there anything specific that the person and teaching of Jesus draw our attention to?

Is the point of the passage clarified or amended in any way, by this?

Contemporary Context

What is our contemporary context?

What is our position in it?

What is the position of the community of God?

How can we understand our contemporary context, by using every available tool of analysis?

How do we make the link between the "two horizons", biblical and contemporary?

Evaluating this Academic Theological Method

This method is rational and seeks to be fair. It seems to be open to adaptation and correction and it has been used for centuries. So what are the emerging critiques?

It works largely at the level of thinking and the mind. It does not involve the whole person, body, soul, mind and strength. It can be detached from everyday life and struggles. Luther said: *"Not reading and speculation but living, dying and being condemned make a real theologian."*

So much time and energy is devoted to the first stage, the biblical "horizon", that there is little time and energy left for the second. The contemporary situation is not given the careful interpretive attention and analysis that is given to the "text".

European/Western theology has developed for long periods in unique conditions and contexts; for example, one religion, not many; relative political stability; common ways of life. It therefore concentrates on issues that are taken as significant in those contexts. Other parts of the world may need to re-prioritise theology in the light of their contexts.

"Theologians" are not representative of the community of faith: men and the middle classes are over-represented. It seems to favour the status quo, and is usually conservative, tending to neglect the masses of those who are oppressed, including the poor, women, children and "others".

The traditional process of theology is very individual and didactic. Lectures, sermons, books, are typical methods. What of the community of faith? It is the "banking model" of education.[34]

Some of the Challenges of Liberation Theology

The writer used as the basis of this section is Jose Miguez (Bonino). The book quoted is *Doing Theology in a Revolutionary Situation*.[35] Like many of his Latin American colleagues he found that traditional western theology did not make practical sense in his contemporary situation. His focus is on an alternative way of doing theology but here we note some of his critiques of traditional theology that have paved the way for alternatives.

God can tend to be portrayed as the *"eternally Present One who renders superfluous the movement of history"* rather than the *"subverter of the status quo"*.[36] Theology has tended to separate temporal/profane and spiritual/sacred history. But there is only one history. Liberation is the term chosen to integrate the two. It is about socio-political liberation, humanization and self-realization. It is also about deliverance from sin that restores fellowship between human beings and between them and God. Genesis is the story of one history inaugurated in Creation as the beginning of *"the human enterprise and Yahweh's saving history"*.[37]

The selectivity of traditional western theology puzzles the Latin Americans. Why have the obvious political motifs and undertones in the life of Jesus remained hidden? Why are events like the Exodus 'spiritu-alised' and wrenched from their historical, social and political contexts?

Why such stress on 'doctrine' and so little on the consequences of doctrine?[38]

The process of theology is inadequate. It stems from the Greek hermeneutic assumption of: *text – principles – action*. But in real life much of the process is reflection that takes place after action and events. The analysis of contemporary life and conditions has preceded the biblical theology of interpretation.[39]

Praxis: to do theology we must take action. "Part theology is impossible." Faith is not a gnosis but a way. It is always a concrete obedience that relies on God's promise and is vindicated in the act of obedience. The powers and structures of society must be addressed in specific ways.[40]

The language of the Gospel is never neutral, although that is what traditional theology assumes. There is a political element to the Messianic hope of the Gospel that is missing from this type of theology. *"Barth in his transcendentalism, Bultman in his existentialism and Moltman in his 'futurism', have submitted to languages that do not take human life and action seriously."*[41] There are no non-partisan languages. All theology must take sides and work out its relation to power.

CHAPTER NOTES

[30] From Penang consultation July 2004
[31] Holt and Company, New York, 1929
[32] See also Mozoomdar, and Keshub Chandra Sen.
[33] See Richard Bauckham, pages 13-19, *The Bible in Politics*.
[34] This important critique comes from Paulo Freire, *The Pedagogy of the Oppressed* (Penguin, 1972)
[35] Fortress Press 1975
[36] Ibid; page 76
[37] Ibid; pages 69-72
[38] Ibid; page 91 onwards
[39] Ibid; page 61 onwards
[40] Ibid; pages 86-95
[41] Ibid; page 77

CHAPTER 17

"A Little Child will Lead Them"

REDISCOVERING CHILDREN AT THE HEART OF MISSION

KEITH WHITE

Introduction

THERE IS a misconception of serious proportions among Christians that 'the Bible says very little about children'. This particular quotation is taken from an otherwise well researched and documented evangelical publication dated December 2000 and it is an attitude that may still be widely prevalent. It is the purpose of this paper to put the matter straight. After a brief survey of biblical material, I suggest the beginnings of a theological framework for our role in God's mission among children at risk.

Let us not underestimate the significance of our task. What if we have misheard or neglected God's revealed teaching about children and childhood? What of the likely effects of such a process on the history and current life and shape of the church? What if by default we have not been salt and light in God's world? What if our vision of the Kingdom of Heaven is a pale reflection of what Jesus revealed?

What is offered here is the tentative sketch of an outline. It has been produced while the responsibilities of caring for children at risk have taken priority over the writing and checking of the manuscript. It comes from the heart as well as the head and from one who has spent much of the last twelve years working on a new Bible, designed for children of every culture who are encountering the Scriptures for the first time.

An Old Testament Cast of Children (from Genesis to Malachi)

Ishmael (Genesis 16) means 'God hears'. His pregnant mother, Hagar, had all but given up hope, but God was infinitely concerned about this single mother and her future son.

Isaac (Genesis 22) prefigured Jesus in the story of the testing of Abraham.

Joseph (Genesis 37) the 17 year-old dreamer was the one through whom his father and the Children of Israel were saved.

Benjamin (Genesis 44 & 45) was the boy through whom reconciliation came between Joseph and his brothers.

Moses (Exodus 1) was saved by the vigilance of his sister **Miriam**.

The story of Exodus begins with the murder of Jewish baby boys, foreshadowing the birth of Christ. The last plague involved the death of firstborn sons.

The climax to the book of Ruth is the birth of a baby, **Obed**, one of the ancestors of Jesus.

Samuel (1 Samuel 3) was the child through whom alone God was able to reveal His will when adults failed. He is a model for human spirituality and obedience.

David (I Samuel 17) was the person through whom it was revealed that God was not dependent on adult power or training. Through a boy the Philistines were routed.

Elijah & Elisha each brought **a widow's son** to life. 1 Kings 17; 2 Kings 4)

A young servant girl was the means of the healing of Naaman, the army commander (2 Kings 5).

Josiah, through whom reformation of politics and religion occurred, was a boy-king (2 Kings 22). He was a boy when the dramatic reforms began (2 Chronicles 34).

Esther, the future queen who would save the Jewish people, was an orphan girl. (Esther 2)

Jeremiah was chosen by God, though he was 'only a child' (Jeremiah 1).

It is not just that these people happened to be children but that some of the most significant acts and revelations of God were through these children. Their faith and actions are critically important in the unfolding and outworking of God's purposes.

Childhood in the Old Testament

The Old Testament is much more than a record of the significance of individual children. Children and childhood are of great significance as part of the whole social life and structure.

Worship was visual and dramatic – equally accessible to children and adults. The Passover assumes children will ask what it means (Exodus 12), and so do the 12 stones set up after being taken from the bed of the river Jordan (Joshua 4). The rituals and practices described in Exodus and Leviticus are a primary way in which God's people will serve and worship Him. There is little if any separation of children from adults. In Ezra 10 when the Law is read out, children are mentioned as part of the crowd, echoing the occasion of the renewal of the Covenant in Joshua 8:35.

Children are seen as a sign of God's blessing all through the Old Testament and yet they are the first to suffer when sin, deceit, war, and famine affect a tribe or city. Achan's children die as a result of his sin (Joshua 7). There are desperately sad and vivid depictions of the suffering of children throughout the Old Testament (Psalm 106; Jeremiah 31; Lamentations 1–2 & 4; Joel 3; Amos 2; Zechariah 1 etc.)

It follows that one of the primary concerns of any responsible adult is the well-being and care of children. In most situations families will provide for them, but when this is not possible because of disease, death, famine or war, then the care of the fatherless is dear to God's heart. (Psalms 10; 146; Isaiah 1, Zephaniah 7 etc.)

God's relationship with His people is portrayed in different ways in the Old Testament but an emerging one (subsequently developed in the N.T.) is as a Father. In Deuteronomy 8 God disciplines those whom He has chosen as a father. In Psalm 27 a child may be abandoned by father and mother but not by God, the Heavenly Father. God's compassion is like that of a father to a child (Psalm 103). The Wisdom literature is written largely as from a father to a son (e.g. Psalm 34; Proverbs 1–7). The Jewish people are often called 'Children of Israel' or Daughters of Zion'.

The mother/child relationship is significantly used as an embodiment of the bond between God and us. There is a beautiful description of the weaned child in Psalm 131 representing the stilled and quietened soul. A mother may forget her child at breast but God will never do so (Isaiah 49:15-16). Isaiah closes with a tender description of childbirth that concludes: *"As a mother comforts her child, so will I comfort you"* (Isaiah 66:13). Hosea movingly relates the early days of the Israelites thus: *"When Israel was a child, I loved him, and out of Egypt I called my son"* (Hosea 11:1).

You will find much food for thought in Ecclesiastes 11–12: 'Remember your Creator in the days of your youth'; Ezekiel and the 'son of man' (1ff). And the Old Testament closes with a renewed relationship across the generations between children and fathers (Malachi 4:6). And that's only a skim through!

Old Testament Themes

But there are three deeply significant themes we have not yet touched and before we leave the Old Testament we must deal with them.

First in Psalm 8 there is a truth that is easily overlooked alongside the immensity of the night sky. Jesus specifically draws attention to it, so that should be good enough for us to stop and take note: *'From the lips of children and infants you have ordained praise because of your enemies to silence the foe and the avenger'* (8:2). Children are ordained and designed to praise God and His glory. They are not consumers or future adults but worshippers of the Creator God. Their ears, eyes, feet, hands and voices have been created to praise God. This is their true nature and purpose. But more than this they have a special role in silencing the enemies of God. When all else fails, it is children (like Samuel and David, for example) who will be the means of moral and spiritual virtue and power. Isn't this remarkable? The child is being portrayed morally and spiritually as the "father of the man".

This leads on to the second great insight in Isaiah 11. The Messianic kingdom is portrayed here vividly: *'The wolf will live with the lamb, the leopard will lie down with the goat, the calf and the bear and the yearling together, and a little child will lead them.'* You see the place of the child? Leading! And it will be a safe environment in which children can play – unlike the urban, war-torn, consumer market – dominated jungle of today. (See also Isaiah 65). The Kingdom of Heaven has children at its heart. We must never lose sight of this if we want to understand the teaching of Jesus, our relationship to God, and our joint mission on earth.

But there is one last crowning role for the child in the Old Testament. Isaiah talks of God's righteous anger against the sin and hypocrisy of humankind. This situation seems unimaginably bleak and hopeless, and yet God gives a sign: *'The virgin will be with child and will give birth to a son, and will call him Immanuel'* (Isaiah 7:14). The culmination of God's saving action is a light to those living in the shadowlands: 'Unto us a child is born. Unto us a son is given. And the government will be on His shoulders ...' (Isaiah 9:6)

The focus is not a warrior king, a wise rabbi or a High Priest but a child. The natural and normal place to look for salvation is everywhere else and to everyone else but the government will rest on this child's shoulders.

And so the scene is set, the stage is ready, for us to venture into the New Testament. 'Little to say about children' indeed? What does this tell us about the way the Scriptures have been read? What else might have been missed? Can we really have been that blind?

The New Testament and Children

It is in the Gospels that we encounter the working out and development of each of these themes from the Old Testament.

There are lots of incidents involving children in the life of Jesus: the daughter of the Canaanite woman (Matthew 15 and Mark 7); the boy with a demon (Matthew, Mark and Luke); the official's son at Capernaum (Jn 4); Jairus' daughter (Matthew, Mark and Luke); the son of the widow at Nain (Luke 7) and the boy who offered Jesus the five loaves and two fish (John 6). Jesus has a heart for children and they are drawn to Him. His preferred method of teaching by story and sign is, like the Old Testament worship and ritual, equally accessible to children and adults.

Four threads

There are four aspects of the Gospel narratives that call for our particular respect and attention.

The first is the birth of Jesus, *the incarnation*. The Gospels of Matthew **141** and Luke devote their opening chapters to this. Matthew quotes the passage from Isaiah about the virgin and child (Isaiah 7:14). The wise men come in search of the child. When they find him, they worship him by kneeling and presenting gifts. The Exodus narrative is recreated and revisited as Herod realises he has been tricked. Once again, young boys are killed. In Luke there is an extensive account of the birth of John the Baptist and Jesus. Luke tells of a sign for the shepherds that replicates the prophecy of Isaiah: *'You will find a baby wrapped in cloths and lying in a manger'* (Luke 2:12). Simeon tells of the significance of the child: *'This child is destined to cause the falling and rising of many in Israel and to be a sign...'* (Luke 2:33) and when those who looked forward to the redemption of Jerusalem came to the prophetess Anna, she spoke about *'the child'* (Luke 2:38).

The word 'child' is repeated in both Gospels at this point in the story again and again. And what is the significance of all this? God has chosen to enter the world, to reveal Himself as a baby and as a child. Perhaps we are so accustomed to Christmas that we do not realise how radical this is. The theologian Nestorius was so upset about the implication of this that he wrote: *'I deny that God is two or three months old!'* Karl Barth, describing the helpless baby wrote: *'This is your God!'* The fullness of the creator God is a tiny child? Is it possible? If so what does it mean?

The hymn writers have pondered the paradox and come up with *'Lo within a manger lies, He who built the starry skies ...'* and other ways of expressing total amazement. If it is difficult to see how the fullness of the godhead could dwell in a human being, how much greater is the challenge to see Almighty God contracted to the span of a baby! From God's point of view there is no problem, but it shakes our preconceptions. A baby is small, weak, dependent and vulnerable, lacks education and training and language. Yes, says God, and you must learn to look and find me in these things, in little ones, in little things. You must learn, to move from the palaces and encounters with the learned and the powerful, to the manger and the child.

The second strand in the Gospels concerns *children and childhood* and requires some work. Turn to Matthew 17 and read through to chapter 21.[42] The story here spans the period from the Transfiguration to the entry of Jesus into the Temple at Jerusalem. (It is told also in Mark 9–11 and Luke 9–19 with many of the same elements.) It contains some of the clearest teaching of Jesus about the nature of the kingdom. What we are going to do now is to seek to understand the mind of Jesus and this means we will have to leave the standard commentaries and assumptions behind!

The first action of Jesus after the Transfiguration is to heal the boy with a demon. Then there is a section on taxation where payment and sonship are explored. Then, in chapter 18, teaching about children, including the famous statement *'unless you change and become like little children, you will never enter the kingdom of Heaven'*, a curse on those who cause harm to children, and the story of the lost sheep applied to children (little ones).

Next comes teaching on forgiveness and divorce prompted by adult questions and concern, and once again Jesus places children in the centre of the kingdom (19:13-15). A rich young ruler is then told to sell everything in order to enter the kingdom (i.e. to become like a child). There is a parable about workers in a vineyard that demonstrates the upside-down nature of the Kingdom, and more teaching about the death of Jesus. Then the mother of James and John wants to claim top places in the Kingdom for her boys! She has completely misunderstood the nature of the Kingdom and what childhood teaches us about it. The two blind men (20: 29-34) do a lot better! Then Jesus enters Jerusalem and crowds welcome Him. In the Temple things carry on as if the Christ had not arrived and the Kingdom of Heaven did not exist. Only children continue to praise Jesus. They are rebuked. But Jesus confirms that these children are doing exactly what they are designed for: to praise and worship God (Psalm 8:2).

What have we discovered? A thread from Transfiguration to the Temple, from one mountain-top to Mount Zion, linking the teaching about the death of Jesus and the Kingdom of Heaven. Children and child-likeness form the linking strand. All the major commentaries miss this and some translators don't help by deciding to take *'nepioi'* (little children) and record it as 'the simple'! (Matthew 11:25, Luke 10:21).

The third strand is about the *Kingdom of Heaven*. And what is Jesus teaching about the Kingdom of Heaven?

Greatness in His kingdom has nothing to do with status, power,

strength, influence, wealth, or the normal assumptions in
society.

You need to change (to repent) to enter the kingdom.

You need to become like little children if you are to enter the
kingdom of Heaven.

Welcoming a little child we welcome the Lord of the Kingdom!

The Kingdom belongs to the childlike...

The Kingdom is in fact not like an earthly kingdom at all! It's the opposite in every way. Upside down! Inside-out! The best way of describing it is not as a place or territory at all but as *"God's way of doing things"*. That's when all the stories of the kingdom fall into place.

The other great paradox of the kingdom concerns when it will be fully realised, or when it started. It is both inaugurated (i.e. it has begun) but also not yet (i.e. it has not been fully realised). In this children help us: for children are both fully human (now) and also not fully developed (not yet). Childhood and the kingdom illuminate each other. No wonder Jesus is seething with anger at the thought of anyone harming a child, made in God's image and sign of His kingdom!

The fourth strand is a powerful and common description of entering the kingdom that we have allowed to become detached from children and childhood. That is the teaching of Jesus to Nicodemus (John 3): *'You must be born again'*. What is Jesus teaching? Exactly the same truth: you've got to repent, to let go of all your adult, culturally-laden preconceptions and become a little baby: to start all over again in Christ. It's not a separate metaphor or teaching: like Matthew, Mark and Luke, John is recording the need for an adult to become like a child: otherwise he or she cannot see the Kingdom of God.

This truth is embedded in John's Gospel in the relationship between Jesus and His Father. This is the dominant description: Father and Son. And this is to be our norm. So when we pray we are to say not 'Almighty God', 'Creator', 'Lord God' but *'Our Father'*. It is the realisation of the hope of the Old Testament. The Gospel of John begins by talking of "children of God" and Jesus' life shows most tenderly and plainly what this means.

In the Gospels and in the Kingdom, if we are to allow God's spirit free rein, children are at the centre – like the boy offering his five loaves and two fish to adult disciples who felt it right to point out to Jesus they weren't enough! The twelve baskets left over afterwards may have helped them understand in this particular case!

And what of the rest of the New Testament? In Romans and Galatians the whole nature of our relationship with God in Christ is worked out: we are adopted into God's family and enabled to know God as 'Abba'. We are to enter into every aspect of the life of Christ and to live as children of the light. And one of the favourite descriptions of the followers of Jesus is 'dear children'. The epistles describe a new and emerging way of living where in Christ there is neither male nor female, Jew nor Gentile, bond nor free!

But now let us begin the real work. What are the implications of all this?

A Christ-centred Framework for Mission

Let's look first at some of the errors to be avoided from past experience before we begin to outline a theological framework for the future.

1   We have made fundamental mistakes about the *kingdom* of God and about mission. We, particularly in Europe, have to separate it from our own culture. Kingdom, empires, colonialism were all about power and territory, conquest. We thought mission was what we did and that God's kingdom depended on *our* activity.

2   We have gone about *theology* in the wrong way. It has been an adult-orientated pursuit. There is tremendous emphasis given to philosophy, doctrine, systematic theology and hermeneutics and very little to stories, paradoxes and signs of the kingdom.

3   We have made mistakes in the *church*. We have got our priorities mixed up. Sometimes we did not distinguish between kingdom and church. Often we underestimated the place and contribution of children and little ones. We honestly did not think we had anything to learn from them!

4   We have contributed to *societies* where adults, power, wealth, possessions seem to count for almost everything. Where Jesus' teaching to sell everything becomes for many impossible to contemplate. And where childlikeness is marred, or squeezed into adulthood by our commercialism and adult programmes of education. Children are second-rate concerns of the political

system. They suffer hugely and the wrath of God and Jesus does not seem to have stirred us into appropriate action.

With this in mind by way of preparation, what of a theological framework for our future mission alongside and among children?

I draw from *Transforming Mission* the work of David J. Bosch, the South African theologian killed in a car crash in 1992, and from the Lausanne Covenant and subsequent Manila statements. They make the life of Jesus a central organising principle. It is in shape and emphasis a Christological framework.

We are, along with every follower of Jesus Christ, called to present our bodies as living sacrifices in His service; to allow the world-view and mind of Christ to permeate our every thought and attitude; to serve Jesus as Lord; to live in new relationships and a new community in such unity and love that people know we are His disciples; to continue His priorities and mission. This is our common calling. But what for those of us committed to work with children and young people at risk?

Let's take six of the major events of His life as our framework and see how far our mandate and tasks become clearer.

1. The Incarnation (the model of our mission)

We acknowledge that Evangelical Protestant theology has tended to be comparatively weak at this point, in its stress on the cross and redemption, and we pledge ourselves to seek out the implications and demands of this astounding event. We rejoice that God entered the world in time and space, that Jesus in His life and teaching brought forgiveness and healing irrespective of role, gender or class.

We rejoice that parenting, families, communities, work, play, all matter to Jesus, so much so that he brought restoration to people and relationships. We rejoice that the New Testament sees such relationships and life as central to our calling as followers of Jesus. We acknowledge the call to follow Jesus, and rejoice that, as we ask the question "What would Jesus do?", we find His ministry such a vivid and simple guide.

We are seeking to continue His life's work in every family, city and street, along each track, mountain, river and well, in every wound and disease. We acknowledge with humility and wonder that the transcendence and divinity of Jesus are revealed distinctively in John's Gospel through His humanity. That though His daily life, with dust on His feet, and thirst in His mouth, he revealed God's grace and glory.

We acknowledge the social and political dimension of the Gospel implicit in the agony, sweat and blood of Jesus, not only on the cross, but also in His life and ministry. We acknowledge that the wrestling and struggle at the heart of the Lausanne Covenant represents a struggle at the heart of the Gospel. Evil is not only in the human heart, but also in the social structures and there is no Gospel without solidarity (incarnation). In all this and more we recognise the implications of the incarnation for our life and calling in Christ. But our life alongside children at risk leads us to shed light on hidden aspects of the incarnation.

Traditionally, Western theological creeds have stressed that Jesus became man (*'homo factus est'*). The Gospel narratives in contrast stress the *child* Jesus. Drawing on Isaiah, the sign in Luke's Gospel that this was indeed God's chosen One, the Messiah, was the fact that a *'baby was lying in a manger'*. The implications of the Incarnation involving a baby and a child have not been fully worked into Western theology. Do the creeds need reformulation? *'Puer factus est'*: he became a boy-child?

This tendency to overlook the significance of the child Jesus, finds its way into the commentaries on His ministry and teaching. The centrality of childhood in understanding and entering His kingdom has been overlooked or marginalized. We have not seen children as signs of the kingdom.

We call upon our Christian brothers and sisters to see that the parent-child relationship is perhaps the most pervasive in describing God's love for each person; Christ Jesus taught us to pray: *'Our Father'*.

A Christian is one who has been born again, has become like a child, and this process is deeply interwoven with the Incarnation: the child Christ in us and we in Him.

2. The Cross (the cost of our mission)

The life and death of Jesus cannot be separated. They are indissolubly linked and meaningful. In Philippians 2 his life and death are summed up: *'being found in appearance as a man, He humbled himself and became obedient* to death, even death on a cross!' Bonhoeffer wrote not long before his execution: 'When Christ calls a man he bids him come and die'. It is the symbol of our salvation through Christ's sacrificial death. It is also the reminder that 'suffering is the divine mode of activity in history' (Schutz) There is no following of Jesus without scars.

As followers of Jesus we live under the shadow of the Cross. It is a constant reminder and emblem of the reality and savage cruelty of human sin, rebellion and suffering. We delude ourselves if we ever minimise the extent of human suffering and degradation. It reminds us of the constant necessity for repentance and re-formation as individuals and as a community of believers. There is no mission without tears. And no righteous action that does not need to be forgiven for the power that works for justice may be unjust tomorrow. The Cross is God's reminder that we cannot save ourselves by human means: our plight is too serious. We are not just lost but dead in our sins.

It also points to the sacrifice of Jesus, the sinless one, that we might be right with God. There is no healing or forgiveness without the shedding of innocent blood. It is a constant challenge to our own motives and commitments: a call to love irrespective of reward or return. It is also a symbol of reconciliation uniting people irrespective of creed, gender or class. It is the place and the point alone where we meet as equals.

Through all this and more we recognise the implications of the Cross for our life in Christ. But as those called to live among and alongside children, we are constrained to cry out on behalf of the silent suffering of children worldwide in every culture and economy. Children are suffering like silent lambs on the altars of our gods.

As adults we have become so obsessed with our own ambitions, fears and agendas, we have allowed generations of children to suffer. Our institutions and structures reflect this. We do not know what we are doing. The prayer of Jesus relates to all, but not least to children: Father, forgive them they know not what they do. The Cross calls us to identify most of all with those who are oppressed and suffer unknowingly, and chronically. The innocence of so many children who suffer in our world finds in Jesus on the Cross, one who understands more than others will ever know.

3. The Resurrection (the mandate for our mission)

We are an Easter people and 'Hallelujah' is our song! Through the resurrection of Jesus the forces of the future, joy, hope and victory, stream into the present.

We are not bitter, angry and consumed by a desire to destroy and exact revenge. Why? Because the Cross has taken that desire away and replaced it with love and because the Empty Tomb opens up whole new horizons and worlds.

We believe there is no situation that cannot be transformed by the power of the risen Lord. And having glimpsed the transforming reality of God's reign we identify and stand against the forces of death, exploitation and destruction. We are not afraid to unmask idols and false gods.

We are prepared to become seeds that die in order that God's life might be revealed in all its glory. We value each person on earth and each relationship in the light of God's love and yet we see beyond human life, beyond the graves and killing fields.

In all this we identify with our brothers and sisters in Christ worldwide but as those alongside and living among children at risk we find ourselves moved to consider the ways in which children speak to us of resurrection. We see the decline of institutional religion in Europe as a sign of hope when we see the spiritual longing of children and young people.

We see in the ability and resilience of children in the face of appalling loss, suffering and humiliation, the desire to work for a better world, as resurrection in action. Children in our world are Easter signs like green shoots after the grip of winter.

4. The Ascension (the incentive for our mission)

We acknowledge that we have too often overlooked the significance of the Ascension of Jesus for our life and God's mission.

We affirm that it is the sign that Jesus Christ is King! That the kingly reign has begun. We acknowledge Jesus as Lord. We acknowledge that we are called to live as the Messiah People, in a world that does not as yet acknowledge Jesus as Lord. We are to resist being squeezed into worldly moulds and ecclesiastical and institutional patterns that distort the values and priorities of Christ.

We recognise there is a rich biblical vision of this new kingdom all through the Scriptures and that we are called to realise it in our lives, our families, our countries, our culture and in the wider world.

We also confess that in the history of mission other visions have unconsciously shaped the living out and proclamation of God's reign. In particular: territory, power and status have been valued more than gift-love and servanthood. We acknowledge that this kingdom demands an inverting of the status quo: bringing the changes portrayed in the Magnificat of Mary!

In particular we acknowledge that children are central in this vision, and that this is a revolutionary contrast to contemporary political kingdoms that have lost touch with the childlike spirit in their preoccupation with adult concerns and solutions.

Children and childhood present us with insights into the nature and dynamics of God's kingdom, especially the 'now' and 'not yet'. This is a creative tension. We see a child and a sacrificed lamb at the heart of that vision. It is an everlasting kingdom where every aspect of creation lives in harmony and without fear or pain. We acknowledge that political short-termism and selfishness conspire to cloud the purity and inspiration of that kingdom.

We commit our lives afresh to the service of Christ the King, the baby, child, Lord and Servant, Saviour and Brother.

5. Pentecost (the power for our mission)

We acknowledge the power of God's Spirit in the life and witness of God's people. The love and fellowship of God's people is part of the message the church proclaims.

This community is distinctive in that it exists for others, to be servants of the wider community by revealing righteousness and justice in action. It is God's avant-garde, a sign of the new kingdom but is not the kingdom.

It is a fellowship of followers of Jesus, on the move, responsive to God's agenda, call and timing. No Christian individual or organisation exists independent of the Spirit's enabling and *koinonia*. We are accountable to Christ through His people.

As those alongside children and living with them we acknowledge that the church has all too often replicated the assumptions and institutions of the culture in which it has been set, at the expense of Christ's example.

Children have not been at the heart of our life together and our worship. Too often, like the infant Jesus, they have been relegated to the stable-like margins. We have agonised over matters like infant baptism, participation in the Lord's Supper, and whether they are saved and at what age, while unaware of the ways in which, like the disciples of Jesus, we have come between children and the love of Jesus.

We have tended to see work with children as outside the mainstream of church life and worship. We recognise the biblical call to refocus our corporate agenda.

6. The Second Coming (the urgency of our mission)

All our work, initiatives and structures, like our celebration of the Lord's Supper, are interim. We live in the period between His first and second comings. We occupy 'until He comes'. We see in part; the kingdom is realised in part. But then we shall see Him face to face and the kingdom will be fully revealed.

We are alert; we listen; we work in the knowledge that He may come at any time. We operate in every part of the world, for that is His command. He has no preferred people or cultures: all are objects of His mercy and love and all peoples will be equally joyful as they participate in the new kingdom.

We live in expectation and hope. This event and vision of God's ultimate reign acts as a powerful magnet aligning our activity with His magnetic field, nature, holiness and justice.

We acknowledge that should Jesus come again today the suffering of millions of children will provoke His burning anger and judgement of those peoples and institutions that oppress them and cause them harm.

And as those living alongside and among children we acknowledge the special place and role that they have in His kingdom. They will lead the worship because this is what they are ordained to do. They will be at the centre, as centuries of marginalisation, victimisation and abuse will be replaced by an experience of perfect freedom and harmony.

Some Implications of the rediscovery of children in mission

This approach and outline has radical, potentially world-shattering implications. Let us list some of the most obvious and begin the task of working out others.

Theology. There have been major challenges to the western tradition of theology in recent decades from women and from non-European peoples and cultures. The old colonial-type edifice is crumbling. We cannot read the Old Testament, see Jesus, or understand the New Testament and Gospel in the same way. How could we have missed the great transcendent truths constricted by the constraints of our narrow assumptions?

But especially how could we ever have seen Jesus as a western male, a sort of Evangelical clergyman? We have begun to understand our Lord and Saviour in fresh and living ways: the Jesus we never knew!

Children have been all but invisible in theology, in its formal sense. The assumption has been that theology is an adult pursuit, and children are given baby food versions! What if we made the teaching of Jesus the starting point of theology:

Doing, not hearing alone ...
Being born again ...
Becoming like children ...?

There would be much that we would 'need to unlearn – all the adult structure and the cumbering years'.

Church. Alongside the shifts in theological understanding and process have come fresh insights into the nature of "church". For centuries the European consensus across denominations has been of institutions usually worshipping in a building with a male leadership. And in Europe this model has reached a crisis point: there is widespread and chronic decline especially among children and young people.

Are there new ways of being church? In their study Anne Wilkinson-Hayes and Stuart Murray[43] look at examples from different parts of the world. And one of their discoveries was that in several cases 'children are very central to the way of being church'. Stuart Christine in Brazil tells of his discovery of the dramatic change in his understanding of church when he saw children at the heart of ministry, life and worship.[44]

We need to redefine the core and margins of the church always reforming. The core is clearly identified in the scriptures: widows, orphans, strangers and the 'little ones'. We have radical work to do if we are to be God's avant-garde.

Society. Ours is a calling to change the world in line with the contours of God's kingdom. We cannot accept the status quo. We will be salt and light at every level: living in a new way, challenging evil, power, and traditions. This is non-negotiable. If children are being harmed we cannot hold back.

We will challenge adult assumptions and preferences: the market forces that corrupt children and childhood. And where do 'Rights' and 'Democracy' figure in this transformed society? Patterns and understandings of families, and parenting need to be rethought. We will be involved personally and corporately, in action and policy, with individuals and institutions, with ideologies and structures.

A Call to Obedience

We did not choose Him; He chose us. He loved us and gave Himself for us. He fills us with His spirit and leads us into His mission. In leading us to be alongside children He entrusts us with the heart of His mission and kingdom. He warns us of the costs and dangers but He promises that as we open our hearts to one child, we welcome Christ himself.

We have an awesome calling to be alongside children at risk, and in the process to reshape the processes, nature and structures of church, mission and society. If we fail, it is not just children who continue to suffer but civilisation as God sees it. Not only will children fail to have their rightful place but Jesus himself will be misunderstood and unrecognised. He will have knocked at the door of our souls and fellowships in vain. But when we welcome a child in His name, we have opened our hearts afresh to Him.

CHAPTER NOTES

42 This passage is discussed in more detail in chapter 20 of this book.

43 S Murray and Anne Wilkinson-Hayes, *Hope from the Margins: New Ways of Being Church* (Cambridge: Grove Books, 2000).

44 See the PEPE project: www.pepe-network.org

CHAPTER 18

The Child in the Midst of the Biblical Witness

KEITH WHITE

Introduction

IT IS always a joy and encouragement when we come to the Bible with a particular question in mind and find that God is ready and waiting to greet us. By His Holy Spirit he has not left us without a witness.

In this unique collection of writings comprising 66 books compiled over 1,500 years, God's purposes towards a huge number of groups and situations is revealed. Thus those in Latin America who sought to understand the place of the poor and oppressed in God's kingdom were able to trace his commitment to them from the earliest pages and stories, especially in the liberation of the Hebrew slaves from Egypt. So it has been with those enquiring about those seen as outsiders or others because of their culture, ethnicity, crimes, brokenness or gender. I personally remember the time when as a sociologist I read Jacques Ellul's great book *The Meaning of the City* which traced the place of cities in God's unfolding purposes from the very first chapters of Genesis to the last pages of Revelation.

One of the results of such a search is to see things more comprehensively and sensitively. Anyone who has tried to understand the place of women in God's mission for example cannot fail to read the Gospel of Luke differently to those who wrote commentaries a few decades ago.

In some ways, reading the Bible making children the starting point for study can be compared to these other perspectives and movements; there are striking similarities. But the emerging field of Child Theology has also found a significant point of departure: a uniqueness, if you like. Put simply it is the fact that Jesus took a little child (not a woman, poor man, gentile), placed him/her in the middle of his disciples and used the child as a key to understanding the Kingdom of Heaven, the very heart of his calling and mission.

But that is to go ahead of ourselves. Before looking at the place of the child and children in the Scriptures, we need to remind ourselves that at the very heart of the Bible we find God himself, revealed in different ways and at different times but supremely and most fully in Jesus Christ. However precious any part of creation is (and children are very dear to God's heart) anything that displaces God will tend to become an idol and in relating to any such created thing we will tend to become guilty of idolatry however indirect and unconsciously. So I would like to stress that all of us must take good care never to think or act in a way that elevates children or childhood in such a way that God is relegated to the background.

1. Children (and young people) as children

The title of this chapter – "biblical witness" – is releasing. More often, we tend to think of "children in the Bible". And there is a big difference. We can indeed look right through the Bible from Genesis to Revelation using a concordance and find lots of references to children and young people. You can do the same thing with plants, mountains, rivers, women, colours, cities and so on. You end up with an impressive list and if you reflect on it you can work your way to some sort of biblical or even theological understanding of the category that you start with. At best you will work towards a theology *of* children, plants, mountains, rivers, women, colours or cities. And that has its place, because God who created all things delights in every part of creation and it is good to have our eyes opened to new aspects of his work of art we think of as the universe.

But biblical witness is about something more than this. It challenges us to see the meaning of each part of creation; its testimony if you like. What is it pointing to? What is the message it is designed to convey to us?

And it doesn't take us long to realise that the Bible itself is crystal clear that everything in creation is designed to point to God in Jesus Christ. Everything is created to praise the Creator: whether trees clapping their hands, seas roaring, or babies crying. This means that in seeking to understand children as part of the biblical witness we are not merely trying to understand better how children are made, what they are like, how they develop (although there is so much that we can learn about these things), but to understand more fully what children reveal to us of God and his purposes and nature.

If you can make this distinction with me, you will immediately grasp the difference between a "theology of childhood" and "child theology". This is not to say that they do not inform each other and overlap but to point out the way in which Child Theology goes beyond the child as a child, in order to see the child in relation to God in Jesus Christ. It may be that a theology of childhood is a useful starting point. An excellent reference book if you are looking for an encyclopaedia of children in the Bible is *Precious in His Sight* by Roy B. Zuck.[45] I always keep it beside me!

We have already provided a summary of how Christian biblical scholars and theologians have interpreted all the references to children in the Bible in Chapter 13. Marcia Bunge, in that paper, offers six categories to summarise the way Christians have understood children. I believe that only if we hold on to them all can we begin to see deeper into the biblical witness to God and his faithfulness, justice and love. But rarely do we manage in church and ministry to hold all of these together. It is not hard to see the problems that arise when we concentrate on only one of these perspectives. If for example we see children as simply gifts of God and sources of joy, we will not take seriously the challenges of motherhood and will tend to have a sentimentalised and romantic idea of children that does not do justice to the suffering and oppression of children worldwide. If on the other hand we see them simply as sinful, parenting and teaching may not be open to what children have to teach as we seek to care for and teach them. There is work here for all of us to do, and these two resources are a real blessing as we set about this task.

2. Children as partners in God's mission

A few years ago I too read right through the Bible, but with a particular purpose in mind.

I was looking to see how, where and why children figured in the Bible. The result was the paper "Rediscovering Children at the Heart of Mission".[46] It was a turning point in my whole ministry and could be said to have given birth to what we now call Child Theology. One insight that turned my whole understanding of children around was that God *"performed some of his most significant acts and revelations through these children. Their faith and actions are critically important in the unfolding and outworking of God's purposes."* [47]

Until then I think I had tended to see children as precious objects of care, teaching and ministry. They remain that still, but what I had missed was the fact that again and again the Bible tells how, when things got really serious, God chose children. It is God's nature to choose the weak things of this world, so no one can boast. So when we see children as partners, we also see ourselves, as adults are always children to God, chosen in our weakness.

This insight helped me to see that it is necessary to ponder deeply the nature of God's mission. He takes the weak things of the world and reveals his strength in and through weakness. Children are largely unconscious of the way in which God is using them: they are not trained agents of the Kingdom. Perhaps God is using us as individuals and a church in ways that we are completely unaware of. Do we stress conscious mission, objectives and outcomes, systems and models, when He prefers to work as quietly as yeast in the dough and a mustard seed in the garden? This discovery has led me both to see my relationship to children differently and also to reflect deeply on what all this has to teach about God, Jesus and the Kingdom of Heaven.

3. Child and childhood as God's way of seeing all humans

Once you start reading the Bible with children in mind you quickly discover that many if not most of the references to children are not actually about children as young human beings at all but ways of describing adults and adult communities. In the Jewish Scriptures there is continuous reference to "the children of Israel" for example and this phrase refers to the whole of the Jewish community, male and female, young and old. Likewise in the New Testament followers of Jesus are often referred to as "little children", for example in the letters of John.

This is not the place to develop this perspective but we can note that it has some important implications. One is that we must be careful in making distinctions between adults and children, lest we obscure the fact that God sees us all as his children. What if childhood, rather than being a temporary phase in human development before what we may think of as maturity or adulthood is, from God's point of view a description of the whole of our lives? When you pray, say, "Our Father": not just while you are little children but as adult believers and followers of Jesus.

Allied to this is the recognition that some of the most important descriptions of what it is to be a Christian relate to processes that we usually associate with children and childhood. Two obvious examples are 'Adoption' and being 'Born Again'. Whatever Paul and Jesus mean when they use these symbols they are not calling adults to cease to be responsible adults; but at the same time it is clear that unless we hold on to the child in the midst we, as adults, lose a vital sign of the Kingdom of God.

4. The Messiah as child

One of the umbilical links between the Old and New Testaments is the child foretold in the prophets, notably Isaiah, and the birth of Jesus. I invite you to ponder afresh the passages in Isaiah which speak of this child (Isaiah 7:14; 9:1-7; 11:1-11) to see what they reveal of God's nature and his Kingdom. And then to read afresh the two birth narratives of Jesus in the Gospels of Matthew and Luke. There is something distinctive and vital about the fact that God is revealing himself, coming among us, as a baby: *"This will be a sign to you: you will find the babe, wrapped in swaddling clothes and lying in a manger."*

Jesus does not refer to his childhood in his adult ministry, and we must be careful not to build theology where he chooses not to do so. But he does draw attention to the importance of the cries of newborn babies in Psalm 8:2. Although we know that salvation comes to us through the life, death and resurrection of Jesus, rather than through his childhood, we should be careful not to overlook Jesus the promised child.

When thinking about this in Malaysia a year or two ago, I preached on the subject "child in the midst" arguing that God had chosen to place a child in the middle of human history and that the immediate reaction was that this divine child was placed in a manger because there was no room for him in the inn. Still I wonder whether we make sufficient room in our theology, biblical studies, worship, and pastoral work for the baby Jesus.

In very practical terms I am suggesting that Christmas is rightly seen as a very special festival, and that it should not simply be seen as a prelude to the later ministry of Jesus. In this little baby God is revealing deep things about himself, and as we grasp them we will see both our Father God, and also little children differently. (I commend to you the book by David Jensen, *Graced Vulnerability*,[48] which takes this as one of its starting points.)

5. Child as representative of Jesus and Kingdom

I have been working with Haddon Willmer for some years on a book that expounds the encounter between Jesus and his disciples in Matthew 18 where Jesus places a child in their midst as a sign of the Kingdom of Heaven. This has led us both to realise that neither we, nor our theological and biblical colleagues have given sufficient attention to what this child in the midst teaches us about Jesus, the way of the Cross and the nature of the Kingdom of Heaven. Jesus is clear that there is a risk of his disciples missing out on the Kingdom all together if they do not heed the sign of the child but subsequent church history does not suggest we have heeded his action, teaching or warnings seriously.

Let me give you a flavour of our exposition. We see the disciples engaged in an argument which is essentially theological about arguably the most important matter of all: what the Kingdom of Heaven means. Jesus has tried to explain the nature of the Kingdom and the way of the Cross in a number of different ways: stories, signs, examples, actions, and specific teaching. But they have not even grasped the most basic idea of this Kingdom. So as he begins his final journey to Jerusalem and the Cross he places a child in their midst to provide a completely unexpected clue or key to the Kingdom.

As we have considered this deeply and at length we have come to believe that the passage has considerable insights for us all into the heart of God, the way of the Cross and how we are to relate to children and to Jesus.

One crucial discovery for us concerns the use of the term "representative". Others have talked about the way Jesus identifies with little children in this and a later incident when he took little children in his arms and blessed them. Clearly there is a close link between children and Jesus. We have come to see the word "representative" as crucially important here. And this has led us to see in a fresh way how Jesus represents us on the Cross. He holds the space open for us so that by his Spirit the time comes when we are really "in him in his death" and therefore raised with him to newness of life. The child and Jesus are not interchangeable, any more than Jesus and his followers are interchangeable, but they and we are representatives.

6. The Child and Systematic Theology

Those of us who have studied systematic theology with a child in mind find that children are usually marginal, if not completely invisible, in all that has been written so far. Others have noticed before that the poor, women and black people have also been noticeably absent in what is written and have started to put that right.

As we begin to re-read this theology we find that new insights are dawning and new questions arise about: Creation, the Fall and Sin, Redemption, Church, Christ, the Kingdom of Heaven, the Resurrection, the Last Days and so on. The most obvious example is the way in which a child helps us to understand the "now" and "not yet" of the Kingdom of Heaven.

CHAPTER NOTES
[45] Grand Rapids: Baker Books, 1996
[46] Published in *Celebrating Children* (Paternoster Press, 2003, pages 189-199)
[47] Ibid; Page 190
[48] Cleveland: Pilgrim Press, 2005

CHAPTER 19

A Reflection on Psalm 8:2

KEITH WHITE[49]

Introduction

THIS GREAT hymn of praise starts and finishes with unforgettable cadences that have given rise, among other inspiring Christian songs, to *How great thou art*! Its alpha is praise and its omega is praise and between these refrains we find the whole of creation: from the tiny little baby to the farthest star; from the human realm to creatures that walk, swim and fly; from the foe and the avenger to heavenly beings. It meant so much to Jesus that when He entered the Temple in Jerusalem as the Chosen One, the Messiah, the Christ, and healed the blind and the lame for the last time, accompanied by the cries of Hosanna from some young people who were watching what He did, he quoted part of the Psalm to the chief priests and teachers of the law.

The flow of the Psalm, so beautifully balanced and expressed when used as a song of worship, is a challenge when scrutinized. Some see it having three stanzas, some two. There are problems of syntax in verses 1 and 2. Jesus and the writer of the letter to the Hebrews both used the Septuagint in which the word *"strength"* in verse 2 is translated *"praise"*. This is not the place to become bogged down in a detailed analysis of the text but it is as well to be aware of some of the pitfalls for the unwary. It is a hymn or paean of praise to the Lord. It is about the whole of creation. It exalts the name of the Lord.

The psalm says something quite astonishing, to the point of incomprehensibility, about children, and sets children in their proper context. Marshal Macluhan in *The Global Village* points out that when we focus on any subject or group we take them from their usual place and bring them into the foreground: this is as true of the scientist as of the artist. Having looked at them in this bright light, we find that they never quite fit the background from which they were originally taken. Things have changed both in the foreground and in the background as a result of our action. As those concerned with, and committed to, children and young people this is a risk about which we must be warned. If we overlook it we may sentimentalise and abstract children from their usual and rightful context. We may set children over against adults; we may divorce their education from the natural world and we may define their rights without an adequately contextualised moral and social framework.

So we are selecting a Psalm where children have a special place but in which at the same time they are set within a proper context, as part of the created order and, even more important, as part of the unending hymn of praise to the name of the Lord that emanates from the dawn of creation.

Children in God's Kingdom

So where do children fit in? What is their place and role in the whole of God's way of doing things?

There are three truths articulated here and we will ponder each in turn.

1. Children are ordained to play a part in the scheme of creation.
2. Their pre-school and pre-language cries are to be heard as praise.
3. They have a role in silencing the foe and the avenger.

1. Children are ordained to play a part in the scheme of creation
That's an interesting word to start with: ordained. We usually associate it with the priesthood and leaders of the church. Here it is applied to suckling babes. And we must understand, articulate and champion that ordination once we are clear about it. It is possible that one of the reasons why the world is not 'fit for children' is because we have lost sight of and

are out of touch with this primary role of children as ordained by the Lord.

> Children are not primarily created to help the economic situation of family and nation.
> Children are not primarily blank pieces of paper on which adults write a script in the name of 'education'.
> Children are not just objects to be entertained by the media.
> Children are not primarily 'adults in waiting' or 'human becomings'.
> Children are not primarily consumers, whether of food, market produce or media images.
> Children are not potential slaves to be branded.

They are *ordained* to join in a hymn of praise which pulses and resounds throughout creation, with its source in the conversation of the Trinity, its development through history and its fulfilment when the Lamb is seen face to face on the throne surrounded by the worshipping congregation that no one can number. Before, as adults, for whatever motives or intentions, we seek to rescue, care for, educate and mould children, we must grasp the Maker's intentions for them.

C.S. Lewis made just such a point at the beginning of his classic work, *A Preface to Paradise Lost*: everything in creation has its unique nature and purpose. Until we understand it we will never be able to respond to it appropriately and in striving oft we mar what's well. Like the Kingdom of Heaven, a child is both now and not yet. The best parents and teachers instinctively appreciate the uniquely creative space nestling within these two poles of reality and existence.

I have been reading around the subject and one of the more harrowing books is *Branded* by Alissa Quart[50]. It is about the buying and selling of teenagers by corporations who seek to groom them into consumers of their particular brands. Descartes started with the premise, *cogito ergo sum*. These corporations posit a consumer rather than a thinker and conspire to batter and brainwash teenagers into submission by destroying their creativity and individuality. It has been dubbed *"corporate paedophilia"*[51].

Once we are clear what children and young people are ordained by

God to be – what is their *"logical service"* (Romans 12:1-2) or *"species-being"* (to use the Marxian concept) then we are able to be genuine advocates for them: to pronounce a resolute and uncompromising 'No!' to the forces that corrupt and undermine the Creator's design and purpose for them.

There is a host of material in the Scriptures that, like this psalm, sets children in their proper context: an environment overarched by the stars, (*"lovely as under starlight waiting Him out of it"*, G.M. Hopkins), and shared with creatures that walk, swim and fly (see Isaiah 11:6-9; 65:20-25). Children are designed to seek out and enjoy warm and enjoyable human relationships (see Zechariah 8:3-8).

When looking at the mission statements and aims of many Christian organizations and groups, as well as international declarations, I have been struck by the assumption they make that we should proceed as quickly and efficiently as possible to prepare children for adulthood whether as producers, parents or citizens. Education is seen as the primary if not exclusive engine of this process. All the time the stark and prophetic warning of Rousseau in his great work, *Emile*, lies virtually unnoticed and unheard: always looking for the man in the child, without considering what he is before he becomes a man.[52]

2. Children's pre-language cries are to be heard as praise

The words for children here are perfectly clear: we are reading of newborn babies and suckling infants. These are primal children, in a state before adult conventions and formal processes of education and socialization have kicked in. Their cries should not be dismissed as meaningless but should be understood as part of the great hymn of praise throughout creation. To 'read' such cries requires a fundamental revolution in adult consciousness and institutions. Frobel studied little children for 15 years or so in coming to realize the subtleties of the communication between mother and baby. Korczak spent his life among children before concluding: *"A baby can hold a very complicated conversation without being able to talk."*[53]

You probably know of the recent research on babies and their babble. Rhythms and sing-songs between parent and child come before real words. Dr Petitto commented, *"there's a marriage between babies' sensitivity to specific rhythms around them, and the fact we give them those rhythms."*[54]

The adult must lay aside conventions and patterns around which the social world is ordered[55] and learn to listen all over again, like someone learning a new language with its strange cadences and inflexions. Isn't it obvious that a baby is uniquely sensitive to rhythms and sounds given the time spent within that rich, resonating mixture of pulse beats and movement we call the mother's womb? Communication continues with movement, rhythm, and song; poetry rather than prose; worship rather than learning by rote.

It follows from this that parents and kindergarten teachers must above all else be skilled, intuitively or by careful training, in listening to and observing the little child. They will need to understand the innate signs and movements of the baby and do so in the context of the natural environment. They will know that bird-song, animal sounds, waves of the sea, rhythms of the stream, movement of branches and leaves, of clouds and skies, are of unending attraction to the developing child; that insects, grubs and animals are natural companions of the little child and that a bee landing on the petal of a flower being swayed by a breeze can become a means of linking the child's inner world to the movement and dance of creation. Play, in its various and subtle forms, is the primary means or context of development, not learning by rote or catechism, though these have their place within the wider context.

One of the great joys since beginning to realize the significance of this passage has been to see parents and teachers coming to realize something more of the significance and meaning of infant babble and children's play. They have come to sense and then understand that the world is full of praise, human and natural, once we are prepared to pause in our attempts to teach and educate and to begin the infinitely more complicated and rewarding process of listening and observing. It is not just that the child is thus given creative space in which to flourish but that the adults receive the blessing of inestimable and unending experiences of real praise.

What a joy to discover that there is a more profound psalm of praise reverberating throughout creation than the Sunday School songs however special and beloved they may be!

3. Children have a role in silencing the Foe and the Avenger
We now reach a statement that has confounded some of the best biblical

scholars and interpreters. I have already noted the problems presented by the Hebrew and Septuagint texts. In my view the NIV represents the most sensible and congruent reading.[56] The challenge in this case is not so much in the words being used but in the assault on our adult assumptions and worldview. How on earth can little suckling babies take on and defeat the powers of darkness?

In the cosmic battle between principalities and powers represented by biblical books like Job, Ezekiel, Romans and Revelation is there a role for the tiny little baby? Isn't the suckling always the object of suffering and trauma, having no influence on the course of War, Famine, Disease and Death?

Commentators have, in the light of this logic, sought to find another way of treating the text. But Calvin, with his immense scholarship and faith in divine providence reminds us in his commentary on the Psalms that God is God! This Psalm is a hymn of praise celebrating the greatness of the Name of the Lord. Is there a problem once we accept that God is sovereign? He chooses (elects) how he will act and who, if anyone, he will use to achieve his purposes. If there is one underlying pattern in history seen through the eyes of faith it is surely the one St. Paul describes in 1 Corinthians 1:20-31: God chooses the weak and despised things of the world. In 2 Corinthians 12:9 this is spelt out beautifully: "My grace is sufficient for you. My strength is made perfect in weakness."

What we have in this Psalm is not therefore a puzzling exception to the way God works but a statement of the essence of his providential nature and purposes. He delights in revealing the true nature and potential of broken reeds, smoking flaxes, widows with their mites, boys with their picnics and leaders like Peter who deny and desert Him. The suckling child could not reveal the way God has chosen to work more clearly and memorably. Israel was chosen, not because it was strong and great, but because it was weak. In Ezekiel 16:4-6 it is described as an abandoned and rejected child with its umbilical cord still uncut, kicking in its blood, despised and rejected. We have, in short found our way to the heart of the Gospel of grace and of God's limitless loving-kindness and mercy.

The ultimate enemy is death and the resulting corruption of human relations issuing from despair of ever experiencing justice, peace and joy. This enemy has been in horrifying and chronic evidence throughout recorded history. Human might, organization, education and civilization can do and have done nothing to tame this enemy. Ozymandias is an unforgettable symbol and reminder of the futility of human empires but every childbirth is another revelation of God's grace and mercy: the triumph of life over death, of hope over despair.

Have you every heard a newborn baby cry? There are echoes of the Messianic promise and hope in that cry. When Jesus was born (with, I always imagine, a cry rather than, as the hymn writers portray it, "silently") the cry of every newborn baby was compressed, just as at the end of his life the sins of the world were upon him. Jurgen Moltman wrote: "With every beginning of a new life, the hope for the reign of peace and justice is given a new chance ... Every new life is also a new beginning of hope for a homeland in this unredeemed world ... children are not lonely metaphors for our hopes ... but of God's hope for us: God wants us, expects us, and welcomes us ... God is 'waiting' for the human person in every child, is 'waiting' for God's echo, resonance and rainbow".[57]

We could go on to delve more deeply into this rich Psalm, to explore the relationship between the suckling babe and the man (verses 2 and 4), between the man and the son of man (verse 4) between the son of man and the heavenly beings (verse 5) and between human rule and divine rule (verses 6 to 9). We have a richly textured backcloth against which to develop our thinking and work among children today.

My plea is that we always heed Macluhan's warning and never sever the link between the child that is the focus of our attention and exploration and the context in which both that child and we live. We share the same environment and owe it to children as well as to our Lord never to abstract children from the created world whether in the name of education, child protection or parenting. This Psalm is a bulwark against all that!

Concluding Reflection

We are only just beginning to discover some of the implications of all this in family, churches, schools and society, because children have been almost invisible to mainstream theologians and theological training until this point of time.

The major corrective to my thinking and work stemmed from the discovery that children were agents of God's providence and purposes, not just recipients of His love and care mediated through parents, teachers and the community of Christ. As I read through the narrative of God's dealings with His people the pattern began to take shape. Here are some of the roles played by children and young people that God chose:

The role of Joseph as a teenager: saving a family and nation
The role of Benjamin: reconciling his brothers and family
The role of Moses the baby and Miriam his sister: saving the
    Hebrews from Egypt
The role of the baby Obed in the Book of Ruth: founding the royal
    line of David and Jesus
The role of Samuel: uncovering the total corruption at the heart of
    God's people
The role of David: rescuing the Israelites from the Philistines
The role of the slave girl: the healing of Naaman
The role of young Esther, the orphan girl: saving her people
The role of the boy-king, Josiah: the reformation of Israel.

The picture should by now have become a lot clearer: it's a description of how God used children to silence and overcome the foe and the avenger. And when we come to the New Testament we should not be too surprised to find that the whole of God's plan of salvation rests on a baby wrapped in swaddling clothes and lying in a manger! In fact that is the very sign that the shepherds are given when they want to know how they will recognize the Saviour, the Messiah.

Let us be clear. These children became adults and were still used of God. We as adults have special responsibilities under God towards children. That's one of the reasons that we are here today. God chooses us and uses us to be advocates, kinsmen-redeemers (like Boaz). But we should never see children simply as objects of our attention and care, as victims needing rescue. We must always be aware that they can also be agents of God's purposes and mediating His love and purposes. They are God's language expressing with particular clarity the nature of His kingdom. They are like God's chosen visual aid, if you see things like this. Like the Heavens, they declare His majesty and glory, not least, and perhaps best, through their infant cries. Perhaps as a result of our brief excursion through the Scriptures you are that more prepared to join in this lovely Psalm from the heart of your being:

"O Lord, our Lord, how majestic is your name in all the earth!
You have set your glory above the heavens.
From the lips of children and infants you have ordained praise
    because of your enemies
To silence the foe and the avenger."

And perhaps you will come to understand why children and young people shouting this Psalm in the Temple at Jerusalem were such anathema to the opponents of Jesus, and such a comfort and encouragement to our Saviour and Lord, as He laid aside His majesty and became obedient even unto death on the Cross, that through His childlike faith and servanthood we might be adopted into His family and come to experience life as sons and daughters of the Living God.

CHAPTER NOTES

[49] From the Houston consultation, May 2004

[50] See the more detailed treatment of this book in Chapter 8.

[51] Quart, 2003: 8

[52] Quoted, Jenks, 1996:2

[53] A Voice for the Child: 23

[54] Guardian: 10.11.2001

[55] A profound resonance here with the kenosis of the Son entering creation as a human being!

[56] See also Robin Maas, 'Christ as the Logos of Childhood", Theology Today, January 2000 Vol. 56, No. 4: 462, for an excellent reading of this text.

[57] Theology Today, January 2000: 603

CHAPTER 20

A Walk with Jesus from Caesarea Philippi to Jerusalem

(MATTHEW 16–21)

KEITH WHITE

Introduction

IN THIS chapter, I invite you to take a walk with Jesus and his disciples from Caesarea Philippi to Jerusalem as he made his last preparations to equip his disciples for ministry, including child ministry.

Caesarea Philippi was on the slopes of Mount Hermon, North of the Sea of Galilee not far from the present day Damascus. The journey we are embarking on with Jesus took him from near the very north of the area in which he ministered to near the south, from a centre of pagan worship to the heart of Jewish celebration and sacrifice. All the time Jesus is heading for the place where the divine cup awaits him. And it is significant that his ministry has a new urgency and focus. He is still announcing and revealing the Kingdom of Heaven but once Peter has declared that he is the Christ, the Son of the living God, Jesus shares with his followers the heart of the Gospel: that he, the Christ, must suffer and be killed before being raised to life and that the Kingdom is completely and utterly different to the kingdoms on earth.

It is difficult to keep track of Jesus' life story when we focus on single verses or passages and so we can miss emerging trends or links. Do you remember what happened immediately after the stunning revelation on the Mount of Transfiguration that confirmed in an unforgettable way the truth of Peter's declaration? The father of a boy who was suffering from seizures, probably a form of epilepsy, confronted Jesus and told him that his disciples hadn't been able to help his boy. They asked Jesus why they were powerless in this situation and, as Jesus explained why, the journey began on which we now embark with them.

When we look at this, we notice that he led by actions and example, not simply by words. That is how we will best teach and equip others. The process is as important as the content of the Gospel. I have argued elsewhere[58] that a theme running right through this climactic period of the ministry of Jesus is that of children and childhood. It seems as if every incident and all teaching is compared and contrasted with childlikeness. I am not going to expound this now but my exposition is set within this understanding of the narrative.

So let's begin our walk with Jesus. For some perhaps the idea of a pilgrimage will resonate, even possibly suggesting for some a forerunner to the Stations of the Cross. I want to share from this passage eight insights into the nature of the Kingdom of Heaven taught by Jesus that are axiomatic in our ministry among children, young people and families.

1. The critical importance of faith[59] and prayer[60]

As far as we can ascertain, it was on Mount Hermon that Peter, James and John saw the transfigured Jesus with Moses and Elijah and it was in the shadow of this snow-capped peak that the father brought his son to Jesus. Jesus healed the boy. The disciples, who had been unable to help, wanted to know why they couldn't rebuke and drive out the demon. Jesus spoke of their lack of faith (Matthew) and the need for prayer (Mark). The two responses form an integrated truth: faith and prayer are inseparable. They are the bedrock of our mission with children and in every setting.

As I have pondered this response of Jesus, it has begun to dawn on me that the overwhelming importance of prayer and faith was not just something that Jesus reiterates in his teaching and mentoring of his followers but was incarnated in his life and ministry. In John's gospel we have the privilege of eavesdropping as Jesus prays. Later we will enter into this wrestling in prayer in the Garden of Gethsemane.

But this was accompanied by the profoundest faith in history. He has just told his followers that he must suffer and die and that he will be raised to life on the third day. Have you stopped to reflect on the faith of Jesus? I'm not sure what the writer to the Hebrews had in mind when he summoned up his great catalogue of the people of faith by referring to the Jesus as the author of our faith (Hebrews 11:2) but, in using a word applied to Jesus as the author of life and salvation, perhaps we should pause to let the significance of this moment in his ministry sink in.

Notice before we move on, the faith of those who brought people to Jesus, including the father of the epileptic boy. We, the body of Christ, have no monopoly of faith. If we think that children's or any ministry in the name of Jesus is possible without faith this is the time to quit! The words *"Have faith in God"* above the door of Mill Grove, my own home, testify to a century of faith: trusting God and relying on His promises. Faith and love go together. We see that beautifully clearly in 1 Corinthians 13:4-8.

Until we can pray *"Thy will be done"* our interventions are loose cannons! We should seek to find the agenda of our Heavenly Father in the life of a child or family. Our primary task is to discover the Missio Dei and to join Him in it, not to seek to enlist His assistance for our own endeavours!

2. The necessity of changing and becoming like little children[61]

By heading south we have now arrived at Capernaum, the well-known town on the shores of Lake Galilee, where Peter's house was situated, and one the centres of the ministry of Jesus. It was the place where he had healed so many as the sun was setting and so fulfilled the prophecy of Isaiah.

So what do we make of this text? The meaning of this teaching is commonly misunderstood. Usually people make a list of the attributes of children (for example: they are trusting, questioning, reliant and dependent on others) and then seek to apply them to adults. We must be very careful if we do this that we don't read our adult and cultural preferences into children! A primary question concerns whether we are prepared to change or not. If we are not, then we are unlikely ever to enter into God's way of doing things. So, let's ask ourselves whether we are allowing Jesus to change us. This is something that is happening to many who have engaged in Child Theology.

Then comes the issue of *becoming like children* and I want to admit that I am becoming steadily less sure what it means as I study its meaning with others across the world. We certainly must avoid sentimentality in our responses and ideas. Perhaps it has something to do with having open and enquiring minds; being ready to learn and to obey, to grow, to change, to wonder. Put practically, it may be about being ready and willing to pray the Lord's Prayer: *"Our Father in Heaven … your way of doing things take precedence, your will be done …"* *"You are the potter: I am the clay."*

3. Welcoming children in the name of Jesus and so welcoming Jesus Himself[62]

We are still in Capernaum, with the fishing boats moving silently across waters of Galilee clearly visible as Jesus speaks.

Some years ago I was asked a question that cut me to the quick. I had already given more than quarter of a century to caring for children at risk in my family home, Mill Grove. The (angry) questioner challenged me: *"Do you really want to be in this ministry?"* I immediately knew from my instinctive defensive reaction that he had touched a raw nerve. The result was a deep pondering of my calling during which I realised that I had reservations and possibly regrets that must have affected my relationship with the children and young people I sought to help. Over time I began to learn what it was really to welcome children in the name of Jesus: to be open to them with my whole being. And I have come to recognise those parents, teachers and carers who have opened their hearts to children; who love and respect the children they are alongside.

The process is similar to that experienced by Jean Vanier and Henri Nouwen. In fact Henri Nouwen's last book *Adam* is a brilliant description of the process involved. For it shows with honesty and reality that our ministry is only Christ-like when it is two-way, when we open ourselves up to the possibility that we are being blessed. Please don't think this welcoming is an easy or painless process!

When we are open to children, really joyful in our ministry, then we will find that we have welcomed Jesus.[63] If so our work is a great privilege. This interpretation is an antidote to a spirituality that focuses on the pilgrimage and identity of self. In such a case, ministry among children might be a way of meeting our own needs rather than theirs.

4. Understanding how abhorrent child abuse is to God[64]

With barely a pause, Jesus changes mood dramatically. It could well be that these words of Jesus are his most angry and condemnatory. And as he speaks he surely points at Galilee. That is where the ripples of the person drowned with a millstone around his neck would forever be lodged in the imaginations of the listeners to his dire warning. It's so hard to read and hear them that we often simply omit them.

Don't you shudder when you hear the numbers of priests in the Roman Catholic Church in America who have been involved in child abuse? In 1962 there was a document written by Cardinal Alfredo Ottaviani, discovered by the British newspaper *The Observer*, that insisted that clergy should be secretive and silent when confronted by sexual abuse within the RC Church. This silence was to include the alleged victim, under threat of excommunication. Can you imagine of how Jesus feels or who can sound the depths of sorrow in the Father heart of God (the title of the hymn by Graham Kendrick)?

But this is not restricted to specific acts of abuse. It includes everything that might cause children (*"little ones"*) to sin. Have you considered the world we have allowed to be created for twenty-first century children and the pressures on them to sin? Think of child soldiers who steal, murder and rape in their hundreds of thousands. Think of the tens of millions of child prostitutes. Think of the children of the rich who grow up to envy the possessions and wealth of others and long to have it. Consider those who are 'branded' around the world by trans-national corporations and marketing machines. Think of corporate and institutional paedophilia. In all these cases and so many more, children are being led into sin. How does God see the modern world developing around us, given His primary concern for children, little ones, the weak and the vulnerable? And where does that leave us?

Question from child at risk:
> "Why do you go to church? You know everything in the Bible, and you are good, so you don't need to go!"

Reply from carer:
> "I go to kneel down and ask God's forgiveness not only for the sins that I know I have committed but also for the systems and institutions that I am allowing to be created and not challenging that cause little ones to sin."

It's a sobering thought.

5. Valuing each child as an individual of inestimable worth[65]

The water of Galilee is still lapping near the feet of Jesus but now it is the hills, particularly to the east, richer in colours and textures as the afternoon turns to dusk, where the listeners now focus their attention. Don't overlook the fact that the story of the one lost sheep in Matthew's Gospel is set in the context of children and little ones and that it begins with a reference to the guardian angels of children. There is also a moral: see that you do not look down on these little ones.

Statistics are powerful and they can stir us with a sense of huge injustice and suffering but in the final analysis it is vital to realise that we are called to be good shepherds who will join in the search for the one lost sheep. I don't know how administrators in children's work cope! I am impressed by those who sponsor an individual child. We must be ready to restructure our lives so that the individual child is loved unconditionally. I have written about this in Celebrating Children.[66]

There have been some varied Christian reactions to the UN Convention on the Rights of the Child but something that underpins the document is a sense of the dignity and worth of each child. It is salutary to reflect on the fact that this is why we are all alive in Christ today: because

God sees each one of us as of eternal value and sent Jesus as the Shepherd to search for us and bring us to our Heavenly home on his shoulders.

6. Allowing children and their families and friends to come to Jesus[67]

Jesus now leaves Capernaum and Galilee and wends his way south along the River Jordan but on the East side known as Transjordania or Perea. He would have passed the place where he was baptised and it is not fanciful to consider that it was near such a spot that this next incident occurs. John the Baptist at first resisted the request of Jesus for baptism before allowing the authority of Jesus to take precedence.

This is one of the eight elements where we probably think we can move on without much need to reflect. Surely we all agree on this point? What controversy could there possibly be? Well, the disciples, having been taught specifically by Jesus all that we have just considered, actually tried to prevent people from bringing children to Jesus! And sadly it is not difficult to find examples of churches and Christians who have, intentionally or not, done this down through the centuries.

We have tended to overestimate our own skills and importance and to underestimate the significance of the direct relationship between children and their Saviour. I was surprised to discover how adults have come between children and Jesus even in the matter of 'Children's Bibles'. What if people bring children to Jesus outside our office hours? What if they have some very strange ideas? What if they need, in our view, education and medical help? Please don't lightly assume that you and I and our ministries have been innocent in all this. But rejoice that when children do find their way to Jesus, he welcomes them and blesses them beyond our comprehension. And let us be thankful for Fröbel, Montessori, Cavalletti and Berryman in all they have taught and modelled.

7. Seeing children as signs of the Kingdom of Heaven[68]

We are still alongside the River Jordan and the final destination of Jesus, the critical event in the unfolding revelation of his kingdom in Jerusalem, is near.

Let me briefly mention just two of the points that dawned on me when I first became aware of Child Theology. First, if children are signs of the Kingdom of Heaven, then we must get rid of all notions of power, territory, possession and hierarchies to enter it. This kingdom is a whole new way of living. It's an upside-down, inside-out and back-to-front world. Put simply it works on almost exactly the opposite principles of the political kingdoms we know from personal experience and history worldwide.

Second, just as the child is both fully human and yet still becoming an adult, so the Kingdom of Heaven is both *'Now and Not Yet.'* You have daily reminders of God's way of doing things whenever you see children at work and play. Is there a better sign of the Kingdom? Is this what the 'Resurrection Mind' is all about, as it refuses to become fixed and finalised, as it remains open to further journeying, revelation and change? It is such a complete contrast with what the disciples and the mother of James and John still had in mind somewhere between the Jordan and Jericho (Matthew 20:20-28).

8. Understanding children's expressions in the context of God's way of doing things[69]

And now, at last Jesus enters the Temple itself. He has come to his Father's House. He has come home. He has come to his own.

In chapter 19, we began to see how the cries of newborn babies can be understood in a whole new light when we trust God's way of doing things, in his purposes and intentions. In the Temple the authorities saw the behaviour of the young people who were singing and shouting as wholly inappropriate. Jesus saw them in a completely different way: they were doing exactly what God had intended.

As we listen really carefully to everything children and young people say and try to reflect on it in the light of God's heart we will find surprising things happening! When children shout and cry in anger we will see sometimes that this is as it should be; they have experienced abuse and injustice. When children see play as more important than formal education, perhaps that is how God sees it too. And when they don't do exactly what we think they ought to in church, is our disapproval representative of God and how He feels? Perhaps their worship is more real than that of many adults. At the very least we should ponder what children are saying rather than ruling it out of court straight away.

Reflection

And so we come to the end of our journey, our walk with Jesus. This period in the life of Jesus is of considerable importance in understanding the Kingdom of Heaven and children and how they relate to each other. There may be no great surprises, but perhaps we are struck by the way Jesus seems to have anticipated modern theories, policies, conventions and legislation. If we are to equip other Christians to join us in ministering to children, then it makes such a difference if we root and ground our teaching in the life and teaching of Jesus. It is a walk, a journey, a pilgrimage that we must all undertake.

Please notice that the focus is not simply on the needs of children, as if ministry is a one-way street. As we draw alongside children with the eyes of Jesus, then we are called to change, to repent. For some of us this may be equivalent to being 'born again'.

The journey from Mount Hermon to Mount Moriah was an epic one for Jesus and, to all those whose eyes and ears are open, the heart of the Kingdom and Gospel have been revealed it. The whole journey is framed by the cries of an epileptic boy and the cries of a group of rowdy young people. Strange that all this has been so hidden from the wise and learned commentators! But then Jesus had already anticipated this: *"I thank you, Father, that You have hidden these things from the wise and understanding and revealed them to babes ... Yes, Father, for such was thy will."* (Matthew 11:25-26) So we have come to the end of this particular journey and find ourselves back at the place where we started. Now we are better placed to understand why the cries of suckling babes are one of the most beautiful, insightful and powerful sounds in creation.

CHAPTER NOTES

58 See chapter 17, pages 141-142
59 Matthew 17:20
60 Mark 9 29
61 Matthew 18:3
62 Matthew 18:5
63 I develop this in greater detail, exploring whether it is in receiving or welcoming children that we become like them, in a book written with Haddon Willmer: to be published
64 Matthew 18:6-9
65 Matthew 18:10-14
66 Miles, G and Wright J-J (Eds); *Celebrating Children*, Paternoster Press, 2003
67 Matthew 19:13-15
68 Matthew 19:14; Mark 10:13-16; Luke 18:15-17
69 Matthew 21:12-16

Part Four
EXPERIMENTS IN CHILD THEOLOGY

IN OUR meetings, participants were encouraged to engage in theological reflection around one or two issues of particular importance to their own cultures. Here we report on the methods used and some of the outcomes. They are not the first or final word on these subjects and maybe 'only' the babblings of theological babes! So, we call them 'experiments'. Like any real experiment, the outcome was unpredictable. Some, if not all, of those reported in this volume are more than averagely provisional and need further work to be really useful. But all have insights and may stimulate further work.

This was a learning process for the organisers as much as for the other participants. Over the years the process has changed and adapted. I have not drawn specific attention to the chronology of this development as there is no certainty that we have 'arrived' at the definitive method or might not at some point return to an earlier approach. Whatever process was used, the key was always to bring a child into a theological discussion, i.e. always to do theological reflection with the child present. Almost always, a child was not physically present but nevertheless was present, in our minds and imaginations. There are no doubt hundreds of ways by which the child may be made present; the chapters here give examples of how we have tried to do it.

The experiments were generally challenging for most participants and I think most found them enjoyable though, on occasion, several confessed they were confused at various points. For most, but not all, the 'penny dropped' before the experiment ended and participants were rewarded with new insights which, on occasion, were reported as life or ministry changing.

Chapter 21 describes the one time in Brazil when we actually were able to put children 'in the midst' and took time to listen and respond directly to them. It was an immensely challenging undertaking but very rewarding. Chapter 22 describes a more typical process for bringing the influence of children to bear on our reflection. The other chapters in this section show how Child Theology has something to say to the whole church, not just the children's department, and is capable of bringing new perspectives to our most cherished doctrines, such as: sin, church, mission and Christology.

Chapters 26, 27 and 28 reflect on significant areas in the life of children: the media, family and education. These are key factors moulding the development of our children who seem to be under constant attack. In particular, chapter 26 focuses on the pervasive influence of the media in western culture. Although the particular child brought into the midst in that discussion was a western child, the issues raised are worldwide. Globalisation is bringing western media, with their concomitant values of materialism and consumerism, into every favela and township and even into rural communities throughout the world. The final chapters from 27 to 29 give examples that have been more fully thought through and have been presented to consultations as 'worked examples' of the process.

CHAPTER 21

Listening to the Urban Child

JAMES GILBERT ET AL

A Consultation in Brazil

THE ITU consultation was conceptualized around the idea of putting the child in the midst of our theological thinking. It was decided in Penang that we should have the experience of visiting Brazilian children at risk.[70] We wanted to ask them what they thought, to listen and to converse with them. We would then reflect upon our visit in our group, before making a return visit to continue the conversation.

In a sense, then, we were to have a conversation within a larger conversation. There was the consultation, an extended theological conversation, and couched within it was the conversation with the children. The theme of the conversations was the child at risk in Brazilian towns and cities.

It may seem odd to describe 'what a consultation might be', but we have found that it is usually not clear to all the participants. A consultation is a purposeful conversation. Though it really doesn't have rules, so to speak, it really only works if a majority of the participants participate throughout the whole consultation. We all know how it is when a late comer tries to enter in the middle of a long conversation. These intrusions can distract from and inhibit the conversation. The problem is not new voices or insights, these are welcomed. Perhaps it is more the tyranny of time, having to go back over old territory to relate what has already been said. Though impossible to prevent, the goal is to reduce this as much as possible.

Another important aspect of the consultation is that it values each participant's input, their differing perspectives and questions. Though there is a leader(s), or facilitator(s), the conversation is only enriched when all the participants live up to their part by participating. This requires both patience and careful facilitation.

Finally, the selection of participants was carefully thought out and a real challenge. We wanted to have about an equal proportion of practitioners and academic theologians (all Christians by nature are theologians).[71] Equally important was the ratio of women to men, as well as those people from differing races and locations from within Brazil. The goal was to try and represent Brazil as best as possible, reflecting its richness and strength of diversity, to enliven and deepen the overall conversation.

The centre of the broader conversation was to be the conversations with the children. That is a way of putting the child in the middle. To facilitate these, we decided to divide the 30 or so participants into five groups, each group visiting a different age group and location. The challenges we put forth for these visits were the following:

Firstly, we did not want the people who work with and care for the children to prepare the children's answers, or guide the children to give the "correct" answers. We wanted as much as possible the conversations to be with the *children* and not with the *children mediated by adults*. To do this we carefully prepared the caretakers of these children beforehand. Though impossible to prevent all such influences we felt we had limited them.

Secondly, we did not want to use the children for our adult agendas. To prevent or avoid this, it would have been much easier to read about a child or children, reflect upon our childhoods – good approaches which have been used by the Child Theology Movement in the past. Yet we felt that as Jesus had brought a live child into the middle of a live theological debate, it would be good to imitate this. If one accepts and believes that a child alongside Jesus may have important things to say to us adults; if God's Word presents children as having perfect praise; if they can and do hear God's voice; and if they are models of the kingdom according to Jesus, then our approach will be respectful, listening to and constructing a conversation, instead of fulfilling an agenda. Of course we had an agenda, which is impossible and not very useful to do away with. More importantly, by this process we could have a real conversation between children and adults. Neither the children nor the adults always had to have an answer.

Thirdly, we did not want the groups to respond with pat answers. We wanted to respect these children as much as possible, which meant that each adult participant realized and accepted that "adult", simplistic or forced answers were not acceptable. Neither were these conversations organized evangelistic opportunities. Though Child Theology is in no way against evangelism, it questions any evangelism that treats people in general, and children specifically, in simplistic ways. It is possible to impose our mission and evangelistic agendas on children and this we strived to avoid.

In summary, the words of children can be words of grace for us and others, if we only listen and respect them. Perhaps in this last phrase lies the centre of our method. It was not invented by us, we believe, but is taken from Jesus teaching his disciples by placing a child at his side, telling them to become like them (Matthew 18:1-5 and parallels). In this text the disciples were having a theological conversation, and Jesus put a child in the middle of it. We hope that in a small way we have imitated Christ in this process.

The following table gives a visual overview of the structure and rhythm of the consultation.

	Monday	Tuesday	Wednesday	Thursday	Friday
Morning	Arrival	Introduction to Child Theology and the program. Paper on the Brazilian context.	Presentations on children and theology.	Presentations on children and theology. Final preparations for second visit.	Final reflection in group and summary.
Afternoon and evening	Introductions. Opening service with special liturgy.	Visits with the children. Time for reflection after the visits.	Group work on the conversations with the children.	Second visit with the children. Evening service with foot washing.	Departure

During the final reflection, we sought to return to where we started the conversation. The final reflection answered the following questions.

> What is the principal theological question taken by your group?
> What is your final theological declaration?
> Who is the single child that you met whom you would like to share
>   with the whole consultation?
> How was the process special for you?

This section has tried to describe the method of the consultation. One could think of the method as a map and that we were on a pilgrimage. A pilgrimage because we had a departure point, a spiritual objective and we had much reflection and struggle along the way. Our hope was to deepen and broaden our understanding of God, His people and the world. To help guide us we brought along some children, specifically, urban Brazilian children at risk. The following section might be considered these children's résumés or curriculum of our guides. This will be followed by five stories of each groups' journey.

GROUP 1
Visit to a PEPE[72] class with children from 4 to 6 years

The group was very well received by our group of small theology teachers from whom we learned so much. They stirred us to reflect deeply during our visit. We felt comfortable among them as they were playing next to us and we were asking ourselves the question "What is good in this neighborhood?". The first answer was the one that attracted our attention most and that was the starting point of our reflection: "The good thing here is Gustavo". After a time of conversation about this question, many different people gave interesting answers and we asked them to illustrate the subject: "If God was the mayor here what would he do?" Aspects that represent union were recurrent in the drawings; there always appeared a scheme of union of two or three figures. In the end, however, when we asked them to give us their drawings, they began to cover their drawings with other colors and to scribble. One child even stopped drawing when we said that. Perhaps they felt exposed or some anguish had been woken there. It was also something for us to think about.

1. What is the principal theological question taken by the group?
   Theology of the glance.
2. What is your final theological declaration?
   The glance of the child is as God's glance, a glance that does not judge, it does not even condemn, and being looked at by them we are transformed into God´s image.
3. Who is the single child that you met that you would like to share with the whole consultation?
   Paul was hospitable and receptive toward us.
4. How was the process special for you?
   The breaking of the paradigm that we were going to offer something to the children. On the contrary, we received and were instructed by them.

GROUP 2
Visit to the children playing in the street of the Slum Capivari

The group had the challenge of hearing children in the community. There was no organized group, the children were found running free in the street and they were playing. Each one of the group talked with a different child. The answers were interesting.

We asked Paulo, a 6-year-old, "If God was the mayor of the city, what would he do?" and "What if you were the mayor?". To the second question, the child answered that he would do the same things that he had listed in the first question. Perhaps he identified with this (imaginative) demonstration of God; in other words, what God would do, it is what I can do.

Another participant asked the same questions to a girl. She answered that God would build an orphanage, because where she lives there are many orphans. She said that she would like to work in that orphanage.

The theological question that motivated the group was "Does God play?" The children taught us in a very spontaneous way that God plays, that he participates in all the fun. Wellington, who is 7 years old, told us that God plays tag and soccer, he plays with animals and tells stories. In a game of soccer God plays all the positions, attack, defense and goalkeeper. God as goalkeeper was not going to let anything pass because he flies! He could be a judge, since he does not make mistakes. The children taught us that theology is something practical, simple, part of daily life. When one plays, body and soul participate in an integrated way. There is no separation between daily life and the sacred. We should always adore and worship God. The children taught us how to break the paradigm in which adoration happens only in the moment of worship. It happens in every moment.

The group of children whom we found consisted only of boys, so we asked about the girls. Kaíque, 9 years of age, answered that God plays with the girls with doll houses. There is no discrimination, since boys and girls are partners of God when they play. In play, a relationship is established with the other. There is interaction, respect, limits and rules. We returned to the thought that theology is part of life, of our day to day activities, and reflected on the Word that became flesh; it became a physical body. A child's space in the church has to express life, freedom, movement, joy, pleasure, and not only words. The city for Wellington, Marcos, Paulinho, and Davi, had to have a place to play, where the persons play together. "God will call more friends", said 10 year old Marcos. It is necessary to have feelings and emotions.

Child Theology must be an instrument for the church and for the people of God to create a new type of relationship between people and with God himself. It should be a way of doing things differently, with more participation, more involvement. There is still much to hear and to learn from the children. This was the beginning of an experience in which God himself mediates our relationship with the child.

1. What is the principal theological question taken by each group?
   The God that plays.
2. What is your final theological declaration?
   God participates in the life of children and plays with them.
3. Who is the single child that you met that you would like to share with the whole consultation?
   Davi was playing with stones and he told us that one day God played with him throwing stones.
4. How was the process special for you?
   That they did not find the idea of God playing with them strange.

GROUP 3
Visit to the children at Belém Home (Vale da Benção)

We tried to begin with a dynamic activity but one of the children simply refused to participate. We began to insist but then we realized that to force participation would be disrespecting a child that we had the intention of helping. She had the right to not participate and that had to be respected.

As for the question "What would be the perfect city?", the children's descriptions always made use of the negative, using the word "not", as in "there will not be this or that", telling about the things that are not good. The answers were more or less like this: "Without theft, without death, without pollution, without violence, without corruption, without drugs, without arms". It called our attention very much to the repeated occurrence of the negative in the description of the city in the Apocalypse of John.

When we brought up the question: "If God was the mayor of the city, how would it be?" The general idea of the answers consisted of: "The city would have love, communion" (they were older children, therefore they had capacity to think more abstractly). Other answers: "If God was a mayor there would not be detours in the city" (the parties in the city are very noisy and fill the night air); "He would give houses to the ones who don't have one"; "The statues would be removed" (there exist several statues of scrap metal of iron in the city, as an effort of the Mayor in self promotion).

A child who was very extroverted and cheerful, when he discovered that Henry was Indian, began to speak with him in Guarani, because he had come from Paraguay (Guarani is the second language of that country). Henry is a Terena Indian and his language is different from the Guarani but even so they managed to communicate.

Afterwards, the children drew the perfect city. A boy explained that in his drawing the person fallen in the street was someone whom he would take care of and take to the hospital. Another boy placed himself in the drawing very satisfied: "Mayor Valdinei". And the name of the city would be Rio de Janeiro. He explained that his city would be completely colorful, because the mayor of the city where he lives paints almost everything with green and yellow (colors of Brazil). In other words, if God was the **187** mayor of the city, He would be going to use all the colors, not only green and yellow.

In this first visit we noted that the theological questions brought by the children concerned the concepts of peace and justice. After that, we discussed these concepts and tried to apply them to the context of the houses. When we placed the children in the middle of our symbolic wheel of reflection, we realized the situations of abuse and violence had revealed their sense of justice. We worked on the following biblical references: Jeremiah 29:4-7 and Isaiah 1:26. From these texts we decided to prepare a playful activity (theater), to present our response to the children.

In the end, we can say that this experience was real because we participated with them, with their reality. It was surprising, because it was not any different than the idea that God plays with them and it was special because they received us, they gave a place for us. We were interrupting their fun to ask them questions but even so they were happy to help us.

1. What is the principal theological question taken by each group?
   Justice and peace.
2. What is your final theological declaration?
   Peace is the result of a process of justice through anguish and pardon.
3. Who is the single child that you met that you would like to share with the whole consultation?
   Samuel in his drawing showed he is concerned with the neighbors, from the necessities that he observed, demonstrated actions of compassion.
4. How was the process special for you?
   The transparency of the children and their possible indifference with so many people visiting the group was distressing for us. And it was surprising to see the potential of the children.

GROUP 4
Visit to the children living in Betânia House
(Blessing Valley)

The group arrived at Betânia House, one of the houses of Children's City, in the Valley of Blessing project. We met in the living room with the social mother and ten children between 8 and 14 years old. We did some fun activities so that our group and the children could get to know each other. We made a circle and sang the song "If this road were mine". Then we replaced the word "road" in the song for "town", so that we could introduce the theme. We asked the children to help us to understand some things and we started to ask questions.

We asked what the perfect city would be like to them and what needed to be done to build it. Some of the answers were:

"Turn the city upside down";
"Have more houses, take out the buildings or make smaller buildings";
"Have a sweet shop for each person";
"Have less pollution";
"Not have thieves";
"Open toy factories";
"It should have everyone working";
"Give more houses to those that don't have one".

The answers to the questions that followed were similar and expressed the idea of a city at peace with its inhabitants and with nature. One child said that in his/her city "the poor and the beggar would be able to go to church". Another said that the children would be allowed to get dirty, sing, dance and sleep. A word that was repeated a lot by the children was "house". They repeated it several times.

At the end of the visit we asked what they would like to know, if they had the opportunity to ask God. We realized that what they said wasn't with the intention of seeking the right answer but it was spontaneous and sincere. Their questions:

Why doesn't God let us go back to our families?
Why doesn't God take the Devil out of the world?
What do we have to do to take the problems out of our life?

After debating we got to the conclusion that the children's questions were related to belonging. They didn't want to stay there in the Valley of Blessing, they wanted to go back to their families. We think that the second question has to do with the problem of evil and human suffering: if God is Almighty, He should take the Devil from the world and in this way children will have no more problems.

We could have worked with the matter of who this God is or the matter of belonging, what makes us part of a family. We chose to work the matter of belonging to a family, particularly to God's family. In the second visit to the house, we shared with the children our thoughts. But we were very surprised with the answer we received from them. When we said good-bye, we asked what would stay in the memory of each one. An older boy said "It was good of you to come here and ask what we think rather than tell us what we have to think".

What is the main theological question brought up by the group?
Belonging to God's family.
What is the group's final theological declaration?
To belong to God's family is to feel taken care of by each other.
Who is the single child that you met who you would like to share with the whole consultation?
Henrique. He changed our adult way of thinking, He showed a critical vision.
How was the process special for you?
At the beginning, the affection and receptivity of the children.

GROUP 5
Visit to the children at the Children's Association of Belém

The structure of the institution and the diversity of the children who attended there were outstanding in this experience. We experienced the solidarity, communion and very real acceptance among the children, which promoted a very fraternal and very calm environment.

The children were very kind to us and they received us very well. All of them were anxious for the visit and for what we were going to talk about with them. To create a relaxed atmosphere we did a fun dynamic activity. Then we asked, "What would a perfect city be like?". We notice that their answers were coming from their longings, from their life experiences. Also the experiences that the children had with God were notable in their answers. Several of them spoke about the wish and the necessity of having a good and pretty house to live in, work, justice, joy, and peace. They raised issues of urban infrastructure: to play in a street without garbage; to take care of the plants; to have no thieves. One of the boys still felt sad because they had killed the horse which he was taking care of. He was always speaking about not killing the animals and that in a perfect city there were animals. Other answers mentioned amusement, parks, joy, pleasure and security. Jesus also was part of their answers – in a perfect city the people have Jesus in their lives. We realized that for them a perfect city has joy, amusement, security, peace, tranquility, belonging {refuge}, relationships and Jesus.

To the question "And what if God was the mayor of Sorocaba?", we got the following answers: There would be no poor people in the streets, patients would be treated, the people would be revived (mostly "Pentecostals"); Life would be healthier. There would be more education, more work. There would be houses for all the homeless and there would be no drugs or other bad things.

At the end, the third question: "And if you could build a new city, what would it be like?"- They would have houses for everyone, food for everyone, more churches, more hospitals. One of them said that it would have more flags of Sorocaba around the city and another said, they would have more evangelical shops where the people could buy CDs and Bibles.

Afterwards, they were asked to draw the "desired city". They talked about their dreams with their drawings and even presented them to us. There was a drawing that showed clearly that the perfect city is under the sovereignty of God. Another had a person throwing a gun in the garbage. Another drawing showed the importance of the presence of nature in the city.

One of the questions that impacted us was one that a boy asked Welinton, "What are you going to do to remember us when you leave? You come on Thursday and then you go away. What are you going to do in order that you do not forget us?"

In the second visit, we made jokes, sang and shared prayer requests with them. In our reflection we remembered Isaiah 11 and saw how the prophecy described the reign of the Messiah and his future government. We encouraged them to pursue their dreams and wishes. We had the opportunity to take a simple snack to them, which helped us in our relationship with them.

It was a short time, but they left deep marks on us regarding the needs of the children we had heard, loved and also how we could learn many biblical truths through them. It was surprising and special that our group observed the reverence of the children, the value that they have because they exist and the necessity of being together with us.

1. What is the principal theological question taken by each group?
   Relationship is a standard of existence in the kingdom.
2. What is your final theological declaration?
   The church is an instrument in the transformation of the city in the existence of effective relationships taking the child as an indicative parameter.
3. Who is the single child that you met that you would like to share with the whole consultation?
   John Vitor is from a privileged economic situation but he is connected deeply with the other children.
4. How was the process special for you?
   To observe the respect of the children for us and the value that they gave to the fact of existence and the need to be with us.

CHAPTER NOTES

70 Children at risk is used here more in a sociological sense than psychologically, though one does not exclude the other. The context of urban Brazil is central to the millions of marginalized children.

71 See Keith White and Haddon Willmer, *An Introduction to Child Theology*, (Child Theology Movement: United Kingdom) page 3. See also, Howard Stone & James O. Duke, *How to think Theologically*, (Fortress Press: Minneapolis) page 1.

72 Programa de Educação Pré-Escolar; see: www.pepe-network.org.

CHAPTER 22

Child Theology and Sin

HADDON WILLMER

AT OUR second meeting, in Cape Town, we conducted a theological experiment on the topic of 'sin'. There are reasons why Child Theology should give attention to the understanding of sin. Sin is taken seriously in Christianity, causing controversy inside and outside the Christian community. And in Christian tradition many issues about the nature and life of children have been intertwined with it.

Christianity is identified by many as analysing the human predicament in terms of sin and as being accusing and punitive as a result. It is especially under criticism in some quarters for the Augustinian tradition, which explains children to a large extent in terms of sin. This is justified doctrinally by understanding original sin as the condition in which all are born, so that sin is expected to manifest itself in even the behaviour of babies. It is alleged that when this view is taken, the upbringing of children will be infected with anxiety and a tendency to punitive coercion, as an attempt to curb or suppress, if not to eradicate, the sinful nature. Historical examples can be found to support this view, which is often generalised into a blanket accusation against Christianity.

However, various contributors in *The Child in Christian Thought*[73] show that there is not an inevitable connection between holding a strong doctrine of original sin and punitive or insensitive upbringing of children. The kind of historical precision in their work builds an apologetic for Christianity, which is welcome but it does not get to a central issue, whether Christian understandings of sin might be rethought in terms that are independent of Augustine and notions of original sin.

In such explorations we find ourselves echoing and working with various theological contributions and experiments. The point is not to be original and thus gain theological glory for ourselves but to walk in the light more fully. And that means walking with others. Almost all discoveries in theology are renewals, not new creations.

Step 1

The first step was for each one of us to identify our starting position in a discussion of sin. We could measure the learning in the seminar by being clear about the baseline from which we started. So the group started by each person writing down three phrases to indicate what they understood by sin. These were private statements: markers for our own use. This took about five minutes.

Step 2

The next step was by an act of deliberate imagination to place two children in the middle of our circle. We were invited to consider two children:

A girl of 13 forced into prostitution;
A boy of 12 forced to be a soldier.

Step 3

The third step was to share stories from African experiences, which would help to make these children more vividly present to us and help us to share insights about them. Many of the group had some story or experience and some shared stories of just such situations from Zimbabwe, Nigeria, the Democratic Republic of Congo and South Africa. From these stories, we were able to identify several themes:

Adults who train and prepare children for evil;
Poverty – evil offers short cuts to riches;
The withdrawal of parental protection;
Children's desire to please allows them to be easily controlled by
    adults.

We must avoid falling into the trap of blaming either social structures or particular personal biographies; the two always co-exist and interact in any given situation. So, economic necessity must be taken into account as well as pride and greed. Even in some desperate situations, there are often some children who resist evil and do not go astray.

Children respond to their immediate perceived needs. What they want is constantly changing according to the circumstances, peer pressure etc. In desperate situations, people respond with what they have for what they see to be the best outcome that ensures survival if possible. But this is not done in a vacuum – there are others struggling with us. We naturally form groups for survival and children get into gangs.

This step took a considerable time, as people told detailed and painful stories.

Step 4

The fourth step was to ask explicitly how the doctrine of *sin* interprets these *children* for us and how these *children* speak to our thinking about *sin*. The theological process works in two directions: the Child interprets sin; sin interprets the child.

These questions were put to an open and freewheeling discussion, in which many issues were explored and disagreements aired. Not surprisingly, there was intense consideration of free will and original sin, of social conditioning and moral responsibility.

Some discovered that the understanding of sin they held became problematic in the presence of these children, especially when sorrow and love committed us to hope for their welfare. So there had to be hard work and constructive new thinking in order to have a serious understanding of sin, but one which would not do cruel violence to the children or deny the Gospel of Jesus Christ for them.

With the assistance of a moderator, the discussion concluded with a quadrilateral diagram (shown below). It indicates a child affected by four forces related to sin. No vote was taken and it is impossible to say what degree of consent it commanded but it was a fruit of shared labour in spiritual and theological thinking and others might like to think along with it.

The child in the middle of our circle is seen as a sinner, falling short of the glory of God, but not primarily because of free decisions made by the child. They are sinners because of what others have done to them, or failed to do for them. They are sinners because of social and cultural conditions, which shape their living and thinking before they are able to make safe judgments of what is of true worth and what is the wise way to live. But can we call people sinners if they have not caused themselves to do wrong, to disobey God's law, or to be disloyal to him? What is sin if it is not a free individual decision?

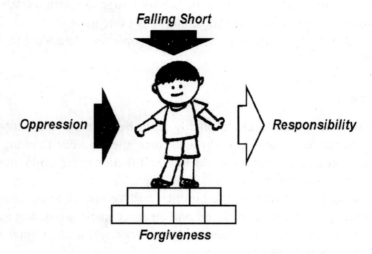

If we take each of these forces that affect the child in turn:

Falling short of the glory of God

Romans 3:23: All have sinned and fall short of the glory of God. The child in prostitution, or in soldiering, fairly obviously falls short of the glory of God. Such humanity does not reflect the glory of the love and life and goodness of God. If the living human being is the glory of God, as Irenaeus said, then these children, already living in some degree in death, fall short of the glory of God. Sin here is a *condition* of being far from God and alienated from his life. Sin is to be recognised in the distorting and destroying of human being and of anything else in God's creation. We are not to postpone taking it seriously as real sin until we can pin down its *cause.* The child as sinner, in a condition of falling short of the glory of God, not surprisingly both suffers and enacts sin.

Oppressor

A second side of the quadrilateral pressing on the child is the sin which makes the child its victim. This is sin that operates through various agents, sometimes individual persons, sometimes groups and organizations, sometimes more general influences, which of course use persons as their agents, even though they are not willed by those people. That a particular child is in prostitution or gun-bearing can be traced back to the sins of commission and omission by various people, organisations and value-systems. When social infra-structure breaks down, there is a large scale sin of omission, which spawns many disordered actions, sins of commission. The agencies of sin need to be recognised and named, analysed and resisted.

Sin as forgiven

The third side of the quadrilateral of forces pressing on the child as sinner is the grace of God in Jesus Christ. In this grace God contradicts sin in the most direct way: the falling short of the glory of God is countered by the revelation of the glory of God in the face of Jesus Christ. The darkness is countered by the light. Sin is seen to be sin here, not simply as the opposite of grace and goodness but as its active enemy. Sin seeks to block grace, to effect death and so stop grace renewing life. But sin is never seen if we merely look at sin, at what has gone wrong and is wrong. Sin can only be known in the light of the goodness and grace of God. Sin is known thanks to God's revelation, by which he contradicts sin, directly speaking against it. God does this not by saying how bad sin is; not by nagging; not by some divine equivalent of investigative journalism, searching out the dirt and giving it publicity over many pages.

God contradicts sin by making clear that it is sin. Sin cannot be seen in its own light, which is in truth darkness. Sin is known only in the light of God, which has better things to do than put sin on display in some courtroom or museum of horrors. The light of God reveals the glory of God. God forgives sin. God condemns sin in the flesh. God ends the reign of sin and frees us from it, so that it does not have dominion. Where sin abounds, grace much more abounds. Jesus is Lord, not sin – anywhere.

This is the Christian faith, the Christian proclamation. It is what Christians believe about all creation and for all creation. And for these children and anyone else who is a sinner.

Sin is truly and accurately identified as sin only in the light of Jesus Christ – only therefore from the vantage point of its having already been contradicted, judged, borne away and overcome by God in Christ. Sin is most truly and fully seen for what it is from within the forgiveness of God. The forgiveness of God cannot be known by anyone simply for himself and his own sin. We are forgiven as we forgive. We cannot truly see the sin of these children unless we look at them forgivingly. And that means not looking at them in the feeble uncertain hopefulness of merely human pity but in the confidence that Jesus is Lord and that God is God, who is for us all.

Taking Responsibility

And so we come to the fourth side of the quadrilateral. Only here may we come to the child and address her as a responsible person. She is responsible not because she is the cause of her condition, but because she may be called within the light of Christ to act responsibly and hopefully as the person she now is, regardless of how she got here; for she is not now being treated as the cause for what she has not caused. Nor is she being treated, depersonalised, as though she is a victimised substance, with no meaningful personal being and as though the language of sin is irrelevant to her. Instead, her personal dignity resides in her being open to the call to take hopeful responsibility from this point forward: the whole situation being seen within the light of the Lordship of Christ.

From this point forward, she is accompanied by people who see her and enter into the reality of her plight but do not blame her for it and are not defeated by it. So she is called and strengthened to take responsibility for herself in the reality of her situation, which is still painful and dangerous and yet has a final horizon of invitation to hope in God. Responding to this invitation means living in truth about sin, not merely the truth of sin as the usurping power but sin as disempowered by the forgiving God.

It may be noted that the four sides, the pressures on the child, are not all of the same kind. Their difference gives a shape and direction to the whole diagram. Sides 1 and 2 press negatively upon the child, they are depressing – just like sin. Sides 3 and 4 are uplifting and open up the way forward. They show God and human being together overcoming sin, in living towards the future.

This understanding of sin interprets the child. It is in tension with some traditional Christian teachings about sin, and it is so partly because 'the child' has been allowed to interpret sin. The picture here of the relation of the nature, the cause and the responsibility for sin is the outcome of trying to respond sensitively and constructively to the reality of these children and others like them. If this is how it is for these children, we may suppose it is similar for all people.

In this discussion, we did not go on to deal with questions which certainly follow, for Evangelical Christians if not others. If this is how sin is interpreted in the presence of the children, what is the truth of atonement and salvation? What implications does it have for how we tell all children the good news of Jesus Christ and invite them to faith? What does conversion mean now?

In the Garden with Jesus: Johanna Chi, age 4 yrs

CHAPTER NOTES
73   Bunge M J, Op cit.

CHAPTER 23

Child Theology and Our Ministry

HADDON WILLMER

MANY READERS will be agents involved in a variety of church-based ministries to children. This means that they have a professional as well as personal commitment to children and possibly, to some extent, have been shaped by their organisational involvement. They are participants in what is a major, long-developed and lively form of organised Christianity. People may complain that the churches still do not give children the priority they merit but, nevertheless, these ministries have a significant mass of resources, personnel and methodologies. They overlap and exist in critical tension and cooperative partnership with religious education.

The first task

For the purpose of this experiment, we asked everyone to imagine themselves in a circle of disciples, not by pretending to be Peter or James or Thaddeus around Jesus in the first century but as participants in the world of organised churchly and para-churchly concern with children.

Wearing this hat, we took stock of who we felt ourselves to be in the culture of this particular form of Christian existence – what are its key features, its encouraging and discouraging aspects, its fruit and its frustrations? In this organisation, what arguments take place (or are suppressed) about its aims, value, spirit and effects, as witness to and service of the kingdom of God?

In these organisations and ministries, we are committed, by virtue of employment if nothing else, to being concerned for children in a Christian way; that is the explicit focus and goal. That is what our mission statements tell us. But such statements may be no more than aspirations: what we would like to be. They may be useful hypocrisies: what we say we are in order to gain power or resource or status. We need also to look at what we *really are* and *really believe* as we wear this hat. There is a difference between professed theology and operative theology in churches and movements. What is the operative theology in these enterprises? What notion of God and his kingdom makes these enterprises tick?

In this short session, groups could not paint a complete picture of child-oriented Christianity. The purpose of the session was to enable us to get into the role of thinking within its framework and as its representatives. Once we were imaginatively inside this role as groups we were ready to move on to the next stage of the experiment.

The second task

In our experiment, we let a child be placed in the midst of this child-oriented Christianity which we were representing. We stood round the child wearing the hat of this kind of Christianity. In this theological experiment, the child was not placed in the midst to be educated or cared for by us. This was not a child at risk nor was it a beautiful child to be wondered at. The child was in the centre in an active role as a clue to the kingdom of God and a call to radical conversion.

The disciples probably thought they were beyond that: they had already left all to follow Jesus, whom they knew to be the Christ. We as active representatives of child-oriented Christianity tend to think we have already been converted with the help of the child in the midst. Has not our Christianity developed over the last two hundred years by deliberately turning towards the child, by conscious child-centredness, by receiving and welcoming the child? Do we not tend to think that it is other kinds of Christianity, not ours, which still needs to be converted by the placing of the child in the midst?

As an experiment, we were to suppose that Jesus might still want to place the child in the midst of our organisations and the arguments about policy, values and theology which are woven into their operation. We were to try not to indulge in criticising other kinds of Christianity which are not child-friendly but to imagine that Jesus had placed the child in our circle as the clue to our entering the Kingdom.

This carried the implication that we may not be as certain to get into the Kingdom as we like to think. Is the child in the midst a call for some specific conversion even in our child-friendly, child-serving ministry? Or, for contemporary child-oriented Christianity, has the story of Jesus placing the child in the centre of the theological argument of disciples become redundant? *As if we have kept this law from our youth up!*

If that is so, then we would not have to place the child in the midst by an act of imagination in a special experimental occasion. Rather, we would see that we live and work in organisations and cultures which have been and are shaped by the child in the midst. So is what we find in our practice already embodied child theology? If we say 'Yes', then this stage of the experiment would be an extension of the first: we would be continuing to (get to) know ourselves as participants in this kind of Christianity, practising the Kingdom. If we say 'No', then this stage would invite us to go beyond the first and be converted so that we might enter the Kingdom.

Another way of focusing this issue would be to ask ourselves this question: *If our organisations and their cultures are child-oriented, generated by receiving the child placed in the midst, what child is in the midst?* Some of our contemporary Christian and secular operations are centred on the child at risk (of what kinds?), others are centred on the child to be evangelised (in various ways), others on the child who has a right to self-fulfilment (perhaps meaning to enjoy life as a consumer), others are centred on the child as the model human being, enjoying a brief moment before adulthood destroys it all. Are any of these the child as placed by Jesus in the midst, as a sign of the kingdom of God? What would happen to our child-orientations if the child in the midst were one placed there by Jesus?

Outcomes

What message, if any, comes out of this experiment for our child-oriented Christianity and its organisations?

What changes if any in our operative theologies are called for?
Is this method useful and effective? How might it be developed?

Some participants found the task of recasting their organization as a group of disciples to be a 'grotesque comparison'. Comments were made about 'power hierarchies' and endless arguments about where power and authority lie. But it's possible that first century disciples might recognise the scenario all too well and might feel, along with some participants, a sense of pain in having colluded with ungodly conversations or processes.

Some found help in distinguishing between the institution and the disciples in it – maybe a 'useful hypocrisy'. Others found it hard to feel a disciple at all in their organization, relying entirely on the local church for this affirmation. Some felt that this process had exposed the lack of influence children had in their organizations, even those organizations or departments expressly focused on children.

Some felt that if a child were actually in the midst there would have to be a change in the boring, irrelevant and frustrating meetings they experienced in their organizations. It would not be right to force adult structures onto children. Perhaps they would meet on the floor and include play and food! There would certainly be less paper and a change in the language used – this may not only refer to less use of jargon and technical words. There would certainly be fewer arguments about the meaning of words! There would probably be more questions and fewer answers. Work might change its meaning. Time might go more slowly.

Apart from meetings, the inclusion of the child might be a unifying force, bringing people together, with a particular impact in inter-faith dialogue. There would probably be a change in the way money was spent.

When Jesus spoke about 'welcoming' children, it was about more than just receiving a guest, as a temporary visitor. It was about making a home, receiving the Gospel, hearing and obeying.

CHAPTER 24

Child Theology and Church

A CONSULTATION in Penang[74] reflected theologically on the church, using the 'child in the midst' as a way of gaining a new perspective. Participants divided into smaller working groups based on the countries they came from so that perhaps there was a degree of cultural uniformity within each group. The reflection was guided by a series of questions as follows, with a summary of the responses that were shared in the subsequent plenary session.

The 'middle' of church

Where is the 'middle' of church? Knowing this seems to be a prerequisite for placing a child in the midst of church. One group even struggled with the word 'middle'! Other groups offered: preaching; the Kingdom of God; the message; family of God; the community of faith; money; the sacraments; liturgy; worship; social action; teachers; perhaps the hierarchy; perhaps the rich influential members.

When music is the centre (dressed up as 'worship') it can seem that the centre of the church is entertainment. Sometimes church seems like a place of refuge, a womb, a safe place. When children are taken out of the 'worship time' it's an admission of failure that we don't know how to train children to worship or provide them with relevant models of worship.

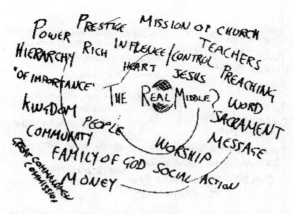

Our 'operative theology' of children and church

'Operative theology' refers to the theology that is actually practiced which may differ from the standard formulations of theology/doctrine espoused by out church or denomination.

Many thought that 'church' is clearly directed to adults more than children, even though there is much interest in and many programmes for children. Children are treated as spiritually inferior because they seem to have fewer of the resources that count in church life. Sometimes children are addressed as a means to an end, e.g. leading children's work is an apprenticeship for future pastors. Sometimes, the church uses children like consumers – they are given packaged programmes. Sometimes they are used as ornaments during special festivals like Christmas and Easter.

These attitudes result not only from doctrine but also from church politics e.g. the focus on activism, on what we are 'doing for Christ' rather than 'fellowshipping in Christ'. Some churches are schizophrenic in their attitude towards children – they are called the 'Junior Church' but not allowed to take part in events like Holy Communion or to vote in Church Meetings.

Changes children might bring

To summarise: there would be a different texture. It might look 'cute' and innocent, colourful and weak.

The buildings and furniture – currently built for adults – would need to change. The buildings and car park would not take all **205**

the land. There would be space to run around. (Why are cars given more space than children in affluent churches?)

The church service and worship would be different: the songs used; more art, colour, drama, and dance. All might sit on the floor or all on chairs so it would become a community church. Children could sit with their families – it would be a bit chaotic, more spontaneous. Godly Play in the church (not just the Sunday School). More movement and physical activity.

The preaching: shorter sermons; more variety; interpretive models of the message – an interpretation to their age categories.

The budget: children allowed to challenge adults; children allowed to participate.

There would be a paradigm shift in the curriculum – it would be relevant to all age groups. It might be more countercultural– first changing families and then society; would look innocent and weak;

Adults would become more caring and nurturing as they realise the vulnerability of children. More emphasis on relationships.

Obstacles to change

Traditionalism is a key problem, whether of the religious or cultural variety. There is a general unwillingness to change. Some feel it is a question of denominational distinctives that must be preserved. Some leaders don't want to take the risk even if they believe in it. Some cultures don't allow adults to worship with children – they are segregated because children are not seen to have arrived. Behind all this is a lack of understanding of the spiritual capacity of children.

Professionalism is another problem that kids' play fouls up. We have to start and end at whatever time. Kids want to keep doing things and be more spontaneous. We need to loosen up what that 1½ hours looks like. But little of this professionalism is given to creative thought to create working models and examples of what kids can do. Churches need to be shown models of God working through kids because people don't know what kids are capable of.

Fear might be an obstacle. We tend to idealize something that we fear. Perhaps we have idealized childhood for this reason. Similarly, there is fear of adolescents and single mothers. The church doesn't know how to handle them.

Could an obsession with novelty be an obstacle? There is a tendency to think that there must always be something new on offer but the best children's books are often repetitive. Children appreciate knowing what is coming. There is value in ritual and liturgy. Spontaneity is good but it isn't everything.

Removing obstacles

There needs to be a rediscovery the Biblical principles of church in the Bible with a reformation of the doctrine of Ecclesiology. This in turn will lead to a shake up of the liturgy. But the changes in church would have to go beyond what happens on Sunday, there would need to be structural and administrative changes.

CHAPTER NOTES
[74] Held in June 2006

CHAPTER 25

Child Theology and Mission

WHEN WE decided to discuss mission in one of our meetings in Asia, we realised that the situation of boys and girls in that continent is often very different; Asian cultures in general have strong gender-based values. Therefore, we organised discussion groups on a gender basis. Each group had the opportunity to meet informally over lunch and then met to consider the following four questions and to complete a sentence using prescribed criteria.

What is our operative theology of mission?

What particular issues arise in the course of mission in our own experience and culture?

What light is shed on theology and the issues identified when a boy (for the male groups) or a girl (for the female groups) child or children are placed in the midst?

What action would you recommend by CTM and others to address these issues?

As a way of distilling the theology around mission, groups were asked to create a single sentence including all the following words: Church; Mission; Kingdom of God; Child. The following sentences were submitted by the groups:

"The church, taking the marginalised child and putting it in its midst embodies the kingdom of God and expresses God's mission here and now"

"The church is to fulfil the mission of building the kingdom of God on earth for and with the child"

"The mission of the church is to live out/actualise the kingdom of
God as signed by the child in the midst"

"The church must receive the child into the kingdom of God to
truly find its mission"

"The child being the centre transforming the church and mission in
order to bring the kingdom of God in its totality."

"In humility and repentance, the church has a mission of living the
kingdom of God with the child in the midst."

Operative theologies of mission

The following phrases capture some of the ideas that participants
thought expressed the church's actual beliefs about mission:

Believer to non-believer; Bringing in the sheaves;

Tomorrow in mind; Faraway;

Cross-cultural; Pervade not invade; Diffusion; Christian identity;

Church planting; Gospel proclamation *and* social action; Sweet
smelling vapour; Lived theology;

Disciple-making; Living in a community

Mission = Missions; Commercial targets; Not disciple making –
focus on numbers; Big is better; Money making;

Leadership development; Picture taking;

Small is beautiful

Problems faced in Mission

Funds, personnel and resources; commercialisation,
commodification and the market approach;

A 'lived theology' perspective; Church as community – sign /
context / unity;

Dealing with new converts – Young children don't know what the
faith is;

Mission, religious rituals and rites;

Social action as a means to an end; Balancing social and
evangelism; Limited understanding of mission – proclamation
only or social action only;

Emphasis on mega-churches and a culture of spiritual voyeurism; instant gratification not future service;

The CLUB – bring in, not send out;

Socio-economic political systems; Want for power in society – societal values vs discipleship;

Ethics and conversions; the power of the cross and resurrection; persecution and discipleship; anti-conversion laws;

Should we focus on 'One-to-one' or a people group?

Lack of collaboration between churches and para-church organisations; Denominational barriers.

Outcomes for Mission

The child leads us to invest in the future and thus we become more concerned with discipleship;

The family comes to the foreground and we begin to appreciate the societal pressure on the family;

We should consider the child's comfort in a huge auditorium;

The Lord's Supper: why should children be excluded and not sharers?

We should adopt inclusive approaches to children in education training and empowering;

We should rethink what following Christ really is, whether primarily conversion to a state *or* a relationship with Jesus; would that also apply to adults as well as children?

Girl Child

Holistic approach in mission to avoid girl-child prostitution;

Promote value of life to avoid abortion of girl children;

Not enough theological reflection on the girl child;

Issues of safety and justice (e.g. less restriction) and their relation;

How to speak of Fatherhood of God in contexts of abuse;

Issues of beauty / self-esteem, value and motherhood.

Boy Child

Emphasising marginalisation – giving importance to boy rather than girl;

Not respecting the Word of God properly. How does the boy learn if the elders don't?

Emphasizing maleness might not be helpful;

Few male role-models in Sunday school;

Encounter of boys with the outdoors – what is comfortable for them?

Jesus loves all the children: Sharon Leow, age 12 yrs

CHAPTER 26

Children, Media and Eschatology

IN THE more affluent parts of the world, the issues that children face are more subtle. The children in affluent societies are rarely sold into prostitution or made to work long hours, for example. But nevertheless, sexual exploitation and slavery to materialism exist. This is not just an issue for affluent countries. In a Child Theology consultation in Africa the participants all agreed that the battle for the minds of young Africans has been lost to the western-dominated media. Children in poor townships show off their mobile phones but might have had no food that day. It is arguable that this has occurred without adults and adult institutions being alert to what has been happening. Media studies have not developed with "a child in the midst"! If Child Theology is to engage with contemporary issues then this is a major issue, *possibly the major issue of our times.*

In one meeting,[75] we were introduced to "Amy" who became the child in the midst for the participants.[76] She speaks of desire. In this case the desire for relationship connected to purchasing something never wanted before. How do we relate this individual biography to our thinking about God?

Amy is a fourteen-year-old who is one of 30 employed as an unpaid "consultant" or "insider" to advise Delia*s (sic.) a clothes company, on how to appeal to her and her friends. Delia*s catalogue has a yearly circulation of 45 million. She typically spends many hours a week testing out new Delia*s products and emailing corporate friends. Her friends then want to buy what she is wearing. She gains a sense of identity both from being valued by the adult professionals in the company and by her peers. She sees herself as a trend spotter and feels "in the know" and "cool" as a consequence. She does most of her "work" in the Americana Manhasset Mall in New York. Amy's parents also wear designer clothes and her mother believes that this activity of hers is educational and empowering. There are tens of thousands of girls like Amy in the USA all owing allegiance and loyalty to the brand that sponsors and "owns" them.[77]

We discussed the following notes as we began to consider the influence of media and the challenge of Child Theology to respond.

Background

If sociology is having trouble trying to keep up with global societal trends because of the pace of change, the challenge is even greater when focusing on children and the media. Among the factors of unique significance in this generation are the following:

There is 24-hour global media coverage available to children from their earliest years until adulthood.

75% of children aged 5-16 years in the UK have a television in their rooms; 38% have their own video; over 80% have their own mobile phone.[78]

Unsupervised access to the Internet, friends, and marketing companies is unparalleled in history. Parents and families are not gatekeepers of the media as they used to be in the era of a single radio, television or telephone.

More time is spent watching TV, videos, on the Internet and mobile phones than at school. Family times together, without the intrusion of the above, are at an all time low. Electronic communication organized globally may now be one of the earliest formative influences in the life of the young child

The presence of the worldwide web and the information society is changing social consciousness to such an extent that sociologists such as Castells argue that class solidarity is being replaced by the quest for an individual identity that can be constructed and re-constructed by the individual concerned as long as they have access to electronic communication and money.

The media are dominated by trans-national corporations owing no loyalty to a particular culture, tradition or value-system other than that of maximizing their own profit through promoting their own brand(s).

Censorship is opposed by "liberal democracies" because it is seen as an infringement of the freedom or rights of the individual adult. Little debate has taken place about whether such an argument is sustainable in a contemporary world when children are assumed to need protection from predators who might abuse them physically and/or sexually but not from the "corporate paedophiles" who seek to groom them as consumers of selected brands.[79]

According to this viewpoint, parents and society should understand children in terms of a market investment for the benefit of adult lives. Parents invest in their children for their own ultimate benefit. We care about children because it helps us get in touch with our own childness. This is commodification. So, why do we have children? Essentially it is a 'lifestyle choice' designed to improve our lives or, at the very least, to make us happy.

Corporations are using children to extract money for their own gain. Of the 27 hours of weekly television watched by children in the USA, one third is advertising. Corporations promote branding (brand loyalty) to children as young as two years old. From the view of the corporation, advertising to the young gives a longer return on the investment.

Questions arising

If this analysis is at all correct then Child Theology may need to start from basic questions and principles. Here are a few that are indicative of the range and importance of what is at stake.

How far could it be argued that the global media have come between children and their families and local cultures (similar to the way that the disciples of Jesus came between families and Jesus)?

What boundaries in media content and coverage are necessary for children to experience "good enough parenting"?

What effect is the sexualisation of relationships and identity having on children and childhood?

What theological insights can be brought to bear on the promotion of the idea that identity is dependent on consumption and possession?

What effects do the media have on the play of children and the nature and role of intermediate objects on which child development depends?

How important is a "narrative framework" (including rites of passage) for the formation of personal and social identity, and how far are such frameworks undermined by the ever-changing, market constructed "post-modern" media contexts and images?

How can Christian adults in families and church provide a creative and nurturing alternative to the dominance of television? What of imagination, wonder, experiences of the sublime in the natural world? What of exercise, physical fitness and hand-eye coordination? What positives are there to be fostered and nurtured in the televisual repertoire?

How far have the media influenced education and what are the likely effects of this on child learning and development?

Discussion
HADDON WILLMER

The ethical evaluation of the branded child has, to this point, been done without theological work or reference. Does Child Theology have anything to say to this analysis or description?

One answer would be, "No, Child Theology is not needed for this. We have seen the need and been given options of how to respond. We understand the issue and don't need to talk further. What we do need is to get on with the response, with specific action steps". If we say, "Yes, Child

Theology needs to speak to this" then we need to consider a more active role for parents. Christian parenting requires an active role in instruction. There can be no passive acceptance or active encouragement of branding. Parents need to step into the power of the home and their roles.

At the same time, we must be careful with the expectations and responsibility we ask parents to carry. Parents themselves are so caught up in the lifestyle that they have no time. But it is not merely time that is at issue – it is their whole personal human formation and horizons that are involved. The whole ethical dimension provides a basis for helpful analysis. Consider debt. It keeps parents busy working all hours to service it and credit card debt is the number one reason college students drop out. This can be linked to marketing and media which in turn reduces their opportunities for relational interaction. An example of an active position is for parents to limit the television viewing habits of their children. The American Paediatric Association recommends that children under two years of age not watch television at all because of the lasting neurological impact.

The church needs to get its own house in order, including getting the child in the midst of the church, before calling out to society. There, the church is viewed sceptically so it must be seen to practice what it preaches. It must check its own ethics toward children. When we consider the child we need to be thinking stewardship rather than property. This includes not paying attention to children just as a means to get adults to church. What the church needs to do is change the message we are giving to people. If this were done in the U.S.A. it would have global impact. Such commodification is not a uniquely US experience even if such direct marketing is unique.

Does each Christian tradition need to take the framework and go deeper within its own sphere to contextualize it? How does this interface with David Sims' work on religion, culture and family?[80] It is critically important to conscientize our culture about what is happening to our children.

One of the implications of analyses such as that by Alissa Quart is that we may be allowing slavery on a historically global scale never witnessed before in history, by which children and young people are being targeted and branded, dispossessed of their culture and kin and made servants of global corporations. There is no reason why such a process cannot be analysed from the perspective of a theologically informed good childhood and alternative ways of living and learning being advocated. Children themselves may well be the leaders in the campaign for change.

The world-wide-web, the most pervasive medium, could be used to bring about change. What has been used for evil could be used for good. There is a failure to censure, to teach values and to have the government to include in the public sector the kinds of things that lead to right conduct.

Media expose, contribute to and express the social ethics of our day. They are not, themselves, the core issue. The media must be addressed in proper perspective to other connected issues. Our challenge is critically to examine media from a theological perspective. Here are two theological issues that could be addressed in this context:

Eschatology and Child Theology

When we describe and analyse problems, get ethicists to work on them and get parents to respond, we work towards a horizon where we expect to reach solutions. We search for those who can do something and expect them to do it. We conceive the problems as solvable. Yet some may only be solvable in the long term, if ever at all. Such problems cause us to ask, "What is the nature of our general human existence?" The whole concept of an eschatological hope speaks to the reality that not all problems have solutions and if we tackle issues as if they do, we will be disappointed. We may conclude that nothing we do works. John 14 reminds us that we will always have trouble in this world and the writer of Hebrews reminds us that we are looking for a city to come *when it comes, not as we compel it*.

We are in an *already-not-yet* kingdom. As the child is placed into the midst of the kingdom we can ask: *"Is the child a sign gift of the kingdom to come?"* In the call to kingdom life, we need to determine what we will strive to accomplish. The biblical call is to strive for justice and deal with present circumstances, to live towards a city that is not here. This is different from living for a city built with our hands. We need to look for solutions for the present age without necessarily striving for solutions for all ages.

Even where there are solutions, the path may not be smooth. For example, whenever there is transition, such as from agrarian to industrial and then from industrial to post–industrial, there is great disruption. Disruption is an abstract general word concealing much suffering, frustration and waste for many real people – including children. Even if the next generation gets into the 'promised land', what vindication and rescue can the present generation find? Do their angels behold the face of the Father in heaven?

Legitimate Theological Representation

Amy in the midst brought with her the world in all its complexity. We could ask "How representative is Amy of the world child?" When we put any child in the midst in this process we claim that the child is representative of all children. The question is whether or not we can allow a uniqueness from which we can talk about similarities and differences at a global level.

Much theological talk speaks of 'child' in generalizing, abstracting or stereotyping language that limits the usefulness of that theology. If a particular child puts us onto something real about the child, it should be attended to regardless of whether that child is representative of many or a few. It is helpful to put different children in the midst. We can ask: Who is this child representative of and who not? Is the subversive power of media shown in a child like Amy in any way typical?

We could ask about the age of the child Jesus put in the midst and how relevant this is to today's teenagers. But it might be better to ask: How did Amy get where she is now? As a toddler was she watching TV, was she babysat? What norms and disciplines, desires and relationships in our culture shaped her? We are told that by age 4 the hardwiring of the brain is 86% complete and by age 10 it is finished. If we know the roots of the trouble, we may better discern what kind of religious and theological preparation we need to give before the teenage years.

Some Christian Education seems to offer a simple "conversionist" decision on how to be safe, preventing young people from seeing kingdom lifestyle choices. In Galatians 4 and 5, Paul gives us a more concrete sensitivity to what is going on in our lives. Flesh is like a predator out to

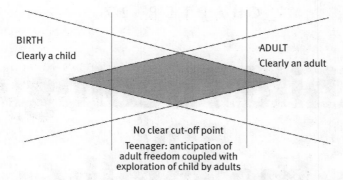

BIRTH
Clearly a child

ADULT
Clearly an adult

No clear cut-off point
Teenager: anticipation of
adult freedom coupled with
exploration of child by adults

get us. The alternative is a call to freedom and love. To say only "God loves you" can turn them into consumers of the love of God. In fact, they are called to choose between living a flesh-driven life and living a spirit-driven life.

However, we still need to identify what a teenager is. Strict exegetes may leave out the teen because there was no "teen" at the writing of the Bible. Although the Jewish bar Mitzvah was at thirteen years old, a boy was not considered a full adult until the age of thirty. This created a cultural ambivalence – an *already-not-yet* scenario not unlike today (see figure).[81]

CHAPTER NOTES

[75] From the consultation in Houston, May 2004

[76] Amy comes from the book, *Branded: The Buying and Selling of Teenagers*, by Alissa Quart (Random House Publishers, 2003)

[77] Source: *Branded*, pages 22–47

[78] Quart, op cit, 2003: xi

[79] Ibid: 8

[80] PhD thesis by David Sims entitled "An Evangelical Theology of Liberation for Affluent American-Evangelical Children (AAEC)."

[81] Readers wishing to follow up this line of thought are referred to *Life Maps: Conversations on the Journey of Faith* by James W. Fowler and Sam Keen (Word Books; 1985, second edition)

CHAPTER 27

Child Theology and the Family

A RECURRING issue at our consultations, particularly in Africa, has been the breakdown in family life that we are currently witnessing and which is perhaps unprecedented, at least on such a global scale. Many factors are contributing to this – warfare, economics, the easy availability of reliable contraception with its concomitant 'liberation' of women (mothers); economic pressures; electronic media; etc.

Several contributors referred to these issues, and some of these theological reflections follow in this chapter.

The Challenge of Child Rearing
JOHN WALL[82]

Jewish, Moslem and other ethicists focus on issues like poverty, war, and marriage. There is little development of Christian ethics of children but such as there are fall into three broad approaches:

Communitarianism
This is a 'top down' model looking at how to deal with the privatisation of child rearing. There is a need to transmit social values, traditions, histories and social goods to children. With this model, the responsibility falls chiefly on parents and church because they are most involved in the day to day.

Who is responsible for raising children today? Over 2,000 years, it has gradually developed into smaller units of responsibility. Families are smaller – nuclear versus extended. Fathers' roles in children's lives are smaller now than ever. The industrial revolution had a significant impact, exacerbated now by the broken family, so that even dedicated fathers have little opportunity to be involved. Mothers are ultimately responsible for the children.

What is good about this model is that it attempts to put children in larger contexts to help them resist the culture around them. The problem is that it puts children at the back of the church or whatever context. It takes away their dignity by trying to find ways to have children learn social values as understood by the adults so that the voice of the child is devalued.

Libertarianism

This is a 'bottom up' effort to see the value of children as gifts. It is a grassroots attempt to allow children to develop and grow on their own terms. The chief responsibility of adults in this model is to provide protection. This is seen through the interest in children having sufficient health care and in the interest in political and economic issues such as the rights of education, the right to be heard and the right to basic needs being met.

Children are the poorest age group in the USA, having overtaken the elderly in the 1970s. The younger they are, the poorer – 1/3 of the homeless in the USA are children. In a market economy and culture where everyone is individualistic and where you only get what you put in, the children lose because they cannot put in. They cannot lobby congress for more money, so how well they do depends on adults.

There are two problems to this model:

It doesn't have a good idea of goals for child rearing. It expects the child, once protected, to reach maturity and social values by itself. What is the kingdom of God we are after? What aim do we have?

It tends to place more emphasis on political and economic solutions than on underlying culture. It is culture that determines a society's basic attitudes and beliefs about children.

Covenantalism

This is a dialectical (not top down, not bottom up) model of integration seeking the integration of children into community. It places a lot of emphasis on marriage and church. The primary cause of child poverty in the USA is the father's disappearance from his children's lives; they were either never a part or they left later. The marriage movement believes the way to deal with children's issues is to strengthen families through strengthening marriages. In history, marriage has been key, especially in gaining the economic and moral commitment of fathers.

Luther and Calvin were the engines behind marriage becoming a public institution. Prior to their efforts, marriage was largely ecclesiastical. They were responding to the social dilemma of the day where women could have trouble ensuring men took the responsibility of fatherhood. Marriage became a social institution that integrated and protected children; the church can function the same way. At the end of the 19th century, Pope Leo XIII in an effort to furnish help ("subsidiarity") promoted the family as a private institution that can only do its work with help from the surrounding society

The one key problem with covenantalism is that it doesn't understand what liberationists do. Children are not just impacted by family but also by what happens outside the family.

In this paper, I propose a fourth model:

Critical Covenantalism

This is an effort to combine the best of the models, bridging historical tradition and the contemporary world. It particularly seeks to balance covenantalism with liberationism, generating a larger 'social covenant' of commitment to children's whole lives. Practical 'consequences' might include the following:

Media. The amount of media exposure is appalling. Parents need to be involved but it is perhaps too easy to blame parents given the pressures they face. How do we contain media? We live in a culture where if we let free market run its course 'everyone wins' but for children that is not so certain. The church needs to speak to the culture.

Fathers. Fathers have a much stronger role than realized. We speak of family in 19th century terms: women and children – the distant fathers merely impregnate. Before then, the emphasis was on women child-bearing with men taking over child-rearing at an early age of the child. It would be good to good to look at previous models and develop new models more appropriate to our culture. Right now, it is difficult for men to be primary caregivers.

Church. Churches have a role with the children in their midst who attend church or live in the local community and they also have a role in changing culture. Churches can put children in the midst of culture in better ways. Child Theology can advance that.

School. Schools have become places of excellence but not as defined by Aristotle (the founder of ethics as known in the west) who would equate excellence with virtue and contribution to social good. Today, excellence means being number one, getting the highest scores. The number one person in schools is the athlete who has visibly beaten the others.

Health. There are presently 10,000,000 children without health care in the United States. We tend not to think of children as having bodies but to think of them in more spiritual and ethereal terms.

The bottom line is a question of culture: how do we put children in the midst of our culture? In the west, we have tended to respond in one of two opposite ways:

we over-romanticise and sentimentalise children,
or we demonise children saying they are evil and in need of civilization.

What we need to do is humanise children. This hearkens back to the earlier discussion on how we view the child.[83] In short, our perspective of the child needs to change and a strong, healthy Child Theology, working with an equally strong and healthy Christian social ethic will allow this humanization to happen.

Child Theology and Family Reconstruction

This issue was also discussed in the Child Theology consultation held in Prague, Czech Republic. Some participants described two common

Christian attitudes to family and society in Eastern Europe. One is the evangelical model (illustrated below) where the family and child are caught in the middle between Christ and church on one side and a world which is evil on the other side. The Child and Family are not at home in the world or the church but are lost in limbo in the middle.

Where is God in this? Is God only in the church and the world is left to the Devil? This seems a poor understanding of God. Is Christ in the church or with the child/family? Christ is seeking and saving the lost. The church should go where Christ goes. Are the family and child torn apart by this difference or can they be a place of redemption, mediation, forming a bridge?

The other Christian model is the Orthodox: that the church and family are in the world and therefore the public schools can teach the child religion. The problem with this model is that the church does not do the work to decide and explain what God means in the world. What does the question of God mean for us here?

This is a practical question which demonstrates the relevance of child theology. Does the place of child and family in the model deny the Kingdom of God? Once we see the child in our mind as God sees the child we might discover the Servant church – serving the needs of the child. How should the church see the child/family in relation to the world? Could it be that in reference to the child and family that the church and the world are out of tune with where God is? We must receive the child where God has placed the child.

If we take this evangelical view of things (given that the world is evil) there could be families and children (just ordinary people) isolated and very frail. In this situation, if the church is not on your side adequately and the world is not on your side adequately then you are in a fix. God in Jesus goes out into the wicked world – into the dark areas. God goes to the area of the lostness. It could be that in Romania the child/family is where Christ is going – and the church should follow him.

When the social infrastructure fails

A discussion of family issues in Africa yielded a different set of challenges such as polygamy and long-term relationships without marriage. Family breakdown is a major problem which takes various forms: death; divorce; single parenthood; rejection of children by step-parents. This presents the church with numerous challenges:

How can we best find the ancient African (or other cultural) path
and identify its merits?

How do we restore the commandment to honour your father and
mother?

How do we restore the father image in relation to God
the Father?

Does the local cultural tradition have anything to offer in the
reconstruction of modern society which is destroying the life of
the child?

What are the merits of western society? (the pernicious influences
are well-described!)

How do we deal with the extended family in respect of the 'living
dead'?

What models of intervention do we have for HIV/AIDS?

Do we have a practical model to help orphans?

How can we best understand the mindset(s) and language(s) of the
child?

How can we help with integrated family development?

What is our attitude to adoption?

By the term 'social infrastructure' we describe a continuum of care in society ranging across family, church, government and non-government agencies. Among the urban poor, this infrastructure is deficient and sometimes has disappeared altogether. For example, one participant recounted how two boys (age 11 and 12 years) from his Bible class were shot by the police. The 'western' Mission Organisation had no message to give and in fact the supervisor refused to attend the funeral, not wishing to become involved.

Such situations raise many questions:

What is our concept of mission? Does it include bringing God's redemptive message to all levels of society?

What is the purpose of salvation? Does it extend beyond the personal?

Who brings the message? Do the messengers need better vetting and training?

How do people in the local context develop an identity? How do we help children to develop a mental picture of themselves in relation to others?

BASIC ISSUE	IMPACT ON CHILDREN	IMPLICATIONS FOR CT
The development of an African hermeneutic	Bible is not made relevant to culture (e.g. low view of children)	Theology that addresses the challenges to the African family
The concept of mission in Africa	At present a lack of focus on children	Help the church to put children in the centre and have a mission to and about children
Understanding the implications and extent of salvation	Children ignored in pre-rational, pre-conversion stages of life and their plight ignored post-conversion; poor teaching and discipleship	Develop models of spirituality for young children
Qualifications and qualities of the messenger	Poor modelling and discipleship (the 'cream' often not assigned to work with children)	Inspire and equip the best messengers to work with children
Concepts of tribalism (-ve) and historical culture (+ve)	Negative stereotyping imposed on them and perpetuated by them	Develop a proper perspective of who children are in Christ and society
Development and visibility of the African identity in global context	Invisible or seen only as victims	Identify the special identity and contribution of children in Christ
The child's mental picture of self and others	See themselves as lesser beings in comparison with other societies and cultures	Provide a substantial underpinning for self-esteem that is not just based on future potential.
Concept of church in relation to mission and community	Children viewed only as targets for evangelism	Develop holistic approaches to involve children in the church.
Non-Christian attitudes to power and control	Ignored, oppressed and exploited	Develop structures that demonstrate the concept of power in the Kingdom of God.
Replacement of traditional religious support systems	Children lack spiritual support e.g child headed households	Develop a coherent and robust Christian theology of the family adequate for such circumstances.

How do we preach the gospel in the midst of poverty? Can we avoid
  the traditional control of resources by Mission organisations?
How do we replace the traditional religious support systems?

The group commenced an analysis of the above issues as shown in the
table opposite.

The Vocation of Parenting
MARCIA J BUNGE[84]

Introduction
Although all children need parental love, some children have no parents
and support for parents is undermined in a number of ways both in contemporary cultures and even within the church.

The Sacred Task of Parenting
Children need parental love. From a biblical perspective, the sacred task
of parenting specifically involves providing for children's basic needs;
expressing positive attitudes toward them; nurturing the faith of children;
helping them use their gifts and talents to love and serve others; and listening to and learning from children.

1. Children need parental love.

2. From a biblical perspective, the primary purpose and task of
    parenting involves:
    • Providing all children with the basic needs of food, shelter and
    affection and recognizing that all children are 'neighbours' and
    that caring for them is part of seeking justice and loving the
    neighbour. (e.g. Exodus, Deuteronomy)
    • Perceiving children as gifts of God and sources of joy who are
    made in the image of God. Therefore: respecting them, enjoying
    them and being grateful for them. (e.g. Genesis, Psalms,
    Jeremiah, John 16, Matthew)
    • Understanding that children are developing beings and moral
    agents in need of instruction and guidance. Therefore: nurturing
    the faith of children; helping them use their gifts and talents to
    love and serve others; and contribute to the common good.
    (e.g. Genesis, Proverbs, Deuteronomy, Ephesians)

• Remembering that children are models of faith for adults, sources or vehicles of revelation and representatives of Jesus. Therefore: listening to and learning from children. (e.g. Gospels)

3. Any strong Christian vision of parenting must be integrally connected to a vibrant and complex theological understanding of children and childhood.

4. The Christian tradition emphasizes the importance of parenting in various ways:
   • The family is a 'little church' (Chrysostom, Bushnell).
   • Parenting is a divine calling or vocation (Luther).
   • Parents are apostles, bishops and priests to their children (Luther).

Ten "Best Practices"

The Christian tradition emphasizes ten practices and responsibilities for nurturing the moral and spiritual lives of children.

1. Reading and discussing the bible and interpretations of it with children;
2. Worshipping with a community and carrying out family rituals and traditions of worship and prayer;
3. Introducing children to good examples, mentors and stories of service and compassion;
4. Participating in service projects with parents or other caring adults and teaching financial responsibility;
5. Singing together and exposing children to the spiritual gifts of music and the arts;
6. Appreciating the natural world and cultivating a reverence for creation;
7. Educating children and helping them discern their vocations;
8. Fostering life-giving attitudes toward the body, sexuality and marriage;
9. Listening to and learning from children;
10. Taking up a Christ-centred approach to discipline, authority and obedience; recognizing that, in the tradition, parental authority is always limited.

The Messiness and Complexity of Family Life
Although children best thrive when they are raised by two loving parents within the covenant of marriage and who carry out these 'best practices', in a fallen world, people and relationships can be damaged.

1. Families are often broken and struggling in various ways, whether with a single or with two parents.
2. The parents of many children are abusive, are seriously ill or have died.
   - Some children are being raised by older siblings, relatives or neighbours.
   - Others have been abandoned or are awaiting adoption.

Implications and potential strategies
The Church must find ways to help all children by supporting parents or primary care-givers in the sacred task of parenting and by ensuring that all children find the love and care that they need.

1. Responsibilities of Church, State and International Organizations:
   - Provide all children and families with safe drinking water, proper nutrition and adequate health care;
   - Help reduce poverty and ensure that all families reach an adequate standard of living;
   - Achieve free and universal education and ensure all children have access to excellent schools and ways to explore and to sharpen their gifts and talents to serve others;
   - Safeguard the natural environment and the diversity of life for the sake of children's quality of life and spiritual growth;
   - Protect children from abuse, neglect and physical punishment;
   - Help reduce infant mortality and the number of orphans, especially by combating diseases such as HIV/AIDS or malaria.
   - Strengthen foster care programmes, improve orphanages and accelerate the process of adoption for children in need.

2. Further Tasks of the Church
- Emphasize the sacred task of parenting in the church and preach and teach on the subject;
- Offer programmes to prevent divorce and support all families;
- Create excellent religious education materials and programmes which:
- Are theologically sound;
- Honour the questions and insights of children themselves;
- Emphasize the importance of parents and primary care-givers in faith development.
- Provide parents and primary care-givers with ideas and resources for nurturing faith at home.
- Listen more attentively to children to learn from them, recognizing the importance of children in the faith journey and spiritual maturation of adults.
- Strengthen theologies of childhood and child theologies.

Our common task in nurturing children:

Caring for children and nurturing their moral and spiritual lives is clearly an important and complex task that requires a cooperative effort among parents, relatives, friends, religious communities, schools, the state and international organizations. All of us, whether or not we are parents ourselves, need to work diligently on many levels and in many ways to protect and to nurture children.

CHAPTER NOTES

[82] See paper: "Let the Little Children Come: Childrearing as Challenge to Contemporary Christian Ethics", John Wall, Rutgers University, Camden, Horizons 31/1 (2004): 64-87. Presented at the Child Theology consultation held in Houston, USA.

[83] See, for example, chapter 13

[84] This essay was originally given by Marcia J Bunge at the International Cutting Edge Conference, September 2005 (Cirencester, UK) and is now published as "The Vocation of Parenting: A Biblically and Theologically Informed Perspective" in *Understanding God's Heart for Children: Toward a Biblical Framework*, edited by Douglas McConnell, Jennifer Orona, Paul Stockley (Colorado Springs: Authentic Publishing, 2007), pp. 53-65

CHAPTER 28

Child Theology and Education

KEITH WHITE

Western Education Systems

Introduction

ON FIRST thinking about education from the perspective of Child Theology we might assume that here is an activity or institution that is non-problematical. That is certainly how it seems to appear in the mission statements and policies of Faith Based Organisations and the CRC.[85] For surely 'the child' is in the centre of the whole process of education? But once we pause to ponder this we realise that it is not that simple. For example, education sometimes appears primarily to be about teachers and adult agendas

Is it 'child-centred' or 'child-focused'? This distinction often seems elusive but it may be of critical importance, particularly to those who have made child-centredness the basis of their engagement with children. Perhaps we can help to define the differences. But as we do so, we need to be aware whether we are taking the child as 'placed by Jesus in the midst' or whether we are dealing with the thinking and feelings evoked by our human reactions to concepts of child and children (that is, child in the midst without reference or relation to Jesus).

People react differently to children. Some are stimulated creatively while others are stimulated to horror. Children don't have in themselves a particular message. It's when Jesus places the child in the midst, with his words, that the child becomes a conveyor of particular meaning.

What follows is an initial attempt to map out some of the ground in a very rudimentary way and it is offered in order that we can at least **231** establish what a map of this subject should look like. We are thinking here not about an exhaustive mapping of every aspect of education but a map that highlights education from the perspective of Child Theology.

The Kingdom of Heaven/God's Way of Doing Things

A starting point would seem to be to ask how far a philosophy (I prefer this term to the more common term "system") of education serves the Kingdom of God and how far it serves other purposes. What would education look like if it started with the actions and teaching about the Kingdom of Heaven? Would it be upside-down, inside-out and back to front compared to what we tend to find at present and in history?

We might do well to ask who or what the existing systems or philosophies of education serve? Do they serve the state and its economy, social control, children, parents and families, church or other purposes and groups? Do we shape the child to fit the system or shape the institution to fit the child? We should be aiming to create an environment in which we help the child become what God intended him/her to be.

There may be other questions that flow immediately from this approach and perhaps we should pause to identify them before proceeding any further. When map-making it is vital to establish the overall intention and perspective of the map before going into detail and, perhaps, Child Theology by its nature helps particularly at this fundamental stage of any analysis.

Church History gives many horrific examples of education supposedly based on the Kingdom of God. They were often totalitarian and oppressive. We may, to some extent, avoid such mistakes by speaking of 'God's way of doing things' rather than earthly power-based structures, such as 'Kingdoms'.

Child

Child Theology must ask what type of child and what philosophy/theology of child does education have in mind. Is it aiming at 'normal' children with others on the periphery? Or does it start with children who have special gifts and needs and thus bring them in from the margins?

And is the concept or understanding of children clear? Are children naturally good as Rousseau seems to maintain in his major work on education, *Emile*? Are children essentially sinful as Augustine, Jonathan

Edwards and many other theologians have argued?

Child Theology cannot be silent at this point. It matters greatly when we start with the child placed by Jesus in the midst. That must surely be every child and Jesus probably sees them differently from the way they are seen by other humans and institutions. How does Jesus see children? Surely he has an adequate understanding of them as created in God's image, as well as the effects of sin and the Fall? The two insights go hand in hand.

What understandings of child do we find in existing models of education? Are they adequate? Is the child a child or a potential adult? We may need to pause here to ask what the child has in common with adults and what the differences between them are. How does education work with this creative tension?

Does education consider the whole child or does it stress the cognitive and physical, rather than the affective and spiritual? If the state is seen as mainly responsible for education should it concern itself with the spiritual?

What do we understand to be the gifts and needs of the growing child that should be received, met and nurtured?

How do children learn best about the things of the Kingdom of Heaven? Catechisms, stories, experiments, play and so on need to be considered. We might do well to see what Jesus preferred.

Teacher

Similarly, Child Theology must ask about teachers.

Are we assuming the teacher is a mature and trained adult? If so what would be the maturity and training that would best equip her for teaching or modelling the Kingdom of Heaven?

Does this teacher have autonomy so that he or she can respond to a child directly and spontaneously or does the teacher have a "script"? If the teacher is operating a programme or curriculum who decides what it is?

Is the teacher and the school an agent of social control? In this case might the teacher actually prevent children from coming to Jesus and presenting an alternative (upside-down) way of living?

Has the teacher 'arrived' in the sense of having no more to learn or are the child and the teacher both children of the same Heavenly Father? **233**

Does it include the child as educator? This is surely a vital aspect of the Kingdom of Heaven: the child is in the midst not just to learn but to be the means of adults learning too. A poem I love by a teacher, Jane Clements, of the Bruderhof Community puts it like this

> "Child, though I take your hand
> and walk in the snow;
> though we follow the track of the mouse together.
> Though we try to unlock the mystery
> of the printed work, and slowly discover
> why two and three makes five
> always, in an uncertain world -
> Child, though I am meant to teach you much,
> what is it, in the end,
> except that together we are
> meant to be children
> of the same Father
> and I must unlearn
> all the adult structure
> and the cumbering years
> and you must teach me
> to look at the earth and the heaven
> with your fresh wonder."

Can non-Christian teachers be the means of introducing children to the Kingdom of Heaven?

School

And a Child Theology reflection on schools might give rise to questions such as these:

Are schools necessary to education as seen from a Child Theology perspective?

If learning is lifelong shouldn't everyone go to school?

Schools should be communities where individual children learn aspects of relationships that develop their awareness of the social nature of their being beyond that learnt in families. Is bullying endemic to schools?

Are there some types of school that are closer to the Kingdom of
Heaven model than others? If so what are they? This may
require a look at philosophies of education. My own interim
conclusion is that Fr?bel offers one of the best models for such
a process of learning. He asked how children learn and studied
mothers and their children for many years. He believed that all
education started with movement: sitting in a circle not lines;
helping the soul of the child to connect with whole of the
Universe; a creative environment, preferably outside, drawing
from the natural world.

Does the age of children in a class or a school matter? Would Child
Theology suggest that little children should be the priority in
the system? If so would kindergartens be given a higher status
than universities, for example?

Does Child Theology have anything to say about church schools?
Home schooling? If so in a contemporary context it needs to
consider all faith-based schooling.

Church and Faith Communities

If education is about lifelong learning and about all of life, not just certain
subjects in a curriculum taught in a school, then the church has a strate-
gic role in education.

Should children's ministry be modelled on secular schools and
their teaching philosophies and methods?

Can churches provide models of learning where the child is in the
midst that pioneer new forms for the state?

What would Child Theology derive from the actions and teaching
of Jesus and the Jewish community of which he was a part?
Festivals, sacraments and worship seem to have played an
important part in the learning process of Israelite children:
When your children ask what it means then tell them. Jesus did
a lot of his teaching at the time of festivals and by making
conscious links.

Does the relationship between the boy who offered his loaves and
fish and Jesus provide any clues about how learning might be
facilitated? The disciples have a role in the story, as told by

John, that comes close to coming between the boy and Jesus. Does the church do this?

Where does family fit into all this? Should it not be seen as part of church and closely linked with all the child's learning? If it does not do so and there is a disjuncture between schooling and church, what does this imply for the learning of the child? Child Theology will need to think carefully about this because its key reference points to date tend to focus on a single child placed by Jesus without reference to the family of the child.

What is the rationale for children's ministry? What is its philosophy whether in local churches or FBOs? Are there any examples of Jesus talking to and interacting with children except in the presence of adults?

Who are the leading lights in children's religious education and whence do they draw their philosophy? Westerhoff, Cavaletti, Berryman are key figures in the West, for example.

There is much in the Bible about children and their development. How does Child Theology draw from and disseminate it?

Changing the system

Before we seek to challenge secular authorities, we must look at our own ministries. Are we pressuring children to be transformed into adults? Much Christian children's work has the aim of producing sound, committed, Christian adults. What about allowing them to be children? (sound and committed!)

There are several challenges for us in the above:

Consider how we may change the environment of children by incorporating community development into Christian child development;

Rethink how adult activities and desires shape worldviews, for example the impact of capitalism on children's lives, where leisure is something you buy (the Gameboy vs. playing on the beach);

Ask ourselves if children's rights are an extension of adult control;

Consider how we relate to gender issues and to children with special gifts and needs (not handicapped);

Ask ourselves why we push children out of adult services. How could we work with children as Jesus would? For example, how do children fit into the communion service?[86]

Be vulnerable enough to explore the world with children and allow them to question our way of doing things;

Be interested in what children are doing. Or, if it is impossible to be interested, perhaps at least notice the child;

Consider whether we might stop talking about the 'Kingdom of Heaven'. Even the disciples had difficulty dealing with the institutional aspects of the notion of 'Kingdom' (Who will sit at your right hand?). The verbal alternative 'Reign of God' is less rigid and offers scope for movement, for change but still has awkward power connotations. Perhaps a better alternative might be: "God's way of doing things."

Discuss how to reorganize our theology, ecclesiology and missiology so that children are always included.

How can we pursue the intrinsic value of children as Jesus saw it?

How can we preserve the qualities that children have: unconditional love, honesty, needing good role models, etc.? What programmes would help this?

How do we do this without romanticizing childhood?

How do we ensure that our Child Theology embraces all children, not just children at risk – children not just in physical danger but also in spiritual danger?

Conclusion

The state's control of the socialisation of the child is most powerfully seen in formal education systems. The primary purpose of education is to move from child to adulthood. 'Kindergartens' have become 'Nursery Schools' where social workers ask: what is the purpose of this activity? (motor skills, social skills?) *Could we not let them play for the sake of playing?* This western model is perceived as universally desirable and we heard of 18 month old babies in Nigeria already in school uniform!

Education reflects the values of society, not only in how the system works, but also in the course material and the standards that are set. Children who can't pass the formal tests are marginalized even if they're gifted in other areas. We heard of a child who was abandoned ten times **237** in one year and, not surprisingly, when he went to school he had major difficulties. He was excluded and diagnosed as having 'Attention Deficit Disorder'. In fact he was not only extremely intelligent but also very resilient. Despite the odds he discovered his gift and became an excellent chef. Clearly, it does no service to a child to grow up without skills that will enable him or her to make a way in society but the system is profoundly ambivalent; it is not wholly good.

Perhaps Child Theology has a particular part to play in supporting churches in the development of new models and communities of learning that can be offered to the state. Whether or not this is so, the placing of Child Theology and education side by side will likely as not have more to teach us as adults about ourselves, society and church than about children.

There are alternatives available. For example, there is an excellent rural education model in India. An extremely informal approach to education is described in Rousseau's novel *Emile* which proposed delaying the teaching of academic subjects and restricting reading to 'Robinson Crusoe'(of value because of its focus on the activities of daily living). Fröbel said *"only as last resort, bring children into a classroom."* Vanstone's *Love's Endeavour, Love's Expense*[87] provides a Christian approach to this issue.

The child in the midst is not placed there by Jesus so that the disciples might gaze at him or her in order to practice a model of mission or education but so that they might learn more about the Kingdom of Heaven and in so doing come to know and receive Jesus in a better and fuller way.

Discussion and Reflection / HADDON WILLMER

On the question of the institutional

The organisations we represent that work with children are not only ministries but to some extent are inevitably institutions, in the sense that they have structures, practices, values and permanence beyond that of the individuals currently staffing them. Whereas institutionalising is a human possibility – we can do it – and it has its uses in an imperfect world, uniqueness has to be respected rather than managed.

Each child simultaneously is unique and susceptible to institutionalisation, because they can fit into certain pigeonholes. Over-institution-alised children are those where the pigeonhole obliterates the unique-ness; but under-institutionalised children are vulnerable, friendless and disordered.

On uniqueness

Nowadays, the uniqueness of each person is axiomatic and politically correct. Theologically it is taken to be grounded in the will of God – the one who knows the fall of the sparrow. That is true and in many contexts it is a truth not to be watered down. Nevertheless, we may ask: is it healthy or natural for children (or ourselves) to make too much of unique-ness, as given in creation? There is a danger of fostering individualistic self-centredness, even narcissism.

Moreover, such a view tends to focus too much on origins, on what we are because of where we come from, whereas the child exists in growing towards the future. The child who does not find a way of moving on is in a bad way. So the question of uniqueness and of identity in the child is con-stantly present but is held, to a degree, in suspense; the answer is to be looked for in the *future*. The uniqueness of the child implies s/he is irre-placeable – and so the child must be respected and its time and place protected, even when it is hard to see that it is significantly different from many other children. Given time, its uniqueness will be shown, because it will be realised in life.

Experiment and protection

An outcome of this future orientation is that the child needs *room* for experiment. But also needs *protection* – not from experiment but to ensure that experiments are kept within limits so that they remain *experiments* and do not turn into *experience*, which defines and confines. Since adult-hood consists in large measure in being defined and confined (e.g. the promise of marriage, commitments to certain kinds of work, projects or causes), the child cannot be permanently saved from it but s/he needs to be *protected* from premature commitments, from being defined and con-fined by experience when there should still be experiments.

Premature experience arising out of reckless experiment is of course the special problem of adolescence. Experiments can be abandoned and left behind without great costs, whereas experience that is wrong in some way carries real moral personal and social costs for the person concerned: it leaves its mark. This distinction between experiment and experience justifies the difference in legal treatment of crime in children and adults.

Experiment and justification by faith

Some Christian theological views of life support not only the experimental approach (*"we do not know what we shall be ..."* 1 John 3.1f, *"leaving things behind, I press on ..."* Phil 3) but also postponing the *definition* of experience to the end, i.e. to God. If we are justified by faith, not by works, then our way of living can be profoundly experimental rather than experiential (in the above sense) to the end. We are judged, not by standards we fully command or have defined out of our knowledge and understanding, but by God who is love, who creates and redeems the whole creation. We live looking forward to the Judgement believing it is not in the end an adverse judgment of condemnation but justification and peace with God, though it will come as extraordinary surprise.

Protecting children from premature adulthood

That the child is experimental is the reason why the child should not be the teacher or the leader, as sometimes seems to be suggested. The child teaches only by not teaching, leads by not leading. There is a deep gulf between respecting children as children and giving children adult roles and duties, which involves adult abdication of responsibility. It is not a way of respecting children to give them adult duties or powers. The abuse of child soldiers who get power they are not ready for (if anyone ever is) is an extreme example. Milder examples, more extensively damaging, are to be found in the market exploitation of children, where their power as consumers makes them the victims of corrupting cultural forces and of the loss which follows from the weakening of good adult models, when pop stars stand high and teachers are despised. Respect for the child preserves the freedom for the child to be conducting experiments for their own growing. This is different from using them in social experiments.

Why do people often remember their childhoods as so different from their later life? We might give a 'Wordsworthian' explanation – they were nearer to God then. But do we want to believe that the longer we live the more life takes us away from that good source and that divine

Companion? It is however clear that we do lose something. I do not think we can avoid this loss, as though we could remain children all our lives. I would prefer to understand the tendency to regard our childhood as we remember it as distinctive from later life, by saying that, seen from the vantage point of age and experience, childhood was a time of experiment.

The transcendence of the child: romantic and theological understandings

Each child has to be respected as a transcendent reality. But what does respecting a transcendent reality mean? Does it mean having an ideal vision of the child, which we insist is the reality, despite appearances and experiences? Or is the transcendent not something above or within the appearance but something rooted in the *whence and whither* of life in time? Transcendence is not the possession or the quality of a child. It is given to the child by God who transcendently hides the life of the child in Christ, beyond all that is done by human agency. Children are vulnerable to being despised or scandalised by others but their angels always are in the Father's presence, gazing on his face (Matthew 18.10).

Children of the World: Poh Kok Chan, age 10 yrs

CHAPTER NOTES

[81] *UN Convention on the Rights of the Child*
[82] Participation in communion is a sensitive issue but John Krenmore asks when was the last time a minister refused communion to a pregnant woman?
[83] Darton, Longman and Todd; 2007

CHAPTER 29

Child Theology and Christology

HADDON WILLMER

'**CHILD THEOLOGY**' is a label for many disparate theological styles, concerns and conversations. I cannot keep up with them all. Over several years now, Child Theology for me has turned out to be a meditation on Matthew 18:1-10, with its parallels in Mark 9.33-37 and Luke 9:46-48. That text is like a hermit's cell, where I have stayed, finding God and the world in a narrow space. From within this cell, I look at christology, thinking about Jesus Christ, which is the crucial core of genuine *Christian* faith in God. This enquiry into the relation of christology and Child Theology is not framed systematically by the categories of conventional or classically formulated christology, though it is not out of harmony with it. Rather, it looks directly and simply at Matt 18 afresh, open to any christological signals to be found there.

Child theology is theology

The disciples argued a major practical theological issue, about greatness in the kingdom of God. Jesus placed a child in the midst, with the expectation that the child's presence would make a difference to the theological argument. In the church today, the child in the midst mostly makes one difference only: her presence says to the adults: "Hush, Hush, talking and thinking about God (theo-logy) is nasty, and not really necessary, children do without it – so let us be like children". That is not what the child meant for Jesus. He expected the child to change theology for the better, not to stifle it. The child would open the disciples to what they were closed against. Taking note of the child would undermine their present idea and the ambitious, anxious and competitive relationships which spawned their false thinking. And more, the child would be a positive clue to entering the kingdom of God.

This much is fairly obvious on a superficial reading of the text, though it does not seem (as far as I know) to have been noticed very often. Frequently, this text is read untheologically. The story serves as a basis for an ethical, spiritual call for humility, to be achieved by 'becoming as the children'. Morality is seen as an attractive, even necessary, escape from theology, which goes with speculation, irrelevancy and unnecessary strife.

In modern times, Jesus has often been preferred to organised Christianity, because in him we find the possibility of walking with God without getting entangled in theology. The untheological Jesus, as we picture him, lived as a free man, the free Son of God, free to be himself to the full, like the boy David, when he has refused Saul's oversized armour and acted in his own integrity. So we often read this text with the light heart of those who have God without theology. But that means, we don't read this text. For there can be no denying that there was an argument here about the kingdom of God – and that is theological. Any talk about the kingdom of God is intrinsically theological. And theology is important because it is thought and talk about, for, with, from and to God. Granted, Jesus was not a professional or academic theologian as we know them now. He talked about the kingdom of God before the long symbiosis of Christianity and university began, while we work largely within the assumption that theology is the product of that symbiosis. But God is, even now, not imprisoned in it, and many people think and talk about God, with practical seriousness, apart from it. Like Pascal, they have to do (Heb 4.13) with the living God, of Abraham, Isaac and Jacob, the God of Jesus Christ, not the God of philosophers and scholars.[88] Theology catches them, as Moses was caught by the sight of the burning bush and found he could not escape (Exodus 3:1ff).

Theology is frightening and arduous, as Moses and the prophets discovered. The working Name of God is given to us, but it is not a Name to be taken lightly on our lips. Glimpsing the reality of the living God makes us sense that theology is more than flesh and blood can stand, so it is no wonder that we try to do with as little theology as possible. Or we look to the preachers, church managers and scholars to make it harmless and undisturbing. Not that they can save us: when they produce theology which seems elitist or irrelevant to life or superficial and manipulative spiritual salesmanship, 'the hungry sheep look up and are not fed',[89] so there is a swing back in a search for the living God. Theology may appear to be either impossible or useless, so we are glad when we see the chance to have God without theology, to enjoy God with the heart and not the mind, with spontaneous action and not coherent thoughtful policy. But Jesus' talking of the kingdom of God calls us not to run away from theology in any form, but to find our way to healthy, serviceable theology, so that we name the Lord without taking it in vain or causing it to be blasphemed (Exodus 20:7; Ezekiel 36:16-32).

Christological signal I: placing the child in the midst

The gospel text is obviously about the child and the kingdom of God. We do not have to go far into it to find that it radiates christological signals. But they are not so obvious.

The first signal is not a word, but an action: Jesus took a child and placed him in the midst of the disciples. The child in the story is anonymous – boy or girl, we do not know. One implication that can be drawn is that this child may stand for any child and every child. Any child may be a sign of the kingdom of God and calls us towards God by simply being there 'in the midst'. This direct universalising of the child is valid and yet is in some tension with another key feature of the story. The child is taken and placed in the midst by Jesus. The child was seen by Jesus as having meaning for the dispute about the kingdom of God. Was Jesus seeing the obvious intrinsic meaning of any child, which is known to all people of intelligence and good will, while the disciples were being unusually obtuse and resistant to the plain truth?

We, as more than modern people, are informed by the Convention on the Rights of the Child and so are in possession of the insight which values each and every child in her own right. Even without theology, without Jesus, we are on the right track. This is the confidence of secular humanism. Christians often are assimilated to secular humanism, at least in reading this story: the child in herself, by herself, is enough to show us what the kingdom of God is like and how to get there. The child belongs by nature to the kingdom of God. We can find the way by 'becoming as the children'. Any child – and there are many around us – could show us the way. The secret is in the child as a natural truth. So it is common in reading this story, to give no weight to the action of Jesus which shapes it. But there would be no story, no theological argument if Jesus had not placed the child.

The placing of the child gives the child immense significance but it also discloses something of Jesus. It is thus relevant to a christological enquiry. And the child is immediately shown to be not just any child, in her individual self-contained being, but a child who is christologically defined. This child could be any child, but it is not any child in and by virtue of her any-ness. The child signs the kingdom of God as Jesus placed her in this argument and gave her this specific ministry. The child in the story is not known to us by her name, which is a basic personal characteristic which every child has the right to possess[90]; but the child is not quite unknown, for she is the child placed by Jesus.

Christians have a presumption in favour of Jesus as a creative One, bringing novelty into the world, opening up something which would otherwise not be available. That is putting it minimally. The New Testament makes more of it: God has spoken to us by his Son, the Word that is God, made flesh and revealing his glory. God surprises us in Christ by proving God-self beyond all our expectations. Yet what God in Christ brings is not pure novelty, for that would involve abolishing the present world and replacing it with something quite different.

The newness Christ brings is also simultaneously the faithfulness of the eternal God. God in Christ reveals recreative, saving grace. What in the world belongs to God has gone missing – now it is found; what has worn itself out in sin and frustration is redeemed; what has gone astray is redirected. The creation is owned by God despite its rebellion. That God is faithful in redemptive action comes to the sinning world as a surprising, almost unbelievable, novelty: when the Lord turned again the captivity of Zion, we were like those who dream (Psalm 126). The salvation of God cannot be comprehended and tamely assimilated to our norms and expectations which have been scaled down to fit what is possible in the world as seen in our faithlessness. God's action in faithfulness to his creation and in undefeated pursuit of his will on earth as in heaven surprises us, and yet it is rooted deep in the origin and source of all things.

This is a grand sweeping idea, which can be expressed in concepts like the johannine Word of God. If the Word through whom all things were created was made flesh, then we can expect to encounter and be drawn into the ever-fresh novelty of the deep-rooted renewal of all things, in the little day by day events that make up the life of the incarnate one. So the little action of Jesus, taking a child and putting her in the midst of the disciples, is not to be passed over as having no meaning. It is not a mere stage setting, building a platform for the teaching of a general truth. It rather calls us to be open to the creative, gracious, saving authority of the teacher and Lord, who, in ordinary daily trivial occurrence, gives us more than is ordinarily available to people like the disciples, people like ourselves.

Jesus invests the child with significance. He embraces and blesses the children (Matthew 19:13) not just for their own well-being but to make them a blessing. Through them, others find the way into the kingdom of God. So though the placing of the child in Matthew 18 is not described as a blessing, it has that value, for here Jesus brought the child within the dynamic process of his ministry. So this story is a christological story from the beginning.

Christological Signal II: Child reiterates Cross

The next christological signal can be picked up in the words of Jesus: Unless you turn and become as the children, you will not enter the kingdom of heaven. Whoever humbles himself as this child, he will be greatest in the kingdom of heaven.

The only way to the kingdom is to come down, to lower oneself. Thus, the meaning of the child in this context reiterates the key instruction Jesus had given to those who would be his disciples: Say No to yourself, take up your cross and follow Me (Matthew 16:24). The way signed by the child and the way opened by the Lord on the way of the Cross are the same. To become as the children does not give us a playful way of faith, over against the Cross which is grimly serious. Rather the call to become as the children reiterates the call to discipleship, because it involves saying No to the acquired, adult self which is precious to us. When the child is seen as socially lowly, with the servants, the child points to a way that is not easy to follow.

So long as it is accepted that the call to becoming as the children reiterates the call to discipleship in the way of the Cross, we may pay attention to the difference between them. Being like children offers no escape from the Cross, but the reiteration is not mere repetition. Saying the same thing in a different way reveals more of the reality. One image enlarges and protects the other. The Cross frightens us with the finality of death: it means total extinction. The child is new life, opening out in hope. The child does not give us an escape from saying No to self as we take up the Cross but it gives it to us as the way to life and hope. If on one side, the child reiterates the call to follow Jesus with the cross, on the other, the child reminds us of resurrection, new life bursting free from the liberating goodness of God to the crucified. Just as life without death is not the Gospel, so is death without life.

Christological Signal III: Reception and representation

The third christological moment in this text is in verse 5: whoever receives one such child in my Name, receives me. In Mark 9:37 and Luke 9:48, the saying is expanded: Whoever receives a child in my name, receives me and whoever receives me, receives the one who sent me. The relation of Jesus to the one who sent him, the Father, is not, however, foreign to Matthew. His 'johannine bolt from the blue' is unforgettable (Matthew 11:25-27). There, child, Son and Father are linked in knowing each other, which is a form of reception.

The text in a few verses encapsulates the pattern of Christian thinking about the kingdom of God. For Jesus the kingdom of God was the concept that framed his life and mission. He talked in many ways about what the kingdom of God is like, and he signed its imminence, just as he himself lived on its threshold in open expectation. But it was given to him to be the servant, sign and messenger of the coming kingdom of God in such a way that its approach is concentrated in his presence (Matthew 12:28). So, to receive Jesus is to receive or be ready for the kingdom of God.

After Jesus, especially as the Church grew in the Roman empire, the kingdom of God faded into the background and Jesus the Lord, the Son of the Father, Saviour, gave shape and centre, image and sensibility to Christianity. Disciples largely gave up talking about the kingdom of God and instead focused on Jesus and God, in time formulating their ideas in christological dogmas. And within that framework, piety and faith often concentrated on Christ. Faith and devotion fanned out from this centre in various directions: soteriological interest in atonement, Franciscan *imitatio Christi*, mystic and pietist devotion and even cults of the Hero-Man. Salvation was a relation with God through Christ, rather than the coming of a kingdom. The language of the kingdom of God survived mostly as a backcloth or a backup for earthly Christian kings and their empires; or its appearance as the kingdom of God was postponed to heaven or to the millennium anticipated only by marginal communities.

In the twentieth century, the kingdom of God has regained some theological, missional and practical salience, not least as a result of deeper historical and social readings of the New Testament and of proper and improper secularising politicisations of the faith. One extreme, kitsch manifestation of this development is in the contemporary western celebrations of Christmas, where the Baby still just holds centre stage, competing with reindeers and commercial advertisements but the kingdom of God is invisible. Christmas in this form is the Baby without the Kingdom and so we have missed the wisdom of the star-sighting seekers from the East, who sought a King. To end up with Jesus without the kingdom of God is to lose the Gospel, just as much as if we hold on to some kingdom which has not been turned upside down by Jesus.

The point of this argument is that Matthew 18:5 must not be separated from the earlier statement. Receiving Christ and so receiving God is not an alternative to entering the kingdom of heaven. The two are one.

This text offers us christology in an unaccustomed, obscured and stimulating form. Reception and sending are two crucial categories. They point to a dynamic movement between Father, Son, human beings and child.

The child is identified as one who can be received in Christ's Name. That implies the converse: that we can act on Christ's behalf, doing his work on the earth, by receiving a child. Receiving children is not outside his interest or unworthy of him. It is not merely that Christ approves the reception of a child. When a child is received, Christ is received. To act as the agent of Christ in his work finds its reward in nothing less than receiving Christ. Christ not merely commands and directs us into the work we have to do but gives himself to us as the reward. Out of this we can make a simple christological statement: Christ is one who is pleased to be represented[91] by the child. It is no surprise that the Lord who became a servant and humbled himself to death on the cross should be glad to be represented in the child, as in the poor and needy (Matthew 25:31–46).

Commonly, when christology gets beyond asking How, or What, Christ is, and asks Who? – it responds in two ways. Jesus Christ is the incarnate Word and Son of the Father, one with the Father and the Holy Spirit. It is the relation in God as Trinity that decisively characterises Jesus Christ. The other way is in the confession of faith that Jesus is Lord: those who believe and confess are related to Christ.

When children are considered, questions arise about how old a child has to be to acknowledge Christ fitly, and what competences are required for them to do so. What kind of catechesis or formation will bring them not merely to say orthodox words about Jesus but to enter into 'saving faith'. The questions can never be settled, because the christology is too narrow to receive the child. Another way is possible: christology can be built by receiving the child by and in whom Jesus Christ is content to be represented. Where does Jesus dwell? In the child whom he places in the midst of people who are concerned about the kingdom of God. Christology is thus not restricted to describing Christ as uniquely related to God, nor as the object of the believer's confession of faith. It witnesses to Christ wherever and as he is represented – which is often under unlikely appearances. Christology answers the question: Lord, when did we see you? (Matthew 25:37). Christ is the one who is received when a child is received in his Name. This does not mean the child becomes Christ or takes his place. Reception is a concept which respects the difference but realises belonging and sharing, overcoming separation, alienation and strangeness. Christ is received when he is represented by an Other. Christ is one who is ready to be represented, so ready and present in the representation that he may be really received in it.

This points the way to a Christology of loving action. The child received is loved in a way appropriate to the child – the love is just. The child received is where Christ is, and is the form and way in which Christ is ready to be received.

There are possibilities of a christology of reception and representation, which link up the child, Christ and the Father. The act of receiving a child in Christ's Name is blessed by God in Christ. The reward for receiving a child is to receive Jesus Christ and the one who sent him. What could be more than that?

I interject a simple pastoral narrative, which is probably clearer and worth more than all this stilted academic writing.

A group of Christians, men and women, talk about their prayer life. A young mother recalls how close she felt to God, and how much she put into prayer, in earlier years when she was single and ardently Christian. Now, she says, my prayer life has taken a nose-dive: I hardly pray at all. Two young children occupy me all day and in the evening I just go to sleep. She feels bad and would like to get back to how it was, because as a Christian, she should have a good prayer life, visible and convincing to herself. With such a devotional life, she would live with the feeling that she was close to God and God to her. But, notwithstanding this loss, she believes it was right to get married and to have children. Yet she goes on bemoaning her loss as though she has never heard the words of Jesus: Whoever receives a child in my Name, receives me, and whoever receives me receives the One who sent me. The word says: You are close to God, God is close to you, though she does not feel it. All she needs to see this, is, first, the concept, the text, to enable her to name and appreciate what is being given to her in her children, and secondly, the grace and strength to go on receiving the children, day by day, which is not without parallels to the way of the cross. It certainly involves saying No to the self that built itself up in the days of single freedom. It calls for faith in the darkness when it is not obvious that God is near. Churches had not put her on to this way of looking at God and Christ, prayer and children and herself. In being unhelped by the church at this point, she is far from alone. Her experience is so common and so overwhelming that the words of Jesus may seem to be a promise too frail to counteract the spiritual numbing she is going through. But there may be tough grace, tough promise here.

It was a mother who raised the question and got the answer. But it is not just for mothers. Fathers may find it harder to face the question and to accept the answer but they too need it. So do all who work with children and all who have responsibility for children – which means all of us, including those who find important excuses to say children are not our business.

Christ comes to and into those who receive a child. Somehow, Christ is present and communicated in and through the child. We might discern parallels with traditional sacramental theology: somehow Christ is received in the bread and wine in the Eucharist. The reception of the child is as concrete and should be as central to Christian faith and practice as is the reception of the bread and wine.

But we should not seek to sacramentalise the child in a churchy way. It is essential that we do not alienate the real child from the actual world, where God is. We should not bring her into the church and set her aside for a special religious function, as we have done with the bread and wine since very near the beginning. At first, the Lord's Supper was rooted in the ordinary eating and drinking of Jesus with people around him. It had meaning: Jesus shared the bread of life, giving himself, in open unecclesiastical settings. Paul demanded of the Corinthians that they discern the Lord's body when they ate and drank in church but what he meant by that was not that they piously imagined they were eating Jesus' personal body, in any form, rather that they respected the whole body of Jesus in all the people he gathered to himself (I Cor.11.17-34). This company which he gathered and owned included poor people whom the rich could look down upon, ignore and shame. It was not a gathering of well-churched people but a cross-section of an ordinary human society. It was because they did not see that the poor were owned by Christ as full members of his body that they did not discern the Lord's body and so, despite their pious doctrine about what they were doing, it was not the Lord's Supper which they ate.

A sacrament of bread and wine could be developed, because it is fairly easy to ecclesiasticise and set apart some bread and wine, while valuing and using most bread and wine in a secular, practical way. Children are not so easily ecclesiaticised and have not become part of the sacramental routine of the church to the same extent. This is so, even where infants are baptised. So the child, who lives, day and night, in the world, hopefully in some sort of family, good or not so good, is still there, for Christians as for others, as an ordinary created being. And it is this ordinary child who is in view when Jesus speaks of her being 'received'. If Jesus Christ is received when a real child is received in his Name, Jesus Christ is not being sacralised within the church-as-religion but is respected in his freedom for the life of the world.

It is a constant temptation for Christianity to show itself to be wholehearted and spiritual by deserting the earth. Seek those things that are above, where Christ is (Colossians 3:1); set your mind on things that are above, not on things on the earth. This kind of teaching seems plain. So plain it makes us forget 1 John 4:20: how can you love God whom you do not see, if you do not love your brother – or this child – whom you do see. Many Christians in their best moments move in the direction, from the earth to what is above. This movement is in line with the direction of a simple and obvious view of the resurrection. The resurrection is treated as though it authorises our forgetting the downward road taken by the Son, coming to earth and living as one of us. The earthly Jesus and the Cross are set in the past: the resurrection opens a new day, a new set of conditions in which we can and should live. But the resurrection is the resurrection of Jesus: he is not left behind, nor is he redundant in the new world opening up in light. Rather, everything Jesus was and did is given afresh to the world by God in raising him from the dead. The content of the resurrected One is the life he lived as the beloved Son of the Father. On earth Jesus called disciples to walk with him into the thick of human affairs, taking up the cross – and receiving a child. A child is new life in and for the earth. The child who will live happily to a hundred is a sign of the city of earth, as it is envisaged in God's creative pleasure (Isa. 65.20).

Jesus taught his disciples to pray: your Kingdom come, on earth as in heaven. That 'as' is a key Gospel conjunction: it links earth to heaven and it means that heaven is not the home for those who despise or are weary of the earth but is the pattern and inspiration for us here. Christians live in the conjunction, 'as in heaven, so on earth' and guard it against all pressures to replace it with something like 'heaven, instead of earth'. The 'as-so' between earth and heaven reflects orthodox christology, as presented, for example, in the Definition of Chalcedon (AD 451). There, the Lord Jesus Christ was acknowledged as one Person, the Son, in two natures, truly God and truly human. The two natures are not mixed up, so that they are confused and changed into something they are not, but they are united 'without division, without separation'. Divinity and humanity are not incompatible realities, pulling apart from each other. In Jesus Christ, each is fully and truly present, realised and revealed; but this fullness is achieved in harmony. Jesus did not merely teach us to pray, 'as in heaven, so on earth', but he had his own being in and with the Father on the same 'as-so' pattern.

Because it is the resurrection of Jesus, resurrection is not a magic escalation to a higher level of existence, but is the validation of everything that was given and opened up in the life of Jesus on earth, when we beheld the glory of the One who was with the Father and came in the flesh (I John 4:2)

Christological Signal IV: Sent

Along with reception, sending and being sent is a pregnant christological image in this text. It has several facets. First, Jesus comes from the One who sent him. To be sent is to be commissioned and to be authorised: Jesus comes as representative or ambassador. When he is received, the Sender is received. Through Jesus we come to the Sender, thus finding the source of his being, and can live from it in our turn. Secondly, to be sent is to be related to the Sender and yet to be separated. The sent one ends up at a distance from the Sender (otherwise there would be no need to use the language of sending). The Son goes into the Far Country. Jesus the Son was aware that the sending Father was 'always with me' and yet he in the world on his own, visibly without the Father. He, the carpenter's son from Nazareth, is seen but the Sender is hidden. People see him in the world in such a way that it is reasonable to ask questions like, "Where does he come from? Where does he get all this wisdom and authority? Where is he going?" The Son is sent by the Father into the world and so into this evident distance from the Father. There are hints in the Gospel narratives that Jesus was aware of both the relation and the distance as two aspects of being sent – and he grappled with the consequences, some of which were painful.

Reconciliation

Thirdly, sending thus raises the question of reception. Is the Son sent into exile, disowned and abandoned? The witness of faith, in Scripture and the church, is that God does not leave his chosen one in Hades, but raises him and gives him glory. The Son is received by the Father. But that is not all. The sent one is received on earth, when little ones are received in his Name. The significant reception of Christ is two sided, in heaven and on earth. It is done by God in raising Christ from the dead and it is done by people. Among them, Christ comes like a child, needing reception, not always finding it, or finding it only in clumsy unfitting ways. The question of faith and unfaith is integral to the being of Christ in the world – will he be received or refused? By sending the Son into the distance, God makes him vulnerable to being received or not received. God, the Sender who is received when the Sent one is received is thus in human hands, the Lord, strangely dependent on an uncertain reception. Jesus is like his disciples when he sent them out on mission, as sheep in the midst of wolves (Matthew 10:16,14).

The sending is the creative initiative of God. It is the act of the Lord, claiming his own (Luke 20.13). Consider what the sending to claim his own means. It not only looks for obedience from those who owe it, but it protects and vindicates his creatures against all false claims and threats against them. Sometimes, Christian interpretations of God's message is one-sidedly legalistic, demanding submission and conformity to God's requirements. The News, which the Bible in its totality witnesses to and opens our eyes for, is Good because the claim of God upon his creatures is shown to be both a call to obedience and a promise that God will deliver his claim to his own.

I will be their God and they shall be my people. The people will be the Lord's, cleaving to him with all their heart and soul and mind and strength, presenting their bodies (their whole present being) as a living sacrifice. The Lord will be their God, holding on to them, rescuing them from all their enemies, up to the last enemy, Death, thus making clear to all the powers that they are his and will not be abandoned to any other (Romans 8:31ff; Colossians 2:15) How shall I give you up, O Ephraim? (Hosea 11:8)

Christianity is more than a religion concerned with moral education and good order; it is faith and hope in God the creator and redeemer, to whom creatures are precious. Therefore it has at its heart the question of the trustworthiness and the future of God. Is God an empty hope? Is God a delusion? Bible reading Christians should not be taken by surprise by contemporary assertions that God is a delusion – though they may raise an eyebrow when the assertion is made as though it is a recent science-based discovery – for it was known to prophets and people of old. Why do you say O Israel that my way is hidden from God and my right is disregarded by my God? (Isaiah 40:27)

The faith of Israel carried this kind of question in itself, and faith found itself by sharing in God's answering the question. God gives the kind of answer which does not make the question redundant, satisfied and thus no longer askable; God's answer is always a response to questions which are real, embedded in the world as the meeting place of God and creatures. God's answer in Christ is that God is God for and not against creation, including human being; but the answer takes a form in Jesus which intensifies the question to the lowest depths. So the claim of God is still being made as a plea for reception and an invitation to the risk of faith and love, and is not imposed as a new regime which sweeps the old defeated order into oblivion. God's answer lies in the sending and the coming of the servant and son of God. He entered into full vulnerability to the practical question of the world as it is: What is God's claim upon creatures? Can and will God make good that claim? Will the claim be made sufficiently good so that creatures can have confidence and joy in acknowledging it?

God makes good his claim to be the Lord of all, against all powers, not by dissolving the world immediately and thus depriving the bullies of their playground with its dark corners, but by living life in it, in such a way that living life is possible and hopeful for creatures. If we are unwilling to go the way of the Sent one and with him, the claim will seem empty. God in Christ makes no offer outside God in Christ. (That statement is not to be read as an assertion about the status of Christianity in competition with other religions, or as insisting on assent to a particular doctrine of atonement as being essential for salvation.) God offers us the possibility of being assured that all is well or all will be well only along the path God takes in Christ, as in all the story of God witnessed to in

Scripture. As we have already said, this is where the answer never silences or gets away from the question, and yet is never defeated or held back by the question.

God's Claim on us

God's claim upon us is exemplified in Jesus. Hence the call: "Come follow me" – and its reiteration in another form: "Receive a child in my name". God's claim on us enters into the depths of the suspicion that it is a delusion: "My God, My God, why have you forsaken me?" – and breaks out beyond it when the Sent Son is not left in Hades but is raised from the dead and when the blessing pronounced at his baptism ("This is my beloved Son in whom I am well pleased") is shown to be a reliable word. God's claim upon us in Jesus is also the enacted revelation of God's claiming of his creation, against all false lords and competing powers, which comprise sin and death. The story of Jesus is good news of God for us, God with us. It is not the story of a singular hero, a person uniquely favoured by God, a supreme individual, with no connection with others. Jesus is sent to the people; his history is one in which he is and is shown to be the first-born of many brethren (Rom 8.29; Heb 2). He comes as one who is to be received, with and through the little ones by whom he is represented. Setting the child in the midst as a clue to the gracious rule of God over all is thus in itself a key christological action and word. The child is a language of God, in which the Word of God speaks.

CHAPTER NOTES

[88] Blaise Pascal *The Memorial*, 23 Nov 1654: God of Abraham, God of Isaac, God of Jacob, not of the philosophers and of the learned ... (http://everything2.com/index.pl?node_id = 1347074)
[89] John Milton, *Lycidas*
[90] Convention on the Rights of the Child, article 7
[91] My understanding of representation is informed by Dorothee Soelle, *Christ the Representative* (1967)